# TALES OF OLD IRELAND

# TALES OF OLD IRELAND

*Edited by Michael O'Mara*

MICHAEL O'MARA BOOKS LIMITED

First published in 1994 by
Michael O'Mara Books Limited, 9 Lion Yard,
Tremadoc Road, London SW4 7NQ

A CIP catalogue record for this book is available from the
British Library


ISBN 1-85479-981-9

Typeset by DP Photosetting, Aylesbury, Bucks
Printed in the United States of America

# Contents

# Foreword

*Tales of Old Ireland* is a selection of stories written during the 19th century and the first few years of the 20th. Although it contains stories by the likes of W.B. Yeats and James Joyce it does not aim to be an anthology of the greatest Irish literature. The purpose of this collection is to evoke an Ireland that has vanished: the largely rural country of peasants who eked out a precarious existence on tiny, rented farms, often of less than an acre.

This Ireland was the poorest country in Europe. It was occupied by the British Army and nearly all the land was controlled by English landlords who rarely set foot on Irish soil. According to the Duke of Wellington, 'There never was a country in which poverty existed to the extent it exists in Ireland.' Half the population lived in windowless mud cabins of one room. The peasants had little or no furniture and usually shared their cabins with their pigs. In the 1840s, Ireland was the most densely populated country in Europe with between eight and nine million people. Famine, which killed more than a million, and emigration took an enormous toll so that even today Ireland has only three and a half million people.

Despite the hardships and repression of the time, the Irish had a gift for being happy. Sir Walter Scott wrote of the Irish in 1825, 'Their natural condition is turned towards gaiety and happiness.' The potato, virtually the only crop of old Ireland, needed hard work only in

Spring and Autumn which left lots of time for the main amusements which were fiddling, dancing, telling stories and drinking poteen, the illegal whiskey of the peasant. The people were simple and poor but good manners and hospitality were everywhere to be found. Sir Walter Scott wrote of the 'perpetual kindness of the Irish cabin; buttermilk, potatoes, a stool is offered, a stone is rolled that your honour may sit down.'

Scott must have heard many a gripping and humorous tale before a peat fire on his travels in Ireland, for story-telling was the great art of the peasant. This gift is clear in the first two stories in this volume, by William Carleton, which reflect the extremes of the day: the first a whimsical tale, full of humour, the second a stark account of sectarian murder. The stories of Thomas Crofton Croker and Gerald Griffin have the sense of ancient folk-tale up-dated. Of course there are stories of priests (by Canon Sheehan and Frank Mathew) who had such influence and the ever-present fiddle has a part to play in the stories of Seamas MacManus and Daniel Corkery. The collection ends with James Joyce's The Dead which so vividly evokes old Dublin.

For many millions of Irish descent around the world, *Tales of Old Ireland* offers an authentic portrait of the land their great-grandparents left for the new worlds. I hope these stories will help them understand the beauties and the horrors that formed the daily lives of their ancestors.

Michael O'Mara

# WILLIAM CARLETON

## Neal Malone

*William Carleton (1794–1869) was educated in the so-called 'hedge schools' – the very roughest of schooling. His stories were published under the title of* Traits and Stories of the Irish Peasantry *(1830).*

THERE never was a greater-souled or doughtier tailor than little Neal Malone. Though but four feet four in height, he paced the earth with the courage and confidence of a giant; nay, one would have imagined that he walked as if he feared the world itself was about to give way under him. Let none dare to say in future that a tailor is but the ninth part of a man. That reproach had been gloriously taken away from the character of the cross-legged corporation by Neal Malone. He has wiped it off like a stain from the collar of a second-hand coat; he has pressed this wrinkle out of the lying front of antiquity; he has drawn together this rent in the respectability of his profession. No. By him who was breeches-maker to the gods – that is, except, like Highlanders, they eschewed inexpressibles – by him who cut Jupiter's frieze jocks for winter, and eke by the bottom of his thimble, we swear that Neal Malone was *more* that the ninth part of a man!

Setting aside the Patagonians, we maintain that two-thirds of mortal humanity were comprised in Neal; and perhaps we might venture to assert that two-thirds of Neal's humanity were equal to six-thirds of another man's. It is right well known that Alexander the Great was a little man, and we doubt whether, had Alexander the Great been bred to the tailoring business, he would have exhibited so much of the hero as Neal Malone. Neal was descended from a fighting family, who had signalized themselves in as many battles as ever any single hero of antiquity fought. His father, his grandfather, and his great-grandfather were all fighting men, and his ancestors in general, up, probably, to Con of the Hundred Battles himself. No wonder, therefore, that Neal's blood should cry out against the cowardice of his calling; no wonder that he should be an epitome of all that was valorous and heroic in a peaceable man, for we neglected to inform the reader that Neal, though 'bearing no base mind', never fought any man in his own person. That, however, deducted nothing from his courage. If he did not fight, it was simply because he found cowardice universal. No man would engage him; his spirit blazed in vain; his thirst for battle was doomed to remain unquenched, except by whisky, and this only increased it. In short, he could find no foe. He has often been known to challenge the first cudgel-players and pugilists of the parish; to provoke men of fourteen stone weight; and to bid mortal defiance to faction heroes of all grades – but in vain. There was that in him which told them that an encounter with Neal would strip them of their laurels. Neal saw all this with a lofty imagination; he deplored the degeneracy of the times, and thought it hard that the descendant of such a fighting family should be doomed to pass through life peaceably, whilst so many excellent rows and riots took place around him. It was a calamity to see every man's head broken but his own; a dismal thing to observe his neighbours go about with their bones in bandages, yet his untouched; and his friends beat black and blue, whilst his own cuticle remained undiscoloured.

'Blur-an'-agers!' exclaimed Neal one day, when half tipsy in the fair, 'am I never to get a bit of fightin'? Is there no cowardly *spalpeen* to stand afore Neal Malone? Be this an' be that, I'm blue-mowlded for want of a batin'! I'm disgracin' my relations by the life I'm ladin'! Will non o' ye fight me aither for love, money or whisky – frind or inimy, an' bad luck to ye? I don't care a *traneen* which, only out o' pure friendship let us have a morsel o' the rale kick-up, 'tany rate. Frind or inimy, I say agin, if you regard me – sure, that makes no differ, only let us have the fight.'

This excellent heroism was all wasted; Neal could not find a single adversary. Except he divided himself like Hotspur, and went to buffets, one hand against the other, there was no chance of a fight; no person to be found sufficiently magnanimous to encounter the tailor. On the contrary, every one of his friends – or, in other words, every man in the parish – was ready to support him. He was clapped on the back until his bones were nearly dislocated in his body, and his hand shaken until his arm lost its cunning at the needle for half-a-week afterwards. This, to be sure, was a bitter business – a state of being past endurance. Every man was his friend – no man was his enemy. A desperate position for any person to find himself in, but doubly calamitous to a martial tailor.

Many a dolorous complaint did Neal make upon the misfortune of having none to wish him ill; and what rendered this hardship doubly oppressive was the unlucky fact that no exertions of his, however offensive, could procure him a single foe. In vain did he insult, abuse, and malign all his acquaintances. In vain did he father upon them all the rascality and villainy he could think of. He lied against them with a force and originality that would have made many a modern novelist blush for want of invention – but all to no purpose. The world for once became astonishingly Christian; it paid back all his efforts to excite its resentment with the purest of charity; when Neal struck it on the one cheek, it meekly turned unto him the other. It could scarcely be expected that Neal would bear this. To have the whole world in friendship with a man is beyond doubt rather an affliction. Not to have the face of a single enemy to look upon would decidedly be considered a deprivation of many agreeable sensations by most people as well as by Neal Malone. Let who might sustain a loss, or experience a calamity, it was a matter of indifference to Neal. They were only his friends, and he troubled neither his head nor his heart about them.

Heaven help us! there is no man without his trials; and Neal, the reader perceives, was not exempt from his. What did it avail him that he carried a cudgel ready for all hostile contingencies? or knit his brows and shook his *kippeen* at the fiercest of his fighting friends? The moment he appeared, they softened into downright cordiality. His presence was the signal of peace; for, notwithstanding his unconquerable propensity to warfare, he went abroad as the genius of unanimity, though carrying in his bosom the redoubtable disposition of a warrior; just as the sun, though the source of light himself, is said to be dark enough at bottom.

It could not be expected that Neal, with whatever fortitude he might bear his other afflictions, could bear such tranquillity like a hero. To say that he bore it as one, would be to basely surrender his character; for what hero ever bore a state of tranquillity with courage? It affected his cutting out! It produced what Burton calls 'a windie melancholie', which was nothing else than an accumulation of courage that had no means of escaping, if courage can, without indignity, be ever said to escape. He sat uneasy on his lap-board. Instead of cutting out soberly, he flourished his scissors as if he were heading a faction; he wasted much chalk by scoring his cloth in wrong places, and even caught his hot goose without a holder. These symptoms alarmed his friends, who persuaded him to go to a doctor. Neal went, to satisfy them; but he knew that no prescription could drive the courage out of him – that he was too far gone in heroism to be made a coward of by apothecary stuff. Nothing in the pharmacopeia could physic him into a pacific state. His disease was simply the want of an enemy, and an unaccountable superabundance of friendship on the part of his acquaintances. How could a doctor remedy this by a prescription? Impossible. The doctor, indeed, recommended blood-letting; but to lose blood in a peaceable manner was not only cowardly, but a bad cure for courage. Neal declined it: he would lose no blood for any man until he could not help it; which was giving the character of a hero at a single touch. His blood was not to be thrown away in this manner; the only lancet ever applied to his relations was the cudgel, and Neal scorned to abandon the principles of his family.

His friends, finding that he reserved his blood for more heroic purposes than dastardly phlebotomy, knew not what to do with him.

His perpetual exclamation was, as we have already stated, 'I'm blue-mowlded for want of a batin'!' They did everything in their power to cheer him with the hope of a drubbing; told him he lived in an excellent country for a man afflicted with his malady; and promised, if it were at all possible, to create him a private enemy or two, who, they hoped to heaven, might trounce him to some purpose.

This sustained him for a while; but as day after day passed, and no appearance of action presented itself, he could not choose but increase in courage. His soul, like a sword-blade, too long in the scabbard, was beginning to get fuliginous by inactivity. He looked upon the point of his own needle, and the bright edge of his scissors, with a bitter pang when he thought of the spirit rusting within him; he meditated fresh insults, studied new plans, and hunted out cunning devices for provoking his acquaintances to battle, until by degrees he began to confound his own brain, and to commit more grievous oversights in his business than ever. Sometimes he sent home to one person a coat with the legs of a pair of trousers attached to it for sleeves, and dispatched to another the arms of the aforesaid coat tacked together as a pair of trousers. Sometimes the coat was made to button behind instead of before; and he frequently placed the pockets in the lower part of the skirts, as if he had been in league with cut-purses.

This was a melancholy situation, and his friends pitied him accordingly.

'Don't be cast down, Neal,' said they; 'your friends feel for you, poor fellow.'

'Divil carry my frinds,' replied Neal; 'sure, there's not one o' yez frindly enough to be my inimy. Tare-an'-ounze, what'll I do? I'm blue-mowlded for want of a batin'!'

Seeing that their consolation was thrown away upon him, they resolved to leave him to his fate; which they had no sooner done than Neal had thoughts of taking to the *Skiomachia* as a last remedy. In this mood he looked with considerable antipathy at his own shadow for several nights; and it is not to be questioned but that some hard battles would have taken place between them, were it not for the cunning of the shadow, which declined to fight him in any position than with its back to the wall. This occasioned him to pause, for the wall was a fearful antagonist, inasmuch that it knew not when it was beaten. But there was still an alternative left. He went to the garden one clear day about noon, and hoped to have a bout with the shade, free from interruption. Both approached, apparently eager for the combat, and resolved to conquer or die, when a villainous cloud, happening to intercept the light, gave the shadow an opportunity of disappearing; and Neal found himself once more without an opponent.

'It's aisy known,' said Neal, 'you haven't the blood in you, or you'd come to the scratch like a man.'

He now saw that fate was against him, and that any further hostility towards the shadow was only a tempting of Providence. He lost his health, spirits, and everything but his courage. His countenance became pale and peaceful-looking; the bluster departed from him; his body shrank up like a withered parsnip. Thrice was he compelled to take in his clothes, and thrice did he ascertain that much of his time would be necessarily spent in pursuing his retreating person through the solitude of his almost deserted garments.

God knows, it is difficult to form a correct opinion upon a situation so paradoxical as Neal's was. To be reduced to skin and bone by the downright friendship of the world, was, as the sagacious reader will admit, next to a miracle. We appeal to the conscience of any man who finds himself without an enemy, whether he be not a greater skeleton than the tailor; we will give him fifty guineas provided he can show a calf to his leg. We know he could not; for the tailor had none, and that was because he had not an enemy. No man in friendship with the world ever has calves to his legs. To sum up all in a paradox of our own invention, for which we claim the full credit of originality, we now assert that MORE MEN HAVE RISEN IN THE WORLD BY THE INJURY OF THEIR ENEMIES THAN HAVE RISEN BY THE KINDNESS OF THEIR FRIENDS. You may take this, reader, in any sense; apply it to hanging if you like it is, still immutably and immovably true.

One day Neal sat cross-legged, as tailors usually sit, in the act of pressing a pair of breeches; his hands were place, backs up, upon the handle of his goose, and his chin rested upon the back of his hands. To judge from his sorrowful complexion, one would suppose that he sat rather to be sketched as a picture of misery, or of heroism in distress, than for the industrious purpose of pressing the seams of a garment. There was a great deal of New Burlington Street pathos in his countenance; his face, like the times, was rather out of joint; 'the sun was just setting, and his golden beams fell, with a saddened splendour, athwart the tailor's —' — the reader may fill up the picture.

In this position sat Neal, when Mr O'Connor, the schoolmaster, whose inexpressibles he was turning for the third time, entered the workshop. Mr O'Connor himself was as finished a picture of misery as the tailor. There was a patient, subdued kind of expression in his face which indicated a very fair portion of calamity; his eye seemed charged with affliction of the first water; on each side of his nose might be traced two dry channels which, no doubt, were full enough while the tropical rains of his countenance lasted. Altogether, to conclude from appearances, it was a dead match in affliction between him and the tailor; both seemed sad, fleshless and unthriving.

'Misther O'Connor,' said the tailor, when the schoolmaster entered, 'won't you be pleased to sit down?'

Mr O'Connor sat; and after wiping his forehead. laid his hat upon the lap-board, put his half-handkerchief in his pocket, and looked upon the tailor. The tailor, in return, looked upon Mr O'Connor; but neither of them spoke for some minutes. Neal, in fact, appeared to be wrapped up in his own misery, and Mr O'Connor in his; or, as we often have much gratuitous sympathy for the distresses of our friends, we question but the tailor was wrapped up in Mr O'Connor's misery, and Mr O'Connor in the tailor's.

Mr O'Connor at length said, 'Neal, are my inexpressibles finished?'

'I am now pressin' your inexpressibles,' replied Neal; 'but, be my sowl, Mr O'Connor, it's not your inexpressibles I'm thinkin' of. I'm not the ninth part of what I was. I'd hardly make paddin' for a collar now.'

'Are you able to carry a staff still, Neal?'

'I've a light hazel one that's handy,' said the tailor; 'but where's the use of carryin' it whin I can get no one to fight wid. Sure, I'm disgracin' my relations by the life I'm ladin'.' I'll go to my grave w'dout ever batin' a man, or bein' bate myself – that's the vexation. Divil the row ever I was able to kick up in my life; so that I'm fairly blue-mowlded for want of a batin'. But if you have patience –'

'Patience!' said Mr O'Connor, with a shake of the head that was perfectly disastrous even to look at – 'patience, did you say, Neal?'

'Ay,' said Neal; 'an', be my sowl, if you deny that I said patience, I'll break your head!'

'Ah, Neal,' returned the other, 'I don't deny it – for though I am teaching philosophy, knowledge, and mathematics every day in my life, yet I'm learning patience myself both night and day. No, Neal; I have forgotten to deny anything. I have not been guilty of a contradiction, out of my own school, for the last fourteen years. I once expressed the shadow of a doubt about twelve years ago, but ever since I have abandoned even doubting. That doubt was the last expiring effort at maintaining my domestic authority – but I suffered for it.'

'Well,' said Neal, 'if you have patience, I'll tell you what afflicts me from beginnin' to endin'.'

'I will have patience,' said Mr O'Connor, and he accordingly heard a dismal and indignant tale from the tailor.

'You have told me that fifty times over,' said Mr O'Connor, after hearing the story. 'Your spirit is too martial for a pacific life. If you follow my advice, I will teach you how to ripple the calm current of your existence to some purpose. Marry a wife. For twenty-five years I have given instructions in three branches viz., philosophy, knowledge and mathematics – I am also well versed in matrimony, and I declare that, upon my misery, and by the contents of all my afflictions, it is my solemn and melancholy opinion that if you marry a wife you will, before three months pass over your concatenated state, not have a single complaint to make touching a superabundance of peace and tranquillity, or a love of fighting.'

'Do you mane to say that any woman would make me afeard?' said the tailor, deliberately rising up and getting his cudget. 'I'll thank you merely to go over the words agin till I thrash you widin' an inch o' your life. That's all.'

'Neal,' said the schoolmaster, meekly, 'I won't fight; I have been too often subdued ever to presume on the hope of a single victory. My spirit is long since evaporated: I am like one of your own shreds, a mere selvage. Do you not know how much my habiliments have shrunk in, even within the last five years? Hear me, Neal; and venerate my words as if they proceeded from the lips of a prophet. If you wish to taste the luxury of being subdued – if you are, as you say, blue-mowlded for want of a beating, and sick at heart of a peaceful exis-tence – why, MARRY A WIFE. Neal, send my breeches home with all haste, for they are wanted – you understand. Farewell!'

Mr O'Connor, having thus expressed himself, departed; and Neal stood with the cudgel in his hand, looking at the door out of which he passed, with an expression of fierceness, contempt, and reflection strongly blended on the ruins of his once heroic visage.

Many a man has happiness within his reach if he but knew it. The tailor had been, hitherto, miserable because he pursued a wrong object. The schoolmaster, however, suggested a train of thought upon which Neal now fastened will all the ardour of a chivalrous tem-perament. Nay, he wondered that the family spirit should have so completely seized upon the fighting side of his heart as to preclude all thoughts of matrimony; for he could not but remember that his relations were as ready for marriage as for fighting. To doubt this would have been to throw a blot upon his own escutcheon. He, therefore, very prudently asked himself, to whom, if he did not marry, should he transmit his courage. He was a single man, and, dying as such, he would be the sole depository of his own valour, which, like Junius's secret, must perish with him. If he could have left it as a legacy to such of his friends as were most remarkable for cowardice, why, the case would be altered; but this was impossible, and he had now no other means of preserving it to posterity than by creating a posterity to inherit it. He saw, too, that the world was likely to become convulsed. Wars, as everybody knew, were certain to break out, and would it not be an excellent opportunity for being father to a colonel, or perhaps a general, that might astonish the world. The change visible in Neal after the schoolmaster's last visit absolutely thunderstruck all who knew him. The clothes which he had rashly taken in to fit his shrivelled limbs were once more let out. The tailor expanded with a new spirit; his joints ceased to be supple, as in the days of his valour; his eye became less fiery, but more brilliant. From being martial, he got desperately gallant; but somehow he could not afford to act the hero and lover both at the same time. This, perhaps, would be too much to expect from a tailor. His policy was better. He resolved to bring all his available energy to bear upon the charms of whatever fair nymph he should select for the honour of matrimony; to waste his spirit in fighting would, therefore, be a deduction from the single purpose in view.

The transition from war to love is by means so remarkable as we might at first imagine. We quote Jack Falstaff in proof of this; or, if the reader be disposed to reject our authority, then we quote Ancient Pistol himself – both of whom we consider as the most finished specimens of heroism that ever carried a safe skin. Acres would have been a hero had he worn gloves to prevent the courage from oozing out at his palms, or not felt such a unlucky antipathy to the 'snug lying in the Abbey'; and as for Captain Bobadil, he never had an opportunity of putting his plan for vanquishing an army into practice. We fear, indeed, that neither his character, nor Ben Jonson's knowledge of human nature, is properly understood; for it certainly could not be expected that a man whose spirit glowed to encounter a whole host could, without tarnishing his dignity, if closely pressed, condescend to fight an individual. But as these remarks on courage may be felt by the reader as an invidious introduction of a subject disagreeable to him, we beg to hush it for the present, and return to the tailor.

No sooner had Neal begun to feel an inclination to matrimony than his friends knew that his principles had veered, by the change now visible in his person and deportment. They saw he had 'ratted' from courage, and joined love. Heretofore his life had been all winter, darkened by storm and hurricane. The fiercer virtues had played the devil with him; every word was thunder, every look lightning; but now all that had passed away – before he was the *fortiter in re*, at present he was the *suaviter in modo*. His existence was perfect spring – beautifully vernal. All the amiable and softer qualities began to bud about his heart; a genial warmth was diffused over him; his soul got green within him; every day was serene; and if a cloud happened to become visible, there was a roguish rainbow astride of it, on which sat a beautiful Iris that laughed down at him, and seemed to say, 'Why the Dickens, Neal, don't you marry a wife?'

Neal could not resist the *afflatus* which descended on him; an ethereal light dwelt, he thought, upon the face of nature; the colour of the cloth which he cut out from day to day was, to his enraptured eye, like the colour of Cupid's wings – all purple; his visions were worth their weight in gold; his dreams, a credit to the bed he slept on; and his feelings, like blind puppies, young, and alive to the milk of love and kindness which they drew from his heart. Most of this delight escaped the observation of the world; for Neal, like your true lover, became shy and mysterious. It is difficult to say what he resembled. No dark lantern ever had more light shut up within itself than Neal had in his soul, although his friends were not aware of it. They knew, indeed, that he had turned his back upon valour; but beyond this their knowledge did not extend.

Neal was shrewd enough to know that what he felt must be love – nothing else could distend him with happiness, until his soul felt light and bladder-like, but love. As an oyster opens when expecting the tide, so did his soul expand at the contemplation of matrimony. Labour ceased to be a trouble to him; he sang and sewed from morning to night; his hot goose no longer burned him, for his heart was as hot as his goose; the vibrations of his head at each successive stitch were no longer sad and melancholy – there was a buoyant shake of exultation in them which showed that his soul was placid and happy within him.

Endless honour be to Neal Malone for the originality with which he managed the tender sentiment! He did not, like your commonplace lovers, first discover a pretty girl, and afterwards become enamoured of her. No such thing; he had the passion prepared beforehand – cut out and made up, as it were, ready for any girl whom it might fit. This was falling in love in the abstract; and let no man condemn it without a trial, for many a long-winded argument could be urged in its defence. It is always wrong to commence business without capital, and Neal had a good stock to begin with. All we beg is, that the reader will not confound it with Platonism, which never marries; but he is at full liberty to call it Socratism, which takes unto itself a wife, and suffers accordingly.

Let no one suppose that Neal forgot the schoolmaster's kindness, or failed to be duly grateful for it. Mr O'Connor was the first person whom he consulted touching his passion. With a cheerful soul he waited on that melancholy and gentleman-like man, and in the very luxury of his heart told him that he was in love.

'In love, Neal!' said the schoolmaster. 'May I inquire with whom?'

'Wid nobody in particular yet,' replied Neal; 'but of late I'm got divilish fond o' the girls in general.'

'And do you call that being in love, Neal?' said Mr O'Connor.

'Why, what else would I call it?' returned the tailor. 'Amn't I fond of them?'

'Then it must be what is termed the Universal Passion, Neal,' observed Mr O'Connor; 'although it is the first time I have seen such an illustration of it as you present in your own person.'

'I wish you would advise me how to act,' said Neal; 'I'm as happy as a prince since I began to get fond o' them an' to think of marriage.'

The schoolmaster shook his head again, and looked rather miserable. Neal rubbed his hands with glee, and looked perfectly happy. The schoolmaster shook his head again, and looked more miserable than before. Neal's happiness also increased on the second rubbing.

Now, to tell the secret at once, Mr O'Connor would not have appeared so miserable, were it not for Neal's happiness; nor Neal so happy, were it not for Mr O'Connor's misery. It was all the result of contrast; but this you will not understand unless you be deeply read in modern novels.

Mr O'Connor, however, was a man of sense, who knew, upon this principle, that the longer he continued to shake his head the more miserable he must become and the more also would he increase Neal's happiness; but he had no intention of increasing Neal's happiness at his own expense, for, upon the same hypothesis, it would have been for Neal's interest had he remained shaking his head there and getting miserable until the day of judgment. He consequently declined giving the third shake, for he thought that plain conversation was, after all, more significant and forcible than the most eloquent nod, however badly translated.

'Neal,' said he, 'could you, by stretching your imagination, contrive to rest contented with nursing your passion in solitude, and love the sex at a distance?'

'How could I nurse and mind my business?' replied the tailor. 'I'll never nurse so as I'll have the wife; and as for 'magination, it depends upon the grain of it whether I can stretch it or not. I don't know that I ever made a coat of it in my life.'

'You don't understand me, Neal,' said the schoolmaster. 'In recommending marriage, I was only driving one evil out of you by introducing another. Do you think that if you abandoned all thoughts of a wife you would get heroic again? – that is, would you take once more to the love of fighting?'

'There is no doubt but I would,' said the tailor; 'if I miss the wife, I'll kick up such a dust as never was seen in the parish, and you're the first man that I'll kick. But now that I'm in love,' he continued, 'sure, I ought to look out for the wife.'

'Ah, Neal!' said the schoolmaster, 'you are tempting destiny. Your temerity be, with all its melancholy consequences, upon your own head.'

'Come,' said the tailor, 'it wasn't to hear you groaning to the tune of *Dhrimmindhoo*, or "The ould woman rockin' her cradle," that I came; but to know if you could help me in makin' out the wife. That's the discoorse.'

'Look at me, Neal,' said the schoolmaster, solemnly; 'I am at this moment, and have been any time for the last fifteen years, a living *caveto* against matrimony. I do not think that earth possesses such a luxury as a single, solitary life. Neal, the monks of old were happy men; they were all fat and had double chins; and, Neal, I tell you, that all fat men are in general happy. Care cannot come at them so readily as at a thin man; before it gets through the strong outworks of flesh and blood with which they are surrounded, it becomes treacherous to its original purpose, joins the cheerful spirits it meets in the system, and dances about the heart in all the madness of mirth; just like a sincere ecclesiastic who comes to lecture a good fellow against drinking, but who forgets his lecture over his cups, and is laid under the table with such success that he either never comes to finish his lecture, or comes often to be laid under the table. Look at me, Neal, how wasted, fleshless, and miserable I stand before you. You know how my garments have shrunk in, and what a solid man I was before marriage. Neal, pause, I beseech you; otherwise you stand a strong chance of becoming a nonentity like myself.'

'I don't care what I become,' said the tailor; 'I can't think that you'd be so unrasonable as to expect that any of the Malones should pass out of the world widout either bein' bate or marrid. Have reason, Mr O'Connor, an' if you can help me to the wife, I promise to take in your coat the next time for nothin'.'

'Well, then.' said Mr O'Connor, 'what would you think of the butcher's daughter, Biddy Neil? You have always had a thirst for blood, and here you may have it gratified in an innocent manner, should you ever become sanguinary again. 'Tis true, Neal, she is twice your size, and possesses three times your strength; but for that very reason, Neal, marry her if you can. Large animals are placid; and heaven preserve those bachelors whom I wish well from a small wife; 'tis such who always wield the sceptre of domestic life, and rule their husbands with a rod of iron.'

'Say no more, Mr. O'Connor,' replied the tailor; 'she's the very girl I'm in love wid, an' never fear but I'll overcome her heart if it can be done by man. Now, step over the way to my house, an' we'll have a sup on the head of it. Who's that calling?'

'Ah! Neal, I know the tones – there's a shrillness in them not to be mistaken. Farewell! I must depart – you have heard the proverb, "Those who are bound must obey." Young Jack, I presume, is

squalling, and I must either nurse him, rock the cradle, or sing comic
tunes for him, though heaven knows with what a disastrous heart I
often sing, "Begone Dull Care," the "Rakes of Newcastle," or "Peas
upon a Trencher." Neal, I say again, pause before you take this leap in
the dark. Pause, Neal, I entreat you. Farewell!'

Neal, however, was gifted with the heart of an Irishman, and
scorned caution as the characteristic of a coward. He had, as it
appeared, abandoned all design of fighting, but the courage still
adhered to him even in making love. He consequently conducted the
siege of Biddy Neil's heart with a degree of skill and valour which
would not have come amiss to Marshal Gerald at the siege of
Antwerp. Locke or Dugald Stewart, indeed, had they been cognisant
of the tailor's triumph, might have illustrated the principle on which
he succeeded – as to ourselves, we can only conjecture it. Our own
opinion is, that they were both animated with a congenial spirit.
Biddy was the very pink of pugnacity, and could throw in a body
blow, or plant a facer, with singular energy and science. Her prowess
hitherto had, we confess, been displayed only within the limited range
of domestic life; but, should she ever find it necessary to exercise it
upon a larger scale, there was no doubt whatsoever, in the opinion of
her mother, brothers and sisters, every one of whom she had suc-
cessfully subdued, that she must undoubtedly distinguish herself.
There was certainly one difficulty which the tailor had not to
encounter in the progress of his courtship: the field was his own; he
had not a rival to dispute his claim. Neither was there any opposition
given by her friends; they were, on the contrary, all anxious for the
match; and when the arrangements were concluded, Neal felt his
hand squeezed by them in succession, with an expression more
resembling condolence than joy. Neal, however, had been bred to
tailoring, and not to metaphysics; he could cut out a coat very well,
but we do not say that he could trace a principle – as what tailor,
except Jeremy Taylor, could?

There was nothing particular in the wedding. Mr O'Connor was
asked by Neal to be present at it; but he shook his head, and told him
that he had not courage to attend it, or inclination to witness any

man's sorrows but his own. He met the wedding-party by accident, and was heard to exclaim with a sigh, as they flaunted past him in gay exuberance of spirits – 'Ah, poor Neal! he is going like one of her father's cattle to the shambles! Woe is me for having suggested matrimony to the tailor! He will not long be under the necessity of saying that he "is blue-mowlded for want of a batin".' The butcheress will fell him like a Kerry ox, and I may have his blood to answer for, and his discomfiture to feel for, in addition to my own miseries.'

On the evening of the wedding-day, about the hour of ten o'clock, Neal – whose spirits were uncommonly exalted, for his heart luxuriated within him – danced with his bridesmaid; after the dance he sat beside her, and got eloquent in praise of her beauty; and it is said, too, that he whispered to her, and chucked her chin with considerable gallantry. The *tête-à-tête* continued for some time without exciting particular attention, with one exception; but that exception was worth a whole chapter of general rules. Mrs Malone rose up, then sat down again, and took off a glass of the native; she got up a second time – all the wife rushed upon her heart – she approached them, and, in a fit of the most exquisite sensibility, knocked the bridesmaid down, and gave the tailor a kick of affecting pathos upon the inexpressibles. The whole scene was a touching one on both sides. The tailor was sent on all fours to the floor; but Mrs Malone took him quietly up, put him under her arm, as one would a lap-dog, and with stately step marched away to the connubial apartment, in which everything remained very quiet for the rest of the night.

The next morning Mr O'Connor presented himself to congratulate the tailor on his happiness. Neal, as his friend shook hands with him, gave the schoolmaster's fingers a slight squeeze, such as a man gives who would gently entreat your sympathy. The schoolmaster looked at him, and thought he shook his head. Of this, however, he could not be certain; for, as he shook his own during the moment of observation, he concluded that it might be a mere mistake of the eye, or perhaps the result of a mind predisposed to be credulous on the subject of shaking heads.

We wish it were in our power to draw a veil, or curtain, or blind of some description over the remnant of the tailor's narrative that is to follow; but as it is the duty of every faithful historian to give the secret causes of appearances which the world in general do not understand, so we think it but honest to go on, impartially and faithfully, without shrinking from the responsibility that is frequently annexed to truth.

For the first three days after matrimony Neal felt like a man who had been translated to a new and more lively state of existence. He had expected, and flattered himself, that the moment this event should take place he would once more resume his heroism, and experience the pleasure of a drubbing. This determination he kept a profound secret – nor was it known until a future period, when he disclosed it to Mr O'Connor. He intended, therefore, that marriage should be nothing more than a mere parenthesis in his life – a kind of asterisk, pointing, in a note at the bottom, to this single exception in his general conduct – a *nota bene* to the spirit of a marital man, intimating that he had been peaceful only for a while. In truth, he was, during the influence of love over him, and up to the very day of his marriage, secretly as blue-moulded as ever for want of a beating. The heroic penchant lay snugly latent in his heart, unchecked and unmodified. He flattered himself that he was achieving a capital imposition upon the world at large – that he was actually hoaxing mankind in general – and that such an excellent piece of knavish tranquillity had never been perpetrated before his time.

On the first week after his marriage there chanced to be a fair in the next market-town. Neal, after breakfast, brought forward a bunch of *shillelaghs*, in order to select the best. The wife inquired the purpose of the selection, and Neal declared that he was resolved to have a fight that day, if it were to be had, he said, for 'love or money'. 'The thruth is,' he exclaimed, strutting with fortitude about the house – ' the thruth is, that I've done the whole of yez – I'm as blue-mowlded as ever for want of a batin'.'

'Don't go,' said the wife.

'I *will* go,' said Neal, with vehemence – 'I'll go if the whole parish was to go to prevint me.'

In about another half-hour Neal sat down quietly to his business, instead of going to the fair.

Much ingenious speculation might be indulged in upon this abrupt termination to the tailor's most formidable resolution; but, for our own part, we will prefer going on with the narrative, leaving the reader at liberty to solve the mystery as he pleases. In the meantime, we say this much – let those who cannot make it out carry it to their tailor; it is a tailor's mystery, and no one has so good a right to understand it – except, perhaps, a tailor's wife.

At the period of his matrimony Neal had become as plump and as stout as he ever was known to be in his plumpest and stoutest days. He and the schoolmaster had been very intimate about this time; but we know not how it happened that soon afterwards he felt a modest, bride-like reluctance in meeting with that afflicted gentleman. As the eve of his union approached, he was in the habit, during the schoolmaster's visits to his workshop, of alluding, in rather a sarcastic tone, considering the unthriving appearance of his friend, to the increasing lustiness of his person. Nay, he has often leaped up from his lap-board, and, in the strong spirit of exultation, thrust out his leg in attestation of his assertion, slapping it, moreover, with a loud laugh of triumph, that sounded like a knell to the happiness of his emaciated acquaintance. The schoolmaster's philosophy, however, unlike his flesh, never departed from him; his usual observation was, 'Neal, we are both receding from the same point; you increase in flesh, whilst I, heaven help me, am fast diminishing.'

The tailor received these remarks with very boisterous mirth, whilst Mr O'Connor simply shook his head, and looked sadly upon his limbs, now shrouded in a superfluity of garments, somewhat resembling a slender thread of water in a shallow summer stream, nearly wasted away, and surrounded by an unproportionate extent of channel.

The fourth month after the marriage arrived. Neal one day, near its close, began to dress himself in his best apparel. Even then, when buttoning his waistcoat, he shook his head after the manner of Mr

O'Connor, and made observations upon the great extent to which it over-folded him.

'Well,' thought he, with a sigh – 'this waistcoat certainly did fit me to a T; but it's wondherful to think how – cloth stretches.'

'Neal,' said the wife, on perceiving him dressed, 'where are you bound for?'

'Faith, for life,' replied Neal, with a mitigated swagger; 'and I'd as soon, if it had been the will of Provid–'

He paused.

'Where are you going?' asked the wife a second time.

'Why,' he answered, 'only to the dance at Jemmy Connolly's; I'll be back early.'

'Don't go,' said the wife.

'I'll go,' said Neal, 'if the whole counthry was to prevint me. Thunder an' lightnin', woman, who am I?' he exclaimed, in a loud but rather infirm voice – 'amn't I Neal Malone, that never met a man who'd fight him! – Neal Malone, that was never beat by MAN! Why, tare-an'-ounze, woman! – whoo! – I'll get enraged some time, an' play the divil! Who's afeard, I say?'

'Don't go,' added the wife a third time, giving Neal a significant look in the face.

In about another half-hour Neal sat down quietly to his business, instead of going to the dance!

Neal now turned himself, like many a sage in similar circumstances, to philosophy – that is to say, he began to shake his head upon principle, after the manner of the schoolmaster. He would, indeed, have preferred the bottle upon principle; but there was no getting at the bottle, except through the wife, and it so happened that by the time it reached him there was little consolation left in it. Neal bore all in silence; for silence, his friend had often told him, was a proof of wisdom.

Soon after this Neal one evening met Mr O'Connor by chance upon a plank which crossed a river. This plank was only a foot in breadth, so that no two individuals could pass each other upon it. We cannot find words in which to express the dismay of both on finding that they absolutely glided past one another without collision.

Both paused, and surveyed each other solemnly; but the astonishment was all on the side of Mr O'Connor.

'Neal,' said the schoolmaster, 'by all the household gods, I conjure you to speak, that I may be assured you live!'

The ghost of a blush crossed the churchyard visage of the tailor.

'Oh!' he exclaimed, 'why the devil did you tempt me to marry a wife?'

'Neal,' said his friend, 'answer me in the most solemn manner possible; throw into your countenance all the gravity you can assume; speak as if you were under the hands of the hangman, with the rope about your neck, for the question is, indeed, a trying one which I am about to put – are you still 'blue-mowlded for want of beating'?'

The tailor collected himself to make a reply; he put one leg out – the very leg which he used to show in triumph to his friend; but, alas, how dwindled! He opened his waistcoat, and lapped it round him, until he looked like a weasel on its hind legs. He then raised himself up on his tip-toes, and, in an awful whisper, replied, 'No!!! the devil a bit I'm blue-mowlded for want of a batin'.'

The schoolmaster shook his head in his own miserable manner; but, alas! he soon perceived that the tailor was as great an adept at shaking the head as himself. Nay, he saw that there was a calamitous refinement, a delicacy of shake, in the tailor's vibrations, which gave to his own nod a very commonplace character.

The next day the tailor took in his clothes, and from time to time continued to adjust them to the dimensions of his shrinking person. The schoolmaster and he, whenever they could steal a moment, met and sympathized together. Mr O'Connor, however, bore up somewhat better than Neal. The latter was subdued in heart and in spirit; thoroughly, completely, and intensely vanquished. His features became sharpened by misery, for a termagant wife is the whetstone on which all the calamities of a hen-pecked husband are painted by the devil. He no longer strutted as he was wont to do; he no longer carried a cudgel as if he wished to wage a universal battle with mankind. He was now a married man. Sneakingly and with a cowardly crawl did he creep along as if every step brought him nearer to the gallows. The schoolmaster's march of misery was far slower that Neal's: the latter distanced him. Before three years passed he had shrunk up so much that he could not walk abroad of a windy day without carrying weights in his pockets to keep him firm on the earth, which he once trod with the step of a giant. He again sought the schoolmaster, with whom, indeed, he associated as much as possible. Here he felt certain of receiving sympathy; nor was he disappointed. That worthy but miserable man and Neal often retired beyond the hearing of their respective wives, and supported each other by every argument in their power. Often have they been heard, in the dusk of evening, singing behind a remote hedge that melancholy ditty, 'Let us both be unhappy together'; which rose upon the twilight breeze with a cautious quaver of sorrow truly heartrending and lugubrious.

'Neal,' said Mr O'Connor, on one of these occasions, 'here is a book which I recommend to your perusal; it is called *The Afflicted Man's Companion*; try if you cannot glean some consolation out of it.'

'Faith,' said Neal, 'I'm for ever obliged to you, but I don't want it. I've had *The Afflicted Man's Companion* too long, and divil an atom of consolation I can get out of it. I have one o' them, I tell you; but be me sowl, I'll not undhertake a pair o' them. The very name's enough for me.' They then separated.

The tailor's *vis vite* must have been powerful, or he would have died. In two years more his friends could not distinguish him from his own shadow – a circumstance which was of great inconvenience to him. Several grasped at the hand of the shadow instead of his; and one man was near paying it five-and-sixpence for making a pair of small-clothes. Neal, it is true, undeceived him with some trouble, but candidly admitted that he was not able to carry home the money. It was difficult, indeed, for the poor tailor to bear what he felt; it is true he bore it as long as he could; but at length he came suicidal, and often had thoughts of 'making his own quietus with his bare bodkin'. After many deliberations and afflictions he ultimately made the attempt; but, alas! he found that the blood of the Malones refused to flow upon so ignominious an occasion. So he solved the phenomenon; although the truth was, that his blood was not 'i' the vein' for 't; none was to be had. What, then, was to be done? He resolved to get rid of life by some process; and the next that occurred to him was hanging. In a solemn spirit he prepared a selvage, and suspended himself from the rafter of his workshop; but here another disappointment awaited him – he would not hang. Such was his want of gravity that his own weight proved insufficient to occasion his death by mere suspension. His third attempt was at drowning, but he was too light to sink; all the elements – all his own energies joined themselves, he thought, in a wicked conspiracy to save his life. Having thus tried every avenue to destruction, and failed in all, he felt like a man doomed to live for ever. Henceforward he shrunk and shrivelled by slow degrees, until in the course of time he became so attenuated that the grossness of human vision could no longer reach him.

This, however, could not last always. Though still alive, he was to all intents and purposes imperceptible. He could now only be heard; he was reduced to a mere essence – the very echo of human existence, *vox et praeterea nihil*. It is true the schoolmaster asserted that he occasionally caught passing glimpses of him; but that was because he had been himself nearly spiritualized by affliction, and his visual ray purged in the furnace of domestic tribulation. By and by Neal's voice lessened, got fainter and more indistinct, until at length nothing but a doubtful murmur could be heard, which ultimately could scarcely be distinguished from a ringing in his ears.

Such was the awful and mysterious fate of the tailor, who, as a hero, could not, of course, die; he merely dissolved like an icicle, wasted into immateriality, and finally melted away beyond the perception of mortal sense. Mr O'Connor is still living, and once more in the fulness of perfect health and strength. His wife, however, we may as well hint, has been dead more than two years.

# WILLIAM CARLETON

## Wildgoose Lodge

I HAD read the anonymous summons, but, from its general import, I
believed it to be one of those special meetings convened for some
purpose affecting the usual objects and proceedings of the body; at
least, the terms in which it was conveyed to me had nothing extraordinary or mysterious in them beyond the simple fact that it was not
to be a general but a select meeting. This mark of confidence flattered
me, and I determined to attend punctually. I was, it was true, desired
to keep the circumstance entirely to myself; but there was nothing
startling in this, for I had often received summonses of a similar nature.
I therefore resolved to attend, according to the letter of my instructions, 'on the next night, at the solemn hour of midnight, to deliberate
and act upon such matters as should then and there be submitted to
my consideration'. The morning after I received this message, I arose
and resumed my usual occupations; but from whatever cause it may
have proceeded, I felt a sense of approaching evil hang heavily upon
me. The beats of my pulse were languid, and an indefinable feeling of
anxiety pervaded my whole spirit; even my face was pale, and my eye
so heavy that my father and brothers concluded me to be ill; an
opinion which I thought at the time to be correct, for I felt exactly
that kind of depression which precedes a severe fever. I could not
understand what I experienced; nor can I yet, except by supposing
that there is in human nature some mysterious faculty by which, in

coming calamities, the dread of some fearful evil is anticipated, and that it is possible to catch a dark presentiment of the sensations which they subsequently produce. For my part, I can neither analyse nor define it; but on that day I knew it by painful experience, and so have a thousand others in similar circumstances.

It was about the middle of winter. The day was gloomy and tempestuous almost beyond any other I remember; dark clouds rolled over the hills about me, and a close, sleet-like rain fell in slanting drifts that chased each other rapidly towards the earth on the course of the blast. The outlying cattle sought the closest and calmest corners of the fields for shelter; the trees and young groves were tossed about, for the wind was so unusually high that it swept in hollow gusts through them with that hoarse murmur which deepens so powerfully on the mind the sense of dreariness and desolation.

As the shades of night fell, the storm, if possible, increased. The moon was half gone, and only a few stars were visible by glimpses, as a rush of wind left a temporary opening in the sky. I had determined, if the storm should not abate, to incur any penalty rather than attend the meeting; but the appointed hour was distant, and I resolved to be decided by the future state of the night.

Ten o'clock came, but still there was no change; eleven passed, and on opening the door to observe if there were any likelihood of its clearing up, a blast of wind, mingled with rain, nearly blew me off my feet. At length it was approaching to the hour of midnight; and on examining a third time, I found it had calmed a little, and no longer rained.

I instantly got my oak stick, muffled myself in my greatcoat, strapped my hat about my ears, and as the place of meeting was only a quarter of a mile distant, I presently set out.

The appearance of the heavens was lowering and angry, particularly in that point where the light of the moon fell against the clouds from a seeming chasm in them, through which alone she was visible. The edges of this chasm were faintly bronzed, but the dense body of the masses that hung piled on each side of her was black and impenetrable to sight. In no other point of the heavens was there any part of the sky visible – a deep veil of clouds overhung the horizon – yet was the light sufficient to give occasional glimpses of the rapid shifting which took place in this dark canopy, and of the tempestuous agitation with which the midnight storm swept to and fro beneath it.

At length I arrived at a long slated house situated in a solitary part of the neighbourhood; a little below it ran a small stream, which was now swollen above its banks, and rushing with mimic roar over the flat meadows beside it. The appearance of the bare slated building in such a night was particularly sombre; and to those, like me, who knew the purpose to which it was usually devoted, it was, or ought to have been, peculiarly so. There it stood, silent and gloomy, without any appearance of human life or enjoyment about or within it. As I approached, the moon once more had broken out of the clouds, and shone dimly upon the wet, glittering slates and windows with a death-like lustre, that gradually faded away as I left the point of observation and entered the folding-door. It was the parish chapel.

The scene which presented itself here was in keeping not only with the external appearance of the house, but with the darkness, the storm, and the hour, which was now a little after midnight. About eighty persons were sitting in dead silence upon the circular steps of the altar. They did not seem to move; and as I entered and advanced, the echo of my footsteps rang through the building with a lonely distinctness, which added to the solemnity and mystery of the circumstances about me. The windows were secured with shutters on the inside; and on the altar a candle was lighted, which burned dimly amid the surrounding darkness, and lengthened the shadow of the altar itself, and those of six or seven persons who stood on its upper steps, until they mingled in the obscurity which shrouded the lower end of the chapel. The faces of the men who sat on the altar-steps were not distinctly visible, yet their prominent and more characteristic features were in sufficient relief, and I observed that some of the most malignant and reckless spirits in the parish were assembled. In the eyes of those who stood at the altar, and whom I knew to be invested with authority over the others, I could perceive gleams of some latent and ferocious purpose, kindled, as I soon observed, into a fiercer expression of

vengeance by the additional excitement of ardent spirits, with which
they had stimulated themselves to a point of determination that
mocked at the apprehension of all future responsibility, either in this
world or the next.

The welcome which I received on joining them was far different
from the boisterous good-humour that used to mark our greetings on
other occasions: just a nod of the head from this or that person, on the
part of those who sat, with a *ghud dhemur tha thu?* in a suppressed voice,
even below a common whisper; but from the standing group, who
were evidently the projectors of the enterprise, I received a convulsive
grasp of the hand, accompanied by a fierce and desperate look, that
seemed to search my eye and countenance, to try if I were a person
not likely to shrink from whatever they had resolved to execute. It is
surprising to think of the powerful expression which a moment of
intense interest or great danger is capable of giving to the eye, the
features, and the slightest actions, especially in those whose station in
society does not require them to constrain nature, by the force of
social courtesies, into habits that conceal their natural emotions. None
of the standing group spoke; but as each of them wrung my hand in
silence, his eye was fixed on mine with an expression of drunken
confidence and secrecy, and an insolent determination not to be
gainsaid without peril. If looks could be translated with certainty, they
seemed to say, 'We are bound upon a project of vengeance, and if you
do not join us, remember that we can revenge.' Along with this grasp
they did not forget to remind me of the common bond by which we
were united, for each man gave me the secret grip of Ribbonism[1] in a
manner that made the joints of my fingers ache for some minutes
afterwards.

There was one present, however – the highest in authority – whose
actions and demeanour were calm and unexcited. He seemed to
labour under no unusual influence whatever, but evinced a serenity so
placid and philosophical that I attributed the silence of the sitting

[1] Ribbonism was a rural protest movement – a secret society, anti-Protestant and
nationalist. Its many arcane rituals emphasized solidarity and loyalty to 'the cause',
however vague. (Editor's note)

group, and the restraint which curbed in the outbreaking passions of those who stood, entirely to his presence. He was a schoolmaster, who taught his daily school in that chapel, and acted also, on Sunday, in the capacity of clerk to the priest – an excellent and amiable old man, who knew little of his illegal connections and atrocious conduct.

When the ceremonies of brotherly recognition and friendship were past, the captain (by which title I shall designate the last-mentioned person) stooped, and raising a jar of whiskey on the corner of the altar, held a wine-glass to its neck, which he filled, and, with a calm nod, handed it to me to drink. I shrunk back, with an instinctive horror at the profaneness of such an act, in the house, and on the altar, of God, and peremptorily refused to taste the proffered draught. He smiled mildly at what he considered my superstition, and added quietly, and in a low voice, 'You'll be wantin' it, I'm thinkin', afther the wettin' you got.'

'Wet or dry,' said I –

'Stop, man!' he replied, in the same tone; 'spake low. But why wouldn't you take the whiskey? Sure, there's as holy people to the fore as you; didn't they all take it? An' I wish we may never do worse nor dhrink a harmless glass o' whiskey to keep the cowld out, any-way.'

'Well,' said I, 'I'll jist trust to God and the consequences for the cowld, Paddy, *ma bouchal*; but a blessed dhrop of it won't be crossin' my lips, *avick*; so no more *gosther* about it – dhrink it yourself, if you like. Maybe you want it as much as I do; wherein I've the patthern of a good big coat upon me – so thick, your sowl, that if it was rainin' bullocks, a dhrop wouldn't get under the nap of it.'

He gave a calm but keen glance at me as I spoke.

'Well, Jim,' said he, 'it's a good comrade you've got for the weather that's in it; but, in the meantime, to set you a dacent patthern, I'll just take this myself;' saying which, with the jar still upon its side, and the forefinger of his left hand in its neck, he swallowed the spirits. 'It's the first I dhrank tonight,' he added; 'nor would I dhrink it now, only to show you that I've heart and spirit to do the thing that we're bound an' sworn to, when the proper time comes;' after which he laid down the glass, and turned up the jar, with much coolness, upon the altar.

During our conversation those who had been summoned to this mysterious meeting were pouring in fast; and as each person approached the altar he received from one to two or three glasses of whiskey, according as he chose to limit himself; but, to do them justice, there were not a few of those present who, in spite of their own desire, and the captain's express invitation, refused to taste it in the house of God's worship. Such, however, as were scrupulous he afterwards recommended to take it on the outside of the chapel door, which they did, as by that means the sacrilege of the act was supposed to be evaded.

About one o'clock they were all assembled except six; at least, so the captain asserted, on looking at a written paper.

'Now, boys,' said he, in the same low voice, 'we are all present except the thraitors whose names I am goin' to read to you; not that we are to count thim thraitors till we know whether or not it was in their power to come. Anyhow, the night's terrible; but, boys, you're to know that neither fire, nor wather is to prevint yees when duly summoned to attind a meeting – particularly whin the summons is widout a name, as you have been told that there is always something of consequence to be done thin.'

He then read out the names of those who were absent, in order that the real cause of their absence might be ascertained, declaring that they would be dealt with accordingly. After this, with his usual caution, he shut and bolted the door, and having put the key in his pocket, ascended the steps of the altar, and for some time traversed the little platform from which the priest usually addresses the congregation.

Until this night I have never contemplated the man's countenance with any particular interest; but as he walked the platform I had an opportunity of observing him more closely. He was slight in person, apparently not thirty, and, on a first view, appeared to have nothing remarkable in his dress or features. I, however, was not the only person whose eyes were fixed upon him at that moment; in fact, every one present observed him with equal interest, for hitherto he had kept the

object of the meeting perfectly secret, and of course we all felt anxious
to know it. It was while he traversed the platform that I scrutinized his
features with a hope, if possible, to glean from them some evidence of
what was passing within him. I could, however, mark but little, and
that little was at first rather from the intelligence which seemed to
subsist between him and those whom I have already mentioned as
standing against the altar, than from any indication of his own. Their
gleaming eyes were fixed upon him with an intensity of savage and
demon-like hope which blazed out in flashes of malignant triumph, as,
upon turning, he threw a cool but rapid glance at them, to intimate
the progress he was making in the subject to which he devoted the
undivided energies of his mind. But in the course of his meditation I
could observe, on one or two occasions, a dark shade come over his
countenance that contracted his brow into a deep furrow, and it was
then, for the first time, that I saw the Satanic expression of which his
face, by a very slight motion of its muscles, was capable. His hands,
during this silence, closed and opened convulsively; his eyes shot out
two or three baleful glances, first to his confederates, and afterwards
vacantly into the deep gloom of the lower part of the chapel; his teeth
ground against each other like those of a man whose revenge burns to
reach a distant enemy; and finally, after having wound himself up to a
certain determination, his features relapsed into their original calm and
undisturbed expression.

At this moment a loud laugh, having something supernatural in it,
rang out wildly from the darkness of the chapel: he stopped, and
putting his open hand over his brows, peered down into the gloom,
and said calmly, in Irish, 'Bee dhu husth; ha nihl anam inh – Hold your
tongue; it is not yet the time.'

Every eye was now directed to the same spot, but in consequence
of its distance from the dim light on the altar, none could perceive the
person from whom the laugh proceeded. It was by this time near two
o'clock in the morning.

He now stood for a few moments on the platform, and his chest
heaved with a depth of anxiety equal to the difficulty of the design he
wished to accomplish.

'Brothers,' said he – 'for we are all brothers – sworn upon all that's blessed an' holy to obey whatever them that's over us, manin' among ourselves, wishes us to do – are you now ready, in the name of God, upon whose althar I stand, to fulfil yer oaths?'

The words were scarcely uttered, when those who had stood beside the altar during the night sprang from their places, and descending its steps rapidly, turned round, and raising their arms, exclaimed, 'By all that's sacred an' holy, we're willin'!'

In the meantime, those who sat upon the steps of the altar instantly rose, and following the example of those who had just spoken, exclaimed after them, 'To be sure – by all that's sacred an' holy, we're willin'!'

'Now, boys,' said the captain, 'aren't yees big fools for your pains? An' one of yees doesn't know what I mane.'

'You're our captain,' said one of those who had stood at the altar, 'an' has yer ordhers from higher quarthers; of coorse, whatever ye command upon us we're bound to obey you in.'

'Well,' said he, smiling, 'I only wanted to thry yees; an' by the oath yees tuck, there's not a captain in the country has as good a right to be proud of his min as I have. Well, yees won't rue it, maybe, when the right time comes; and for that same rason every one of yees must have a glass from the jar – thim that won't dhrink it in the chapel can dhrink it widout; an' here goes to open the door for them.'

He then distributed another glass to every man who would accept it, and brought the jar afterwards to the chapel door, to satisfy the scruples of those who would not drink within. When this was performed, and all duly excited, he proceeded:

'Now, brothers, you are solemnly sworn to obey me, and I'm sure there's no thraithur here that ud parjure himself for a thrifle; but I'm sworn to obey them that's above me, manin' still among ourselves; an' to show you that I don't scruple to do it, here goes!'

He then turned round, and taking the Missal between his hands, placed in upon the altar. Hitherto every word was uttered in a low, precautionary tone; but on grasping the book, he again turned round, and looking upon his confederates with the same Satanic expression which marked his countenance before, exclaimed, in a voice of deep determination:

'By this sacred an' holy book of God, I will perform the action which we have met this night to accomplish, be that what it may; an' this I swear upon God's book an' God's althar!'

On concluding he struck the book violently with his open hand.

At this moment the candle which burned before him went suddenly out, and the chapel was wrapped in pitchy darkness; the sound as if of rushing wings fell upon our ears; and fifty voices dwelt upon the last words of his oath with wild and supernatural tones, that seemed to echo and to mock what he had sworn. There was a pause, and an exclamation of horror from all present; but the captain was too cool and steady to be disconcerted. He immediately groped about until he got the candle, and proceeding calmly to a remote corner of the chapel, took up a half-burned turf which lay there, and after some trouble, succeeded in lighting it again. He then explained what had taken place; which indeed was easily done, as the candle happened to be extinguished by a pigeon which sat directly above it. The chapel, I should have observed, was at this time, like many country chapels, unfinished inside, and the pigeons of a neighbouring dovecote had built nests among the rafters of the unceiled roof; which circumstance also explained the rushing of the wings, for the birds had been affrighted by the sudden loudness of the noise. The mocking voices were nothing but the echoes, rendered naturally more awful by the scene, the mysterious object of the meeting, and the solemn hour of the night.

When the candle was again lighted, and these startling circumstances accounted for, the persons whose vengeance had been deepening more and more during the night rushed to the altar in a body, where each, in a voice trembling with passionate eagerness, repeated the oath; and as every word was pronounced, the same echoes heightened the wildness of the horrible ceremony by their long and unearthly tones. The countenances of these human tigers were livid with suppressed rage; their knit brows, compressed lips, and kindled

eyes fell under the dim light of the taper with an expression calculated
to sicken any heart not absolutely diabolical.

As soon as this dreadful rite was completed, we were again startled
by several loud bursts of laughter, which proceeded from the lower
darkness of the chapel; and the captain, on hearing them, turned to the
place, and reflecting for a moment, said in Irish, 'Gutsho nish, avohelhee
– Come hither now, boys.'

A rush immediately took place from the corner in which they had
secreted themselves all the night; and seven men appeared, whom we
instantly recognized as brothers and cousins of certain persons who
had been convicted some time before for breaking into the house of
an honest poor man in the neighbourhood, from whom, after having
treated him with barbarous violence, they took away such firearms as
he kept for his own protection.

It was evidently not the captain's intention to have produced these
persons until the oath should have been generally taken; but the
exulting mirth with which they enjoyed the success of his scheme
betrayed them, and put him to the necessity of bringing them forward
somewhat before the concerted moment.

The scene which now took place was beyond all power of
description; peals of wild, fiend-like yells rang through the chapel, as
the party which stood on the altar, and that which had crouched in the
darkness, met; wringing of hands, leaping in triumph, striking of sticks
and firearms against the ground and the altar itself, dancing and
cracking of fingers, marked the triumph of some hellish determination. Even the captain for a time was unable to restrain their fury; but
at length he mounted the platform before the altar once more, and,
with a stamp of his foot, recalled their attention to himself and the
matter in hand.

'Boys,' said he, 'enough of this, and too much; an' well for us it is
that the chapel is in a lonely place, or our foolish noise might do us no
good. Let thim that swore so manfully jist now stand a one side, till the
rest kiss the book, one by one.'

The proceedings, however, had by this time taken too fearful a
shape for even the captain to compel them to a blindfold oath. The

first man he called flatly refused to answer until he should hear the nature of the service that was required. This was echoed by the remainder, who, taking courage from the firmness of this person, declared generally that until they first knew the business they were to execute none of them would take the oath. The captain's lip quivered slightly, and his brow again became knit with the same hellish expression which I have remarked gave him so much the appearance of an embodied fiend; but this speedily passed away, and was succeeded by a malignant sneer, in which lurked, if there ever did in a sneer, 'a laughing devil', calmly, determinedly atrocious.

'It wasn't worth yer whiles to refuse the oath,' said he mildly; 'for the truth is, I had next to nothing for yees to do. Not a hand, maybe, would have to rise; only jist to look on; an' if any resistance would be made, to show yourselves; yer numbers would soon make them see that resistance would be no use whatever in the present case. At all evints, the oath of secrecy must be taken, or woe be to him that will refuse that; he won't know the day, nor the hour, nor the minute when he'll be made a spatchcock ov.'

He then turned round, and placing his right hand on the Missal, swore, 'In the presence of God, and before His holy altar, that whatever might take place that night he would keep secret from man or mortal, except the priest, and that neither bribery, nor imprisonment, nor death would wring it from his heart.'

Having done this, he again struck the book violently, as if to confirm the energy with which he swore, and then calmly descending the steps, stood with a serene countenance, like a man conscious of having performed a good action. As this oath did not pledge those who refused to take the other to the perpetration of any specific crime, it was readily taken by all present. Preparations were then made to execute what was intended; the half-burned turf was placed in a little pot; another glass of whiskey was distributed; and the door being locked by the captain, who kept the key as parish clerk and master, the crowd departed silently from the chapel.

The moment those who lay in the darkness during the night made their appearance at the altar, we knew at once the persons we were to visit; for, as I said before, they were related to the miscreants whom one of those persons had convicted, in consequence of their midnight attack upon himself and his family. The captain's object in keeping them unseen was that those present, not being aware of the duty about to be imposed on them, might have less hesitation about swearing to its fulfilment. Our conjectures were correct, for on leaving the chapel we directed our steps to the house in which this devoted man resided.

The night was still stormy, but without rain; it was rather dark, too, though not so as to prevent us from seeing the clouds careering swiftly through the air. The dense curtain which had overhung and obscured the horizon was now broken, and large sections of the sky were clear, and thinly studded with stars that looked dim and watery, as did indeed the whole firmament; for in some places black clouds were still visible, threatening a continuance of tempestuous weather. The road appeared washed and gravelly; every dyke was full of yellow water, and every little rivulet and larger stream dashed its hoarse music in our ears; every blast, too, was cold, fierce, and wintry, sometimes driving us back to a standstill, and again, when a turn in the road would bring it in our backs, whirling us along for a few steps with involuntary rapidity. At length the fated dwelling became visible, and a short consultation was held in a sheltered place between the captain and the two parties who seemed so eager for its destruction. The firearms were now loaded, and their bayonets and short pikes, the latter shod and pointed with iron, were also got ready. The live coal which was brought in the small pot had become extinguished; but to remedy this, two or three persons from a remote part of the county entered a cabin on the wayside, and under pretence of lighting their own and their comrades' pipes, procured a coal of fire – for so they called a lighted turf. From the time we left the chapel until this moment a profound silence had been maintained; a circumstance which, when I considered the number of persons present, and the mysterious and dreaded object of their journey, had a most appalling effect upon my spirits.

At length we arrived within fifty perches of the house, walking in a compact body, and with as little noise as possible; but it seemed as if the very elements had conspired to frustrate our design, for on advancing within the shade of the farm hedge, two or three persons found themselves up to the middle in water, and on stooping to ascertain more accurately the state of the place, we could see nothing but one immense sheet of it, spread like a lake over the meadows which surrounded the spot we wished to reach.

Fatal night! The very recollection of it, when associated with the fearful tempests of the elements, grows, if that were possible, yet more wild and revolting. Had we been engaged in any innocent or bene-volent enterprise, there was something in our situation just then that had a touch of interest in it to a mind imbued with a relish for the savage beauties of nature. There we stood, about a hundred and thirty in number, our dark forms bent forward, peering into the dusky expanse of water, with its dim gleams of reflected light, broken by the weltering of the mimic waves into ten thousand fragments; whilst the few stars that overhung it in the firmament appeared to shoot through it in broken lines, and to be multiplied fifty-fold in the gloomy mirror on which we gazed.

Over us was a stormy sky, and around us a darkness through which we could only distinguish, in outline, the nearest objects, whilst the wind swept strongly and dismally upon us. When it was discovered that the common pathway to the house was inundated, we were about to abandon our object and return home. The captain, however, stooped down low for a moment, and almost closing his eyes, looked along the surface of the waters, and then raising himself very calmly, said, in his usual quiet tone, 'Yees needn't go back, boys; I've found a way; jist follow me.'

He immediately took a more circuitous direction, by which we reached a causeway that had been raised for the purpose of giving a free passage to and from the house during such inundations as the present. Along this we had advanced more than half way, when we discovered a breach in it, which, as afterwards appeared, had that night been made by the strength of the flood. This, by means of our sticks and pikes, we found to be about three feet deep and eight yards broad.

Again we were at a loss how to proceed, when the fertile brain of the captain devised a method of crossing it.

'Boys,' said he, 'of coorse you've all played at leap-frog; very well, strip and go in, a dozen of you, lean one upon the back of another from this to the opposite bank, where one must stand facing the outside man, both their shoulders agin one another, that the outside man may be supported. Then we can creep over you, an' a dacent bridge you'll be, anyway.'

This was the work of only a few minutes, and in less than ten we were all safely over.

Merciful heaven! how I sicken at the recollection of what is to follow! On reaching the dry bank, we proceeded instantly, and in profound silence, to the house. The captain divided us into companies, and then assigned to each division its proper station. The two parties who had been so vindictive all the night he kept about himself; for of those who were present they only were in his confidence, and knew his nefarious purpose – their number was about fifteen. Having made these dispositions, he, at the head of about five of them, approached the house on the windy side, for the fiend possessed a coolness which enabled him to seize upon every possible advantage. That he had combustibles about him was evident, for in less than fifteen minutes nearly one-half of the house was enveloped in flames. On seeing this, the others rushed over to the spot where he and his gang were standing, and remonstrated earnestly, but in vain. The flames now burst forth with renewed violence, and as they flung their strong light upon the faces of the foremost group, I think hell itself could hardly present anything more Satanic than their countenances, now worked up into a paroxysm of infernal triumph at their own revenge. The captain's look had lost all of its calmness, every feature started out into distinct malignity; the curve in his brow was deep, and ran up to the root of the hair, dividing his face into two segments, that did not seem to have been designed for each other. His lips were half open, and the corners of his mouth a little brought back on each side, like those of a man expressing intense hatred and triumph over an enemy who is in the death-struggle under his grasp. His eyes blazed from beneath his knit eyebrows with a fire that seemed to be lighted up in the infernal pit itself. It is unnecessary and only painful to describe the rest of his gang. Demons might have been proud of such horrible visages as they exhibited; for they worked under all the power of hatred, revenge, and joy; and these passions blended into one terrible scowl, enough almost to blast any human eye that would venture to look upon it.

When the others attempted to intercede for the lives of the inmates, there were at least fifteen guns and pistols levelled at them.

'Another word,' said the captain, 'an' you're a corpse where you stand, or the first man who will dare to spake for them. No, no, it wasn't to spare them we came here. "No mercy" is the password for the night, an' by the sacred oath I swore beyant in the chapel, any one among yees that will attempt to show it will find none at my hand. Surround the house, boys, I tell ye, I hear them stirring. "No quarther – no mercy" is the ordher of the night.'

Such was his command over these misguided creatures, that in an instant there was a ring round the house to prevent the escape of the unhappy inmates, should the raging element give them time to attempt it; for none present durst withdraw themselves from the scene, not only from an apprehension of the captain's present vengeance or that of his gang, but because they knew that, even had they then escaped, an early and certain death awaited them from a quarter against which they had no means of defence. The hour now was about half past two o'clock. Scarcely had the last words escaped from the captain's lips, when one of the windows of the house was broken, and a human head, having the hair in a blaze, was descried, apparently a woman's, if one might judge by the profusion of burning tresses, and the softness of the tones, notwithstanding that it called, or rather shrieked, aloud for help and mercy. The only reply to this was the whoop from the captain and his gang of 'No mercy – no mercy!' and that instant the former and one of the latter rushed to the spot, and ere the action could be perceived, the head was transfixed with a bayonet and a pike, both having entered it together. The word mercy was divided in her mouth; a short silence ensued; the head hung down on the window, but was instantly tossed back into the flames!

This action occasioned a cry of horror from all present, except the gang and their leader, which startled and enraged the latter so much that he ran towards one of them, and had his bayonet, now reeking with the blood of its innocent victim, raised to plunge it in his body, when, dropping the point, he said in a piercing whisper that hissed in the ears of all, 'It's no use now, you know; if one's to hang, all will hang; so our safest way, you persave, is to lave none of them to tell the story. Ye may go now, if you wish; but it won't save a hair of your heads. You cowardly set! I knew if I had tould yees the sport, that none of yees, except my own boys, would come, so I jist played a thrick upon you; but remimber what you are sworn to, and stand to the oath ye tuck.'

Unhappily, notwithstanding the wetness of the preceding weather, the materials of the house were extremely combustible; the whole dwelling was now one body of glowing flame; yet the shouts and shrieks within rose awfully above its crackling, and the voice of the storm, for the wind once more blew in gusts and with great violence. The doors and windows were all torn open, and such of those within as had escaped the flames rushed towards them, for the purpose of further escape, and of claiming mercy at the hands of their destroyers; but whenever they appeared, the unearthly cry of 'No mercy' rung upon their ears for a moment, and for a moment only, for they were flung back at the points of the weapons which the demons had brought with them to make the work of vengeance more certain.

As yet there were many persons in the house whose cry for life was strong as despair, and who clung to it with all the awakened powers of reason and instinct. The ear of man could hear nothing so strongly calculated to stifle the demon of cruelty and revenge within him as the long and wailing shrieks which rose beyond the elements in tones that were carried off rapidly upon the blast, until they died away in the darkness that lay behind the surrounding hills. Had not the house been in a solitary situation, and the hour the dead of night, any person sleeping within a moderate distance must have heard them, for such a cry of sorrow rising into a yell of despair was almost sufficient to have awakened the dead. It was lost, however, upon the hearts and ears that heard it; to them – though, in justice be it said, to only comparatively a few of them – it was as delightful as the tones of soft and entrancing music.

The claims of the surviving sufferers were now modified: they supplicated merely to suffer death by the weapons of their enemies; they were willing to bear that, provided they should be allowed to escape from the flames; but no – the horrors of the conflagration were calmly and malignantly gloried in by their merciless assassins, who deliberately flung them back into all their tortures. In the course of a few minutes a man appeared upon the side-wall of the house, nearly naked; his figure, as he stood against the sky in horrible relief, was so finished a picture of woe-begone agony and supplication that it is yet as distinct in my memory as if I were again present at the scene. Every muscle, now in motion by the powerful agitation of his sufferings, stood out upon his limbs and neck, giving him an appearance of desperate strength, to which by this time he must have been wrought up; the perspiration poured from his frame, and the veins and arteries of his neck were inflated to a surprising thickness. Every moment he looked down into the flames which were rising to where he stood; and as he looked, the indescribable horror which flitted over his features might have worked upon the devil himself to relent. His words were few.

'My child,' said he, 'is still safe; she is an infant, a young crathur that never harmed you nor any one – she is still safe. Your mothers, your wives, have young innocent childher like it. Oh, spare her! – think for a moment that it's one of your own! – spare it, as you hope to meet a just God; or if you don't, in mercy shoot me first – put an end to me before I see her burned!'

The captain approached him coolly and deliberately. 'You'll prosecute no one now, you bloody informer,' said he; 'you'll convict no more boys for takin' an ould gun an' pistol from you, or for givin' you a neighbourly knock or two into the bargain.'

Just then, from a window opposite him, proceeded the shrieks of a woman, who appeared at it with the infant in her arms. She herself was almost scorched to death; but with the presence of mind and humanity of her sex, she was about to put the little babe out of the window. The captain noticed this, and with characteristic atrocity, thrust, with a sharp bayonet, the little innocent, along with the person who endeavoured to rescue it, into the red flames, where they both perished. This was the work of an instant. Again he approached the man, 'Your child is a coal now,' said he, with deliberate mockery; 'I pitched it in myself, on the point of this' – showing the weapon – 'an' now is your turn' – saying which he clambered up, by the assistance of his gang, who stood with a front of pikes and bayonets bristling to receive the wretched man, should he attempt, in his despair, to throw himself from the wall. The captain got up, and placing the point of his bayonet against his shoulder, flung him into the fiery element that raged behind him. He uttered one wild and terrific cry as he fell back, and no more. After this, nothing was heard but the crackling of the fire and the rushing of the blast; all that had possessed life within were consumed, amounting either to eleven or fifteen persons.

When this was accomplished, those who took an active part in the murder stood for some time about the conflagration; and as it threw its red light upon their fierce faces and rough persons, soiled as they now were with smoke and black streaks of ashes, the scene seemed to be changed to hell, the murderers to spirits of the damned rejoicing over the arrival and the torture of some guilty soul. The faces of those who kept aloof from the slaughter were blanched to the whiteness of death; some of them fainted, and others were in such agitation that they were compelled to lean on their comrades. They became actually powerless with horror. Yet to such a scene were they brought by the pernicious influence of Ribbonism.

It was only when the last victim went down that the conflagration shot up into the air with most unbounded fury. The house was large, deeply thatched, and well furnished; and the broad red pyramid rose up with fearful magnificence towards the sky. Abstractedly it had sublimity, but now it was associated with nothing in my mind but blood and terror. It was not, however, without a purpose that the captain and his gang stood to contemplate its effect. 'Boys,' said he, 'we had betther be sartin that all's safe; who knows but there might be some of the sarpents crouchin' under a hape o' rubbish, to come out an' gibbet us tomorrow or next day; we had betther wait awhile, anyhow, if it was only to see the blaze.'

Just then the flames rose majestically to a surprising height. Our eyes followed their direction; and we perceived, for the first time, that the dark clouds above, together with the intermediate air, appeared to reflect back, or rather to have caught, the red hue of the fire. The hills and country about us appeared with an alarming distinctness; but the most picturesque part of it was the effect or reflection of the blaze on the floods that spread over the surrounding plains. These, in fact, appeared to be one broad mass of liquid copper; for the motion of the breaking waters caught from the blaze of the high waving column, as reflected in them, a glaring light, which eddied and rose and fluctuated as if the flood itself had been a lake of molten fire.

Fire, however, destroys rapidly. In a short time the flames sank – became weak and flickering – by and by they shot out only in fits – the crackling of the timbers died away – the surrounding darkness deepened – and, ere long, the faint light was overpowered by the thick volumes of smoke that rose from the ruins of the house and its murdered inhabitants.

'Now, boys,' said the captain, 'all is safe – we may go. Remember, every man of you, what you've sworn this night on the book an' altar of God – not on a heretic Bible. If you perjure yourselves, you may hang us; but let me tell you, for your comfort, that if you do, there is them livin' that will take care the lase of your own lives will be but short.'

After this we dispersed, every man to his own home.

Reader, not many months elapsed ere I saw the bodies of this captain, whose name was Patrick Devaun, and all those who were actively concerned in the perpetration of this deed of horror, withering in the wind, where they hung gibbeted near the scene of their nefarious villainy; and while I inwardly thanked Heaven for my own narrow and almost undeserved escape, I thought in my heart how seldom, even in this world, justice fails to overtake the murderer, and to enforce the righteous judgement of God – and 'whoso sheddeth man's blood, by man shall his blood by shed.'

This tale of terror is, unfortunately, too true. The scene of hellish murder detailed in it lies at Wildgoose Lodge in the county of Louth, within about four miles of Carrickmacross, and nine of Dundalk. No such multitudinous murder has occurred, under similar circumstances, except the burning of the Sheas in the county of Tipperary. The name of the family burned in Wildgoose Lodge was Lynch. One of them had, shortly before this fatal night, prosecuted and convicted some of the neighbouring Ribbonmen, who visited him with severe marks of their displeasure in consequence of his having refused to enrol himself as a member of their body.

The language of the story is partly fictitious; but the facts are pretty closely such as were developed during the trial of the murderers. Both parties were Roman Catholics. There were, if the author mistake not, either twenty-five or twenty-eight of those who took an active part in the burning hanged and gibbeted in different parts of the county of Louth. Devaun, the ringleader, hung for some months in chains, within about a hundred yards of his own house, and about half a mile from Wildgoose Lodge. His mother could neither go into or out of her cabin without seeing his body swinging from the gibbet. Her usual exclamation on looking at him was, 'God be good to the sowl of my poor marthyr!' The peasantry, too, frequently exclaimed, on seeing him, 'Poor Paddy!' – a gloomy fact that speaks volumes.

# SAMUEL LOVER

## The Gridiron

*Samuel Lover (1797–1868) was a novelist and painter who also composed over three hundred songs. His first book was highly successful:* Legends and Stories of Ireland *(1831). He aimed at expressing Irish character in a truly Irish way.*

A CERTAIN old gentleman in the west of Ireland, whose love of the ridiculous quite equalled his taste for claret and fox-hunting, was wont, upon certain festive occasions when opportunity offered, to amuse his friends by drawing out one of his servants who was exceedingly fond of what he termed his 'thravels', and in whom a good deal of whim, some queer stories, and, perhaps more than all, long and faithful services, had established a right of loquacity.

He was one of those few trusty and privileged domestics, who, if his master unheedingly uttered a rash thing in a fit of passion, would venture to set him right.

If the squire said, 'I'll turn that rascal off,' my friend Pat would say, 'Throth you won't, sir'; and Pat was always right, for if any altercation arose upon the subject-matter in hand, he was sure to throw in some good reason, either from former service – general good conduct – or the delinquent's 'wife and childher', that always turned the scale.

But I am digressing. On such merry meetings as I have alluded to, the master, after making certain 'approaches', as a military man would say, as the preparatory steps in laying siege to some extravaganza of his servant, might, perchance, assail Pat thus:

'By the by, Sir John' (addressing a distinguished guest), 'Pat has a very curious story, which something you told me to-day reminds me of. You remember, Pat' (turning to the man, evidently pleased at the notice paid to himself) – 'you remember that queer adventure you had in France?'

'Throth I do, sir,' grins forth Pat.

'What!' exclaims Sir John, in feigned surprise. 'Was Pat ever in France?'

'Indeed he was,' cries mine host; and Pat adds, 'Ay, and farther, plase your honour.'

'I assure you, Sir John,' continues mine host, 'Pat told me a story once that surprised me very much, respecting the ignorance of the French.'

'Indeed!' rejoins the baronet. 'Really, I always supposed the French to be a most accomplished people.'

'Throth, then, they're not, sir,' interrupts Pat.

'Oh, by no means,' adds mine host, shaking his head emphatically.

'I believe, Pat, 'twas when you were crossing the Atlantic?' says the master, turning to Pat with a seductive air, and leading into the 'full and true account' – (for Pat had thought fit to visit North Amerikay, for 'a raison he had', in the autumn of the year ninety-eight).

'Yes, sir,' says Pat, 'the broad Atlantic,' a favourite phrase of his, which he gave with a brogue as broad almost as the Atlantic itself.

'It was the time I was lost in crassin' the broad Atlantic, comin' home,' began Pat, decoyed into the recital; 'whin the winds began to blow, and the sae to rowl, that you'd think the *Colleen Dhas* (that was her name) would not have a mast left.

'Well, sure enough, the masts went by the board at last, and the pumps was choaked (divil choak them for that same), and av coorse the wather gained an us, and throth, to be filled with water is neither good for man or baste; and she was sinkin' fast, settlin' down, as the sailors calls it, and faith I never was good at settlin' down in my life, and I liked it then less nor ever. Accordingly we prepared for the worst, and put out the boat, and got a sack o' bishkits, and a cashk o' pork, and a kag o' wather, and a thrifle o' rum aboord, and any other little mathers we could think iv in the mortial hurry we wor in – and, faith, there was no time to be lost, for my darlint, the *Colleen Dhas*, went down like a lump o' lead, afore we wor many strokes o' the oar away from her.

'Well, we dhrifted away all that night, and next mornin' we put up a blanket an the ind av a pole as well as we could, and thin we sailed illigant, for we dar'n't show a stitch o' canvas the night before, bekase it was blowin' like murther, savin' your presence, and sure it's the wondher of the word we worn't swallyed alive the ragin' sae.

'Well, away we wint for more nor a week, and nothin' before our two good-looking eyes but the canophy iv heaven, and the wide ocean – the broad Atlantic – not a thing was to be seen but the sae and the sky; and though the sae and the sky is mighty purty things in themselves, throth they're no great things whin you've nothin' else to look at for a week together – and the barest rock in the world, so it was land, would be more welkim.

'And then, sure enough, throth, our provisions began to run low, the bishkits, and the wather, and the rum – throth that was gone first of all – God help uz! – and oh! it was thin that starvation began to stare us in the face. ' "Oh, murther, murther, captain, darlint," says I, ' "I wish we could see land anywhere," says I.

' "More power to your elbow, Paddy, my boy," says he, ' "for sitch a good wish, and, throth, it's myself wishes the same."

' "Oh," says I, ' "that it may plaze you, sweet queen in heaven – supposing it was only a dissolute island," says I, "inhabited wid Turks, sure they wouldn't be such bad Christhans as to refuse uz a bit and a sup."

' "Whisht, whisht, Paddy,' says the captain; "don't be talkin' bad of any one," says he; "you don't know how soon you may want a good word put in for yourself, if you should be called to quarthers in th' other world all of a suddent," says he.

' "Thrue for you, captain, darlint," says I – I called him darlint, and made free wid him, you see, bekase disthress makes uz all equal – "thrue for you, captain, jewel – God betune uz and harm, I owe no man any spite" – and, throth, that was only thruth.

'Well, the last bishkit was sarved out, and, by gor, the wather itself was all gone at last, and we passed the night mighty cowld. Well, at the brake o' day the sun riz most beautiful out o' the waves, that was as bright as silver and as clear as cryshthal.

'But it was only the more crule upon uz, for we wor beginnin' to feel terrible hungry; when all at wanst I thought I spied the land – by gor, I thought I felt my heart up in my throat in a minnit, and "Thundher and turf, captain," says I, "look to leeward," says I.

' "What for?" says he.

' "I think I see the land," says I. So he ups with his bring-'um-near (that's what the sailors call a spy-glass, sir), and looks out, and, sure enough, it was.

' "Hurrah!" says he, "we're all right now; pull away, my boys," says he.

' "Take care you're not mistaken," says I; "maybe it's only a fog-bank, captain, darlint," says I.

' "Oh, no," says he, "it's the land in airnest."

' "Oh, then, whereabouts in the wide world are we, captain?" says I; "maybe it id be in Roosia or Proosia, or the Garman Oceant," says I.

' "Tut, you fool," says he, for he had that consaited way wid him – thinkin' himself cleverer nor any one else – "tut, you fool," says he; "that's France," says he.

' "Tare an ouns," says I, "do you tell me so? And how do you know it's France it is, captain, dear?" says I.

' "Bekase this is the Bay o' Bishky we're in now," says he.

' "Throth, I was thinkin' so myself," says I, "by the rowl it has; for I often heerd av it in regard o' that same"; and, throth, the likes av it I never seen before nor since, and, with the help o' God, never will.

'Well, with that my heart begun to grow light, and when I seen my life was safe, I began to grow twice hungrier nor ever – so says I, "Captain, jewel, I wish we had a gridiron."

' "Why, then," says he, "thundher and turf," says he, "what put a gridiron into your head?'

' "Bekase I'm starvin' with the hunger,' says I.

' "And sure, bad luck to you," says he, "you couldn't ate a grid-iron," says he, "barrin you wor a pelican o' the wilderness," says he.

' "Ate a gridiron!" says I. "Och, in throth, I'm not such a gommoch all out as that, anyhow. But sure if we had a gridiron we could dress a beefsteak," says I.

' "Arrah! but where's the beefsteak?" says he.

' "Sure, couldn't we cut a slice aff the pork?" says I.

' "By gor, I never thought a' that," says the captain. "You're a clever fellow, Paddy," says he, laughin'.

' "Oh, there's many a thrue word said in joke," says I.

' "Thrue for you, Paddy," says he.

' "Well, then," says I, "if you put me ashore there beyant" (for we were nearin' the land all the time), "and sure I can ask thim for to lind me the loan of a gridiron," says I.

' "Oh, by gor, the butther's comin' out o' the stirabout in airnest now," says he. "You gommoch," says he, "sure I towld you before that's France – and sure they're all furriners there," says the captain.

' "Well," says I, "and how do you know but I'm as good a furriner myself as any o' thim."

' "What do you mane?" says he.

' "I mane," says I, "what I towld you, that I'm as good as furriner myself as any o' thim."

' "Make me sinsible," says he.

' "By dad, maybe that's more nor me, or greater nor me, could do," says I; and we all began to laugh at him, for I thought I'd pay him off for his bit o' consait about the Garman Oceant.

' "Lave aff your humbuggin'," says he. "I bid you, and tell me what it is you mane at all, at all."

' "Parly-voo frongsay?" says I.

' "Oh, your humble sarvant," says he. "Why, by gor, you're a scholar, Paddy."

' "Throth, you may say that," says I.

' "Why, you're a clever fellow, Paddy," says the captain, jeerin' like.

' "You're not the first that said that," says I. "whether you joke or no."

' "Oh, but I'm in airnest," says the captain. "And do you tell me, Paddy," says he, "that you spake Frinch?"

' "Parly-voo frongsay?" says I.

' "By gor, that bangs Banagher, and all the world knows Banagher bangs the devil. I never met the likes o' you, Paddy," says he. "Pull away, boys, and put Paddy ashore, and maybe we won't get a good bellyful before long."

'So, with that, it was no sooner said nor done – they pulled away and got close into shore in less than no time, and run the boat up in a little creek; and a beautiful creek it was, with a lovely white sthrand, an illigant place for ladies to bathe in the summer; and out I got, and it's stiff enough in my limbs I was afther bein' cramped up in the boat, and perished with the cowld and hunger; but I conthrived to scramble an, one way or the other, towards a little bit iv a wood that was close to the shore, and the smoke curlin' out of it, quite timpting like.

' "By the powdhers o' war, I'm all right," says I; "there's a house there" – and sure enough there was, and a parcel of men, women, and childher, ating their dinner round a table quite convanient. And so I wint up to the dure, and I thought I'd be very civil to thim, as I heerd the Frinch was always mighty p'lite intirely – and I thought I'd show them I knew what good manners was.

'So I took off my hat, and making a low bow, says I, "God save all here," says I.

'Well, to be sure, they all stopt ating at wanst, and begun to stare at me, and faith they almost looked me out of countenance – and I thought to myself it was not good manners at all – more be token from furriners, which they call so mighty p'lite; but I never minded that, in regard of wantin' the gridiron; and so says I, "I beg your pardon," says I, "for the liberty I take, but it's only bein' in disthress in regard of ating," says I, "that I make bowld to throuble yez, and if you could lind me the loan of a gridiron," says I, "I'd be entirely obleeged to ye."

'By gor, they all stared at me twice worse nor before, and with that, says I (knowing what was in their minds), "Indeed it's thrue for you," says I; "I'm tathered to pieces, and God knows I look quare enough, but it's by raison of the storm," says I, "which dhruv us ashore here below, and we're all starvin'," says I.

'So then they began to look at each other agin, and myself, seeing at wanst dirty thoughts was in their heads, and that they tuk me for a poor beggar comin' to crave charity – with that, says I, "Oh! not at all," says I, "by no manes; we have plenty o' mate ourselves, there below, and we'll dhress it," says I, "if you would be plased to lind us the loan of a gridiron," says I, makin' a low bow.

'Well, sir, with that, throth, they stared at me twice worse nor ever, and faith I began to think that maybe the captain was wrong, and that it was not France at all, at all; and so says I – "I beg pardon, sir," says I, to a fine ould man, with a head of hair as white as silver – "maybe I'm undher a mistake," says I, "but I thought I was in France, sir; aren't you furriners?" says I – "Parly-voo frongsay?"

'"We, munseer," says he.

'"Then would you lind me the loan of a gridiron," says I, "if you plase?"

'Oh, it was thin that they stared at me as if I had siven heads; and faith myself began to feel flusthered like, and onaisy – and so, says I, making a bow and scrape agin, "I know it's a liberty I take, sir," says I, "but it's only in the regard of bein' cast away, and if you plase, sir," says I, "Parly-voo frongsay?"

'"We, munseer," says he, mighty sharp.

'"Then would you lind me the loan of a gridiron?" says I, "and you'll obleege me."

'Well, sir, the old chap begun to munseer me, but the divil a bit of a gridiron he'd gie me; and so I began to think they were all neygars, for all their fine manners; and, throth, my blood began to rise, and says I, "By my sowl, if it was you was in disthress," says I, "and if it was to ould Ireland you kem, it's not only the gridiron they'd give you if you ax'd it, but something to put an it too, and a dhrop of dhrink into the bargain, and cead mille failte."

'Well, the word cead mille failte seemed to stchreck his heart, and the ould chap cocked his ear, and so I thought I'd give him another offer, and make him sinsible at last; and so says I, wanst more, quite slow, that he might undherstand – "Parly – voo – frongsay, munseer?"

' "We, munseer," says he.

' "Then lind me the loan of a gridiron," says I, "and bad scran to you."

'Well, bad win' to the bit of it he'd gi' me, and the ould chap begins bowin' and scrapin', and said something or other about a long tongs.

' "Phoo! – the devil sweep yourself and tongs," says I, "I don't want a tongs at all, at all; but can't you listen to raison," says I – "Parly-voo frongsay?"

' "We, munseer."

' "Then lind me the loan of a gridiron," says I, "and howld your prate."

'Well, what would you think but he shook his owld noddle, as much as to say he wouldn't; and so says I, "Bad cess to the likes o' that I ever seen – throth if you were in my country, it's not that-a-way they'd use you; the curse o' the crows on you, you ould sinner," says I; "the divil a longer I'll darken your dure."

'So he seen I was vexed, and I thought, as I was turnin' away, I seen him begin to relint, and that his conscience throubled him; and says I, turnin' back. "Well, I'll give you one chance more – you owld thief – are you a Chrishthan at all, at all? – are you a furriner," says I, "that all the world calls so p'lite? Bad luck to you; do you undherstand your own language? – Parly-voo frongsay?" says I.

' "We, munseer," says he.

' "Then, thundher and turf," says I, "will you lind me the loan of a gridiron?"

'Well, sir, the divil resave the bit of it he'd gi' me – and so with that, "The curse o' the hungry on you, you owld negardly villain," says I; "the back o' my hand and the sowl o' my foot to you; that you may want a gridiron yourself yet," says I; "and wherever I go, high and low, rich and poor shall hear o' you," says I; and with that I lift them there, sir, and kem away – and in throth it's often since that I thought that it was remarkable.'

# JOHN BANIM

## The Stolen Sheep

*John Banim (1798–1842) was born in Kilkenny and wrote many tales of old Ireland. His most famous collection of stories was* Tales of the O'Hara Family *written with his brother Michael. He was particularly successful in depicting poor Irish farmers and labourers.*

THE Irish plague, called typhus fever, raged in its terrors. In almost every third cabin there was a corpse daily. In every one, without an exception, there was what had made the corpse – hunger. It need not be added that there was poverty, too. The poor could not bury their dead. From mixed motives, of self-protection, terror, and bene-volence, those in easier circumstances exerted themselves to admin-ister relief in different ways. Money was subscribed (then came England's munificent donation – God prosper her for it!), wholesome food, or food as wholesome as a bad season permitted, was provided; and men of respectability, bracing their minds to avert the danger that threatened themselves, by boldly facing it, entered the infected house, where death reigned almost alone, and took measures to cleanse and purify the close-cribbed air and the rough, bare walls.

In the early progress of the fever, before the more affluent roused themselves to avert its career, let us cross the threshold of an individual peasant. His young wife lies dead; his second child is dying at her side; he has just sunk into a corner himself, under the first stun of disease,

long resisted. The only persons of his family who have escaped con-
tagion, and are likely to escape it, are his old father, who sits weeping
feebly upon the hob, and his first-born, a boy of three or four years
who, standing between the old man's knees, cries also for food.

We visit the young peasant's abode some time after. He has not
sunk under 'the sickness'. He is fast regaining his strength, even
without proper nourishment; he can creep out of doors and sit in the
sun. But in the expression of his sallow and emaciated face there is no
joy for his escape from the grave, as he sits there alone, silent and
brooding. His father and surviving child are still hungry – more
hungry, indeed, and more helpless than ever; for the neighbours who
had relieved the family with a potato and a mug of sour milk are now
stricken down themselves, and want assistance to a much greater
extent than they can give it.

'I wish Mr Evans was in the place,' cogitated Michaul Carroll; 'a
body could spake forn'ent him, and not spake for nothin' for all that
he's an Englishman; and I don't like the thoughts o' goin' up to the
house to the steward's face – it wouldn't turn kind to a body. May be
he'd soon come home to us, the masther himself.'

Another fortnight elapsed. Michaul's hope proved vain. Mr Evans
was still in London; though a regular resident on his small Irish estate
since it had come into his possession, business unfortunately – and he
would have said so himself – now kept him an unusually long time
absent. Thus disappointed, Michaul overcame his repugnance to
appear before the 'hard' steward. He only asked for work, however.
There was none to be had. He turned his slow and still feeble feet into
the adjacent town. It was market-day, and he took up his place among
a crowd of other claimants for agricultural employment, shouldering a
spade, as did each of his companions.

Many farmers came to the well-known 'stannin',' and hired men at
his right and at his left, but no one addressed Michaul. Once or twice,
indeed, touched perhaps by his sidelong looks of beseeching misery, a
farmer stopped a moment before him, and glanced over his figure; but
his worn and almost shaking limbs giving little promise of present
vigour in the working field, worldly prudence soon conquered the

humane feeling which started up towards him in the man's heart, and, with a choking in his throat, poor Michaul saw the arbiter of his fate pass on.

He walked homeward, without having broken his fast that day. 'Bud, *musha*, what's the harm o' that,' he said to himself; 'only here's the ould father, an' *her* pet boy, the weenock, without a pyatee either. Well, *asthore*, if they can't have the pyatees, they must have betther food – that's all; ay' – he muttered, clenching his hands at his sides, and imprecating fearfully in Irish – 'an' so they must.'

He left his house again, and walked a good way to beg a few potatoes. He did not come back quite empty-handed. His father and his child had a meal. He ate but a few himself; and when he was about to lie down in his corner for the night, he said to the old man across the room:

'Don't be a-cryin' to-night, father, you and the child there; bud sleep well, and ye'll have the good break'ast afore ye in the mornin'.'

'The good break'ast, *ma-bauchal*?[1] A-then, an' where 'ill id come from?'

'A body promised it to me, father.'

'*Avich!* Michaul, an' sure it's fun you're making of us, now, at any rate. Bud, the good night, a *chorra*,[2] an' my blessin' on your head, Michaul; an' if we keep trust in the good God, an' ax His blessin' too, mornin' and evenin', gettin' up an' lyin' down, He'll be a friend to us at last: that was always an' ever my word to you, poor boy, since you was at the years o' your own weenock, now fast asleep at my side; an' it's my word to you now; *ma-bauchal;* an' you won't forget id; and there's one sayin' the same to you, out o' heaven, this night – herself, an' her little angel-in-glory by the hand, Michaul *a-vourneen*.

Having thus spoken in the fervent and rather exaggerated, though everyday, words of pious allusion of the Irish poor man, old Carroll soon dropped asleep, with his arms round his little grandson, both overcome by an unusually abundant meal. In the middle of the night he was awakened by a stealthy noise. Without moving, he cast his eyes

[1]. My boy.
[2] Term of endearment.

round the cabin. A small window, through which the moon broke brilliantly, was open. He called to his son, but received no answer. He called again and again: all remained silent. He arose, and crept to the corner where Michaul had lain down. It was empty. He looked out through the window into the moonlight. The figure of a man appeared at a distance, just about to enter a pasture-field belonging to Mr Evans.

The old man leaned back against the wall of the cabin, trembling with sudden and terrible misgivings. With him the language of virtue which we have heard him utter, was not cant. In early prosperity, in subsequent misfortunes, and in his late and present excess of wretchedness he had never swerved in practice from the spirit of his own exhortations to honesty before men, and love for, and depen- dence upon God, which, as he had truly said, he had constantly addressed to his son since his earliest childhood. And hitherto that son had, indeed, walked by his precepts, further assisted by a regular observance of the duties of his religion. Was he now about to turn into another path? to bring shame on his father in his old age? to put a stain on their family and their name, 'the name that a rogue or a bould woman never bore'? continued old Carroll, indulging in some of the pride and egotism for which an Irish peasant is, under his circum- stances, remarkable. And then came the thought of the personal peril incurred by Michaul; and his agitation, incurred by the feebleness of age, nearly overpowered him.

He was sitting on the floor, shivering like one in an ague fit, when he heard steps outside the house. He listened, and they ceased: but the familiar noise of an old barn door creaking on its crazy hinges came on his ear. It was now day-dawn. He dressed himself, stole out cautiously, peeped into the barn through a chink of the door, and all he had feared met full confirmation. There, indeed, sat Michaul, busily and earnestly engaged, with a frowning brow and a haggard face, in quartering the animal he had stolen from Mr Evans's field.

The sight sickened the father – the blood on his son's hands, and all. He was barely able to keep himself from falling. A fear, if not a dislike, of the unhappy culprit also came upon him. His unconscious impulse was to re-enter their cabin unperceived, without speaking a word; he succeeded in doing so; and then he fastened the door again and undressed, and resumed his place beside his innocent grandson.

About an hour afterwards, Michaul came in cautiously through the still open window, and also undressed and reclined on his straw, after glancing towards his father's bed, who pretended to be asleep. At the usual time for arising, old Carroll saw him suddenly jump up, and prepare to go abroad. He spoke to him, leaning on his elbow.

'And what *hollg*[1] is on you now, *ma-bauchal*?'

'Going for the good break'ast I promised you, father dear.'

'An' who's the good Chrishthan 'ill give id to us, Michaul?'

'Oh, you'll know that soon, father: now, a good-bye' – he hurried to the door.

'A good-bye, then, Michaul; bud, tell me, what's that on your hand?'

'No-nothin',' stammered Michaul, changing colour, as he hastily examined the hand himself; 'nothin' is on id: what could there be?' (Nor was there, for he had very carefully removed all evidence of guilt from his person; and the father's question was asked upon grounds distinct from anything he then saw.)

'Well, *avich*, an' sure I didn't say anything was on it wrong; or anything to make you look so quare, an' spake so sthrange to your father, this mornin'; – only I'll ax you, Michaul, over agin, who has took such a sudd'n likin' to us, to send us the good break'ast – an' answer me sthraight, Michaul – what is id to be, that you call it so *good*?'

'The good mate, father' – he was again passing the threshold.

'Stop!' cried his father; 'stop, an' turn fornent me, Mate? – the good mate? – What 'ud bring mate into our poor house, Michaul? Tell me, I bid you again an' again, who is to give id to you?'

'Why, as I said afore, father, a body that — '

'A body that thieved id, Michaul Carroll!' added the old man, as his son hesitated, walking close up to the culprit; 'a body that thieved id, an' no other body. Don't think to blind me, Michaul. I am ould, to be

[1] What are you about.

sure; but sense enough is left in me to look round among the neighbours, in my own mind, an' know that none of 'em that has the will has the power to send us the mate for our break'ast in an honest way. An' I don't say, outright, that you had the same thought wid me when you consented to take it from a thief – I don't mean to say that you'd go to turn a thief's recaiver, at this hour o' your life, an' afther growin' up from a boy to a man widout bringin' a spot of shame on yourself, or on your weenock, or on one of us. No; I won't say that. Your heart was scalded, Michaul, an' your mind was darkened, for a start; an' the thought o' getting comfort for the ould father an' for the little son made you consent in a hurry, widout lookin' well afore you, or widout lookin' up to your good God.'

'Father, father, let me alone! don't spake them words to me,' interrupted Michaul, sitting on a stool, and spreading his large and hard hands over his face.

'Well, thin, an' I won't, *avich*; I won't; – nothin' to throuble you, sure: I didn't mean id; – only this, *a-vourneen*, don't bring a mouthful o' the bad, unlucky victuals into this cabin; the pyatees, the wild berries o' the bush, the wild roots o' the arth, will be sweeter to us, Michaul; the hunger itself will be sweeter; an' when we give God thanks afther our poor meal, or afther no meal at all, our hearts will be lighter, and our hopes for to-morrow sthronger, *avich-ma-chree*, than if we faisted on the fat o' the land, but couldn't ax a blessin' on our faist.'

'Well, thin, *I* won't, either, father; I won't: an' sure you have your way now. I'll only go out a little while from you – to beg; or else, as you say, to root down in the ground, with my nails, like a baste-brute, for our break'ast.'

'My *vourneen* you are, Michaul, an' my blessin' on your head; yes, to be sure, *avich*, beg, an' I'll beg wid you – sorrow a shame is in that – no, but a good deed, Michaul, when it's done to keep us honest. So come; we'll go among the Christhthans together. Only, before we go, Michaul, my own dear son, tell me – tell one thing.'

'What, father?' Michaul began to suspect.

'Never be afraid to tell me, Michaul Carroll, *ma-bauchal*? I won't – I can't be angry wid you now. You are sorry; an' your Father in heaven

forgives you, and so do I. But you know, *avich*, there would be danger
in quitting the place widout hiding every scrap of anything that could
tell on us.'

'Tell on us! What can tell on us?' demanded Michaul; 'what's in the
place to tell on us?'

'Nothin' in the cabin, I know, Michaul, but –'

'But what, father?'

'Have you left nothing in the way, out there?' whispered the old
man, pointing towards the barn.

'Out there? Where? What? What do you mean at all, now, father?
Sure you know it's your ownsef has kep me from as much as laying a
hand on it.'

'Ay, to-day mornin'; bud you laid a hand on it last night, *avich*, an'
so –'

'*Curp-an-duoul!*' imprecated Michaul – 'this is too bad, at any rate;
no, I didn't – last night – let me alone, I bid you, father.'

'Come back again, Michaul,' commanded old Carroll, as the son
once more hurried to the door: and his words were instantly obeyed.
Michaul, after a glance abroad, and a start, which the old man did not
notice, paced to the middle of the floor, hanging his head and saying
in a low voice, 'Hushth now, father – it's time.'

'No, Michaul, I will not hushth; an' it's not time; come out with
me to the barn.'

'Hushth!' repeated Michaul, whispering sharply: he had glanced
sideways to the square patch of strong morning sunlight on the ground
of the cabin, defined there by the shape of the open door, and saw it
intruded upon by the shadow of a man's bust leaning forward in an
earnest posture.

'Is it in your mind to go back into your sin, Michaul, an' tell me you
were not in the barn, at daybreak, the mornin'?' asked his father, still
unconscious of a reason for silence.

'Arrah, hushth, ould man!' Michaul made a hasty sign towards the
door, but was disregarded.

'I saw you in id,' pursued old Carroll sternly 'ay, and at your work
in id, too.'

'What's that you're sayin', ould Peery Carroll?' demanded a well-known voice.

'Enough to hang his son,' whispered Michaul to his father, as Mr Evans's land-steward, followed by his herdsman and two policemen, entered the cabin. In a few minutes afterwards the policemen had in charge the dismembered carcase of the sheep, dug up out of the floor in the barn, and were escorting Michaul, handcuffed, to the county gaol, in the vicinity of the next town. They could find no trace of the animal's skin, though they sought attentively for it; and this seemed to disappoint them and the steward a good deal.

From the moment that they entered the cabin, till their departure, old Carroll did not speak a word. Without knowing it, as it seemed, he sat down on his straw bed, and remained staring stupidly around him, or at one or another of his visitors. When Michaul was about to leave the wretched abode, he paced quickly towards his father, and holding out his ironed hands, and turning his cheek for a kiss, said, smiling miserably, 'God be wid you, father dear.'

Still the old man was silent, and the prisoner and all his attendants passed out on the road. But it was then the agony of old Carroll assumed a distinctness. Uttering a fearful cry, he snatched up his still sleeping grandson, ran with the boy in his arms till he overtook Michaul; and, kneeling down before him in the dust, said:

'I ax pardon o' you, *avich* – won't you tell me I have id afore you go? An' here, I've brought little Peery for you to kiss; you forgot *him, a-vourneen.*'

'No, father, I didn't,' answered Michaul, as he stooped to kiss the child; 'an' get up, father, get up; my hands are not my own, or I wouldn't let you do that afore your son. Get up, there's nothin' for you to throuble yourself about; that is, I mean, I have nothin' to forgive you: no, but everything to be thankful for, an' to love your for; you were always an' ever the good father to me; an' —'

The many strong and bitter feelings which till now he had almost perfectly kept in, found full vent, and poor Michaul could not go on. The parting from his father, however, so different from what it had promised to be, comforted him. The old man held him in his arms and wept on his neck. They separated with difficulty.

Peery Carroll, sitting on the roadside after he lost sight of the prisoner, and holding his screaming grandson on his knees, thought the cup of his trials were full. By his imprudence he had fixed the proof of guilt on his own child; that reflection was enough for him, and he could indulge it only generally. But he was yet to conceive distinctly in what dilemma he had involved himself as well as Michaul.

The policemen came back to compel his appearance before the magistrate; and when the little child had been disposed of in a neighbouring cabin, he understood, to his consternation and horror, that he was to be the chief witness against the sheep-stealer. Mr Evans's steward knew well the meaning of the words he had over-heard him say in the cabin, and that if compelled to swear all he was aware of, no doubt would exist of the criminality of Michaul in the eyes of a jury.

''Tis a sthrange thing to ax a father to do,' muttered Peery, more than once as he proceeded to the magistrate's; 'it's a very sthrange thing.'

The magistrate proved to be a humane man. Notwithstanding the zeal of the steward and the policemen, he committed Michaul for trial, without continuing to press the hesitating and bewildered old Peery into any detailed evidence; his nature seemed to rise against the task, and he said to the steward:

'I have enough of facts for making out a committal; if you think the father will be necessary on the trial, subpœna him.'

The steward objected that Peery would abscond, and demanded to have him bound over to prosecute, on two sureties, solvent and respectable. The magistrate assented; Peery could name no bail; and consequently he also was marched to prison, though prohibited from holding the least intercourse with Michaul.

The assizes soon came on. Michaul was arraigned; and, during his plea of 'not guilty', his father appeared, unseen by him, in the gaoler's custody, at the back of the dock, or rather in an inner dock. The trial excited a keen and painful interest in the court, the bar, the jury-box, and the crowds of spectators. It was universally known that a son had stolen a sheep, partly to feed a starving father; and that out of the mouth of that father it was now sought to condemn him.

'What will the old man do?' was the general question which ran through the assembly; and while few of the lower orders could contemplate the possibility of his swearing to the truth, many of their betters scarcely hesitated to make out for him a case of natural necessity to swear falsely.

The trial began. The first witness, the herdsman, proved the loss of the sheep and the finding of the dismembered carcass in the old barn. The policemen and the steward followed to the same effect, and the latter added the allusions which he had heard the father make to the son upon the morning of the arrest of the latter. The steward went down from the table. There was a pause, and complete silence, which the attorney for the prosecution broke by saying to the crier deliberately, 'Call Peery Carroll.'

'Here, sir,' immediately answered Peery, as the gaoler led him by a side door out of the back dock to the table. The prisoner started round; but the new witness against him had passed for an instant into the crowd.

The next instant old Peery was seen ascending the table, assisted by the gaoler and by many other commiserating hands, near him. Every glance fixed on his face. The barristers looked wistfully up from their seats round the table; the judge put a glass to his eye and seemed to study his features attentively. Among the audience there ran a low but expressive murmur of pity and interest.

Though much emaciated by confinement, anguish, and suspense, Peery's cheeks had a flush, and his weak blue eyes glittered. The half-gaping expression of his parched and haggard lips was miserable to see. And yet he did not tremble much, nor appear so confounded as upon the day of his visit to the magistrate.

The moment he stood upright on the table he turned himself fully to the judge, without a glance towards the dock.

'Sit down, sit down, poor man,' said the judge.

'Thanks to you, my lord, I will,' answered Peery, 'only, first I'd ax

you to let me kneel, for a little start'; and he accordingly did kneel, and
after bowing his head, and forming the sign of the cross on his forehead, he looked up, and said, 'My Judge in heaven above, 'tis you I
pray to keep me to my duty, afore my earthly judge, this day – amen'
– and then, repeating the sign of the cross, he seated himself.

The examination of the witness commenced, and humanely proceeded as follows – the counsel for the prosecution taking no notice of
the superfluity of Peery's answers.

'Do you know Michaul, or Michael, Carroll, the prisoner at the
bar?'

'Afore that night, sir, I believed I knew him well; every thought of
his mind, every bit of the heart in his body: afore that night, no living
creatur could throw a word at Michaul Carroll, or say he ever forgot
his father's renown, or his love of his good God; an' sure the people
are afther telling you by this time how it came about that night – an'
you, my lord – an' ye, gintlemen – an' all good Christhthans that hear
me; – here I am to help to hang him – my own boy, and my only one
– but, for all that, gintlemen, ye ought to think of it; 'twas for the
weenock and the ould father that he done it; – indeed, an'deed, we
hadn't a pyatee in the place; an' the sickness was among us, a start
afore; it took the wife from him, and another babby; an' id had himself
down, a week or so beforehand; an' all that day he was looking for
work, but couldn't get a hand's turn to do; an' that's the way it was;
not a mouthful for me an' little Peery; an', more betoken, he grew
sorry for id, in the mornin', an' promised me not to touch a scrap of
what was in the barn, – ay, long afore the steward and the peelers came
on us, – but was willin' to go among the neighbours an' beg our
breakfast, along wid myself, from door to door, sooner than touch it.'

'It is my painful duty,' resumed the barrister, when Peery would at
length cease, 'to ask you for closer information. You saw Michael
Carroll in the barn that night?'

'*Musha* – The Lord pity him and me – I did, sir,'

'Doing what?'

'The sheep between his hands,' answered Peery, dropping his head,
and speaking almost inaudibly.

'I must still give you pain, I fear; stand up, take the crier's rod, and if you see Michael Carroll in court lay it on his head.'

'*Och, musha, musha*, sir, don't ax me to do that!' pleaded Peery, rising, wringing his hands, and for the first time weeping – 'och, don't, my lord, don't, and may your own judgment be favourable, the last day.'

'I am sorry to command you to do it, witness, but you must take the rod,' answered the judge, bending his head close to his notes, to hide his own tears; and, at the same time, many a veteran barrister rested his forehead on the edge of the table. In the body of the court were heard sobs.

'Michaul, *avich*! Michaul, *a corra-ma-chree*!' exclaimed Peery, when at length he took the rod, and faced round to his son, 'is id your father they make to do it, *ma-bauchal*?'

'My father does what is right,' answered Michael, in Irish.

The judge immediately asked to have his words translated; and when he learned their import, regarded the prisoner with satisfaction.

'We rest here, my lord,' said the counsel, with the air of a man freed from a painful task. The judge instantly turned to the jury-box:

'Gentlemen of the jury, that the prisoner at the bar stole the sheep in question, there can be no shade of moral doubt. But you have a very peculiar case to consider. A son steals a sheep that his own famishing father and his own famishing son may have food. His aged parent is compelled to give evidence against him here for the act. The old man virtuously tells the truth, and the whole truth, before you and me. He sacrifices his natural feelings – and we have seen that they are lively – to his honesty, and to his religious sense of the sacred obligations of an oath. Gentlemen, I will pause to observe that the old man's conduct is strikingly exemplary, and even noble. It teaches all of us a lesson. Gentlemen, it is not within the province of a judge to censure the rigour of the proceedings which have sent him before us. But I venture to anticipate your pleasure that, notwithstanding all the evidence given, you will be enabled to acquit the old man's son, the prisoner at the bar. I have said there cannot be the shade of a moral doubt that he has stolen the sheep, and I repeat the words. But, gentlemen, there is a legal doubt, to the full benefit of which he is entitled. The sheep has not been identified. The herdsman could not venture to identify it (and it would have been strange if he could) from the dismembered limbs found in the barn. To his mark on its skin, indeed, he might have positively spoken; but no skin has been discovered. Therefore, according to the evidence, and you have sworn to decide by that alone, the prisoner is entitled to your acquittal. Possibly, now that that prosecutor sees the case in its full bearing, he may be pleased with this result.'

While the jury, in evident satisfaction, prepared to return their verdict, Mr Evans, who had but a moment before returned home, entered the court, and becoming aware of the concluding words of the judge, expressed his sorrow aloud that the prosecution had ever been undertaken, that circumstances had kept him uninformed of it, though it had gone on in his name; and he begged leave to assure his lordship that it would be his future effort to keep Michaul Carroll in his former path of honesty, by finding him honest and ample employment, and, as far as in him lay, to reward the virtue of the old father.

While Peery Carroll was laughing and crying in a breath, in the arms of his delivered son, a subscription, commenced by the bar, was mounting into a considerable sum for his advantage.

# THOMAS CROFTON CROKER

## Daniel O'Rourke

*Thomas Crofton Croker (1798–1854) was born in Cork. He was famous as a folklorist and was the author of* Fairy Legends and Traditions of the South of Ireland *(1825). He also wrote* The Adventures of Barney Mahony *and* My Village versus Our Village.

PEOPLE may have heard of the renowned adventures of Daniel O'Rourke, but how few are there who know that the cause of all his perils, above and below, was neither more nor less than his having slept under the walls of the Phooka's tower! I knew the man well; he lived at the bottom of Hungry Hill, just at the right-hand side of the road as you go towards Bantry.

An old man was he at the time that he told me the story, with grey hair and a red nose: and it was on June 25, 1813, that I heard it from his own lips, as he sat smoking his pipe under the old poplar tree, on as fine an evening as ever shone from the sky. I was going to visit the caves in Dursey Island, having spent the morning at Glengariff.

'I am often *axed* to tell it, sir,' said he, 'so that this is not the first time. The master's son, you see, had come from beyond foreign parts in France and Spain, as young gentlemen used to go, before Buonaparte or any such was heard of; and sure enough there was a dinner given to all the people on the ground, gentle and simple, high and low, rich and poor. The *ould* gentlemen were the gentlemen, after all, saving your honour's presence. They'd swear at a body a little, to be sure, and maybe give one a cut of a whip now and then, but we were no losers by it in the end; and they were so easy and civil, and kept such rattling houses, and thousands of welcomes; and there was no grinding for rent, and few agents; and there was hardly a tenant on the estate that did not taste of his landlord's bounty often and often in the year; – but now it's another thing: no matter for that, sir, for I'd better be telling you my story.

'Well, we had everything of the best, and plenty of it; and we ate, and we drank, and we danced, and the young master by the same token danced with Peggy Barry, from the Bohereen – a lovely young couple they were, though they are both low enough now. To make a long story short, I got, as a body may say, the same thing as tipsy almost, for I can't remember ever at all, no ways, how it was I left the place: only I did leave it, that's certain. Well, I thought, for all that, in myself, I'd just step to Molly Cronohan's, the fairy-woman, to speak a word about the bracket heifer that was bewitched; and so as I was crossing the stepping-stones of the ford of Ballyasheenough, and was looking up at the stars and blessing myself – for why? it was Lady-day – I missed my foot, and souse I fell into the water. "Death alive!" thought I, "I'll be drowned now!"

'However, I began swimming, swimming, swimming away for the dear life, till at last I got ashore, somehow or other, but never the one of me can tell how, upon a *dissolute* island.

'I wandered and wandered about there, without knowing where I wandered, until at last I got into a big bog. The moon was shining as bright as day, or your fair lady's eyes, sir (with your pardon for mentioning her), and l looked east and west, and north and south, and every way, and nothing did I see but bog, bog, bog; – I could never find out how I got into it; and my heart grew cold with fear, for sure and certain I was that it would be my *berrin* place. So I sat down upon a stone, which, as good luck would have it, was close by me, and I began to scratch my head and sing the *Ullagone* – when all of a sudden the moon grew black, and I looked up, and saw something for all the world as if it was moving down between me and it, and I could not tell what it was. Down it came with a pounce, and looked at me full in the face; and what was it but an eagle? as fine a one as ever flew from the kingdom of Kerry.

'So he looked at me in the face, and says he to me, "Daniel O'Rourke," says he. "how do you do?"

' "Very well, I thank you, sir," says I; "I hope you're well"; wondering out of my senses all the time how an eagle came to speak like a Christian.

' "What brings you here, Dan?" says he.

' "Nothing at all, sir," says I; "only I wish I was safe home again."

' "Is it out of the island you want to go, Dan?" says he.

' "'Tis, sir," says I; so I up and told him how I had taken a drop too much; and fell into the water; how I swam to the island; and how I got into the bog and did not know my way out of it.

' "Dan," says he after a minute's thought, "though it is very improper for you to get drunk on Lady-day, yet as you are a decent sober man, who 'tends mass well, and never flings stones at me nor mine, nor cries out after us in the fields – my life for yours," says he; "so get up on my back, and grip me well for fear you'd fall off, and I'll fly you out of the bog."

' "I am afraid," says I, "your honour's making game of me; for who ever heard of riding a-horseback on an eagle before?"

' "'Pon the honour of a gentleman," says he, putting his right foot on his breast, "I am quite in earnest; and so now either take my offer or starve in the bog; besides, I see that your weight is sinking the stone."

'It was true enough as he said, for I found the stone every minute going from under me. I had no choice; so thinks I to myself, faint heart never won fair lady, and this is fair persuadance: – "I thank your honour," says I, "for the loan of your civility, and I'll take your kind offer."

'I therefore mounted upon the back of the eagle, and held him tight enough by the throat, and up he flew in the air like a lark. Little I knew the trick he was going to serve me. Up, up, up – God knows how far up he flew.

' "Why, then," said I to him – thinking he did not know the right road home – very civilly, because why? – I was in his power entirely; – "sir," says I, "please your honour's glory, and with humble submission to your better judgment, if you'd fly down a bit, you're now just over my cabin, and I could be put down there, and many thanks to your worship."

' "*Arrah*, Dan," said he, "do you think me a fool? Look down in the next field, and don't you see two men and a gun? By my word it would be no joke to be shot this way, to oblige a drunken blackguard that I picked up off of a *could* stone in a bog."

' "Bother you," said I to myself, but I did not speak out, for where was the use? Well, sir, up he kept flying, flying, and I asking him every minute to fly down, and all to no use.

' "Where in the world are you going, sir?" says I to him.

' "Hold your tongue, Dan," says he; "mind your own business, and don't be interfering with the business of other people."

' "Faith, this is my business, I think," says I.

' "Be quiet, Dan," says he; so I said no more.

'At last where should we come to but to the moon itself. Now you can't see it from this, but there is, or there was in my time, a reaping-hook sticking out of the side of the moon, this way' (drawing the figure thus on the ground with the end of his stick).

' "Dan," said the eagle, "I'm tired with this long fly; I had no notion 'twas so far."

' "And my lord, sir," said I, "who in the world *axed* you to fly so far – was it I? Did not I beg, and pray, and beseech you to stop half an hour ago?'

' "There's no use talking, Dan," said he, "I'm tired bad enough, so you must get off and sit down on the moon until I rest myself."

' "Is it sit down on the moon?" said I; "is it upon that little round thing, then? why then, sure, I'd fall off in a minute, and be *kilt* and split, and smashed all to bits: you are a vile deceiver – so you are."

' "Not at all, Dan," said he; "you can catch fast hold of the reaping-hook that's sticking out of the side of the moon, and 'twill keep you up."

' "I won't then," said I.

' "Maybe not," said he quite quiet. "If you don't, my man, I shall just give you a shake, and one slap of my wing, and send you down to the ground, where every bone in your body will be smashed as small as a drop of dew on a cabbage-leaf in the morning."

' "Why, then, I'm in a fine way," said I to myself, "ever to have come along with the likes of you"; and so giving him a hearty curse in Irish, for fear he'd know what I said, I got off his back with a heavy heart, took a hold of the reaping-hook, and sat down upon the moon; and a mighty cold seat it was, I can tell you that.

'When he had me there fairly landed, he turned about on me, and said, "Good-morning to you, Daniel O'Rourke," said he, "I think I've nicked you fairly now. You robbed my nest last year" ('twas true enough for him, but how he found it out is hard to say), "and in return you are freely welcome to cool your heels dangling upon the moon like a cockthrow."

' "Is that all, and is this the way you leave me, your brute you?" says I. "You ugly unnatural *baste*, and is this the way you serve me at last? Bad luck to yourself, with your hook'd nose, and to all your breed, you blackguard."

' "'Twas all to no manner of use; he spread out his great big wings, burst out a-laughing, and flew away like lightening. I bawled after him to stop; but I might have called and bawled for ever without his minding me. Away he went, and I never saw him from that day to this – sorrow fly away with him! You may be sure I was in a disconsolate condition, and kept roaring out for the bare grief, when all at once a door opened right in the middle of the moon, creaking on its hinges as if it had not been opened for a month before – I suppose they never thought of greasing 'em – and out there walks – who do you think but the man in the moon himself? I knew him by his bush.

' "Good-morrow to you, Daniel O'Rourke," said he: "how do you do?"

' "Very well, thank your honour," said I. "I hope your honour's well."

' "What brought you here, Dan?" said he. So I told him how I was a little overtaken in liquor at the master's, and how I was cast on a *dissolute* island, and how I lost my way in the bog, and how the thief of an eagle promised to fly me out of it, and how instead of that he had fled me up to the moon.

'"Dan," said the man in the moon, taking a pinch of snuff, when I was done, "you must not stay here."

'"Indeed, sir," says I, "'tis much against my will I'm here at all; but how am I to go back?"

'"That's your business," said he, "Dan: mine is to tell you that here you must not stay, so be off in less than no time."

'"I'm doing no harm," says I, "only holding on hard by the reaping-hook lest I fall off."

'"That's what you must not do, Dan," says he.

'"Pray, sir," says I, "may I ask how many you are in family that you would not give a poor traveller lodging: I'm sure 'tis not so often you're troubled with strangers coming to see you, for 'tis a long way."

'"I'm by myself, Dan," says he; "but you'd better let go the reaping-hook."

'"Faith, and with your leave," says I, "I'll not let go the grip, and the more you bids me, the more I won't let go – so I will."

'"You had better, Dan," says he again.

'"Why, then, my little fellow," says I, taking the whole weight of him with my eye from head to foot, "there are two words to that bargain; and I'll not budge, but you may if you like."

'"We'll see how that is to be," says he; and back he went, giving the door such a great bang after him (for it was plain he was huffed) and I thought the moon and all would fall down with it.

'Well, I was preparing myself to try strength with him, when back again he comes with the kitchen cleaver in his hand, and without saying a word, he gives two bangs to the handle of the reaping-hook that was keeping me up, and *whap!* it came in two.

'"Good-morning to you, Dan," says the spiteful little old black-guard when he saw me cleanly falling down with a bit of the handle in my hand: "I thank you for your visit, and fair weather after you, Daniel."

'I had not time to make any answer to him, for I was tumbling over and over, and rolling and rolling at the rate of a fox-hunt. "God help me," says I, "but this is a pretty pickle for a decent man to be seen in at this time of night; I am now sold fairly."

'The word was not out of my mouth, when whiz! what should fly by close to my ear but a flock of wild geese, all the way from my own bog of Ballyasheenough, else how should they know *me*? The *ould* gander, who was their general, turning about his head, cried out to me, "Is that you, Dan?"

' "The same," said I, not a bit daunted now at what he said, for I was by this time used to all kinds of *bedevilment*, and, besides, I knew him of *ould*.

' "Good-morrow to you," says he, "Daniel O'Rourke; how are you in health this morning?"

' "Very well, sir," says I, "I thank you kindly," drawing my breath, for I was mightily in want of some. "I hope your honour's the same."

' "I think 'tis falling you are, Daniel," says he.

' "You may say that, sir," says I.

' "And where are you going all the way so fast?" said the gander.

'So I told him how I had taken the drop, and how I came on the island, and how I lost my way in the bog, and how the thief of an eagle flew me up to the moon, and how the man in the moon turned me out.

' "Dan," said he, "I'll save you; put out your hand and catch me by the leg, and I'll fly you home."

' "Sweet is your hand in a pitcher of honey, my jewel," says I, though all the time I thought in myself that I don't much trust you; but there was no help, so I caught the gander by the leg, and away I and the other geese flew after him as fast as hops.

'We flew, and we flew, and we flew, until we came right over the wide ocean. I knew it well, for I saw Cape Clear to my right hand sticking up out of the water.

' "Ah! my lord," said I to the goose, for I thought it best to keep a civil tongue in my head anyway, "fly to land, if you please."

' "It is impossible, you see, Dan," said he, "for a while, because you see we are going to Arabia."

' "To Arabia?" said I; "that's surely some place in foreign parts, far away. Oh, Mr Goose! why then, to be sure, I'm a man to be pitied among you."

' "Whist, whist, you fool," said he, "hold your tongue; I tell you Arabia is a very decent sort of place, as like West Carbery as one egg is like another, only there is a little more sand there."

'Just as we were talking a ship hove in sight, scudding so beautiful before the wind: "Ah! then, sir," said I, "will you drop me on the ship, if you please?"

' "We are not fair over it," said he.

' "We are," said I.

' "We are not," said he, "If I dropped you now, you would go splash into the sea."

' "I would not," says I: "I know better than that, for it's just clean under us, so let me drop now at once."

' "If you must, you must," said he. "There, take your own way"; and he opened his claw, and faith he was right – sure enough I came down plump into the very bottom of the salt sea! Down to the very bottom I went, and I gave myself up then for ever, when a whale walked up to me, scratching himself after his night's sleep, and looked me full in the face, and never the word did he say, but lifting up his tail he splashed me all over again with the cold salt water, till there wasn't a dry stitch upon my whole carcass; and I heard somebody saying – 'twas a voice I knew too – "Get up, you drunken brute, off of that"; and with that I woke up, and there was Judy with a tub full of water, which she was splashing all over me, – for, rest her soul! though she was a good wife, she never could bear to see in drink, and had a bitter hand of her own!

' "Get up," said she again; "and of all places in the parish would no place *sarve* your turn to lie down upon but under the *ould* walls of Carrigaphooka? an uneasy resting I am sure you had of it."

'And sure enough I had; for I was fairly bothered out of my senses with eagles, and men of the moon, and flying ganders, and whales, driving me through bogs, and up to the moon, and down to the

bottom of the green ocean. If I was in drink ten times over, long
would it be before I'd lie down in the same spot again, I know that."

# GERALD GRIFFIN

## The Dilemma of Phadrig

*Gerald Griffin (1803–1840) was born at Limerick. He was a writer of great promise who died young. 'The Dilemma of Phadrig' with its delight in old Irish superstitions is one of his most characteristic offerings. He wrote many stories and novels but in 1838 he burned all his manuscripts and entered the Christian Brothers and devoted himself to teaching in the North Monastery, Cork.*

'There's no use in talken about it, Phadrig. I know an' I feel that all's over wit me. My pains are all gone, to be sure – but in place o' that, there's a weight like a quern stone down upon my heart, an I feel it blackenen within me. All I have to say is – think o' your own Mauria when she's gone, an be kind to poor Patcy.'

'Ah, darlen, don't talk that way – there's hopes yet – what'll I do, what'll the child do witout you?'

'Phadrig, there's noan. I'm goen fast, an if you have any regard for me, you won't say anythin that'll bring the thoughts o' you an him between me an the thoughts o' heaven, for that's what I must think of now. An if you marry again –'

'Oh, Mauria, honey, will you kill me entirely? Is it *I'll* marry again?'

'– If it be a thing you should marry again,' Mauria resumed, without taking any notice of her husband's interruption, 'you'll bear in mind that the best mother that ever walked the ground will love her own above another's. It stands with raisin an natur. The gander abroad will pull a strange goslen out of his own flock; and you know yourself, we could never get the bracket hen to sit upon Nelly O'Leary's chickens, do what we could. Everything loves its own. Then, Phadrig, if you see the floury potaties – an the top o' the milk – an the warm seat be the hob – an the biggest bit o' meat on a Sunday goen away from Patcy – you'll think o' your poor Mauria, an do her part by him; just quietly, and softly, an without blamen the woman – for it is only what's nait'rel, an what many a stepmother does without thinking o' themselves. An above all things, Phadrig, take care to make him mind his books and his religion, to keep out o' bad company, an study his readin-made-aisy, and that's the way he'll be a blessing an a comfort to you in your old days, as I once thought he would be to me in mine.'

Here her husband renewed his promises in a tone of deep affliction.

'An now for yourself, Phadrig. Remember the charge that's upon you, and don't be goen out venturen your life in a little canvas canoe, on the bad autumn days, at Ballybunion; nor wit foolish boys at the Glin and Tarbert fairs' – an don't be so wake-minded as to be trusten to card-drawers, an fairy doctors, an the like; for it's the last word the priest said to me was, that you were too superstitious, and that's a great shame an a heavy sin. But tee you! Phadrig, dear, there's that rogue of a pig at the potaties over –'

Phadrig turned out the grunting intruder, bolted the hurdle-door, and returned to the bedside of his expiring helpmate. That tidy housekeeper, however, exhausted by the exertion which she had made to preserve, from the mastication of the swinish tusk, the fair produce of her husband's conacre of white-eyes, had fallen back on the pillow and breathed her last.

Great was the grief of the widowed Phadrig for her loss – great were the lamentations of her female friends at the evening wake – and great was the jug of whisky-punch which the mourners imbibed at the mouth, in order to supply the loss of fluid which was expended from the eyes. According to the usual cottage etiquette, the mother of the deceased, who acted as mistress of the ceremonies, occupied a capacious hay-bottomed chair near the fireplace – from which she only rose when courtesy called on her to join each of her female acquaintances as they arrived, in the death-wail which (as in politeness bound) they poured forth over the pale piece of earth that lay coffined in the centre of the room. This mark of attention, however, the old lady was observed to omit with regard to one of the fair guests – a round-faced, middle-aged woman, called Milly Rue – or Red Milly, probably because her head might have furnished a solution of the popular conundrum, 'Why is a red-haired lady like a sentinel on his post?'

The fair Milly, however, did not appear to resent this slight, which was occasioned (so the whisper went among the guests) by the fact that she had been an old and neglected love of the new widower. All the fiery ingredients in Milly's constitution appeared to be comprehended in her glowing ringlets – and those, report says, were as ardent in hue as their owner was calm and regulated in her temper. It would be a cold morning, indeed, that a sight of Milly's head would not warm you – and a hot fit of anger which a few tones of her kind and wrath-disarming voice would not cool. She dropped, after she had concluded her 'cry', a conciliating curtsey to the sullen old lady, took an unobtrusive seat at the foot of the bed, talked of the 'notable' qualities of the deceased, and was particularly attentive to the flaxen-headed little Patcy, whom she held in her lap during the whole night, cross-examining him in his reading and multiplication, and presenting him, at parting, in token of her satisfaction at his proficiency, with a copy of *The Seven Champions of Christendom*, with a fine marble cover and pictures. Milly acted in this instance under the advice of a prudent mother, who exhorted her, 'whenever she thought o' maken presents, that way, not to be layen her money out in cakes or gingerbread, or things that would be ett off at wanst, an no more about them or the giver – but to give a strong toy, or a book, or somethen that would last, and bring her to mind now and then, so as that when a person 'ud ask where they got that, or who gev it, they'd say, "from Milly Rue," or "Milly gev it, we're obleest to her," an' be talken an thinken of her when she'd be away.'

To curb in my tale, which may otherwise become restive and unmanageable – Milly's deep affliction and generous sympathy made a serious impression on the mind of the widower, who more than all was touched by that singularly accidental attachment which she seemed to have conceived for little Patcy. Nothing could be farther from his own wishes than any design of a second time changing his condition; but he felt that it would be going a grievous wrong to the memory of his first wife if he neglected this opportunity of providing her favourite Patcy with a protector, so well calculated to supply her place. He demurred a little on the score of true love, and the violence which he was about to do his own constant heart – but like the bluff King Henry, his conscience – 'aye – his conscience,' – touched him, and the issue was that a roaring wedding shook the walls which had echoed to the wail of death within the few preceding months.

Milly Rue not only supplied the place of a mother to young Patcy, but presented him in the course of a few years with two merry play-fellows, a brother and a sister. To do her handsome justice, too, poor Mauria's anticipations were completely disproved by her conduct, and it would have been impossible for a stranger to have detected the stepson of the house from any shade of undue partiality in the mother. The harmony in which they dwelt was unbroken by any accident for many years.

The first shock which burst in with a sudden violence upon their happiness was one of a direful nature. Disease, that pale and hungry fiend who haunts alike the abodes of wealth and of penury; who brushes away with his baleful wing the bloom from beauty's cheek, and the balm of slumber from the pillow of age; who troubles the hope of the young mother with dreams of ghastliness and gloom, and fears that come suddenly, she knows not why nor whence; who sheds his poisonous dews alike on the heart that is buoyant and the heart that is broken; this stern and conquering demon scorned not to knock, one summer morning, at the door of Phadrig's cow-house, and to lay his iron fingers upon a fine milch-cow, a sheeted-stripper which con-stituted (to use his own emphatic phrase) the poor farmer's 'substance', and to which he might have applied the well-known lines which run nearly as follows:

> She's straight in her back, and thin in her tail;

> She's fine in her horn, and good at the pail;
> She's calm in her eyes, and soft in her skin;
> She's a grazier's without, and a butcher's within.

All the 'cures' in the pharmacopoeia of the village apothecary were expended on the poor animal, without any beneficial effect; and Phadrig, after many conscientious qualms about the dying words of his first wife, resolved to have recourse to that infallible refuge in such cases – a fairy doctor.

He said nothing to the afflicted Milly about his intention, but slipped out of the cottage in the afternoon, hurried to the Shannon side near Money Point, unmoored his light canvas-built canoe, seated himself in the frail vessel, and fixing his paddles on the *towl-pin*, sped away over the calm face of the waters towards the isle of Scattery, where the renowned Crohoore-na-Oona, or Connor-of-the-Sheep, the Mohammed of the cottages, at this time took up his residence. This mysterious personage, whose prophecies are still commented on among the cottage circles with looks of deep awe and wonder, was much revered by his contemporaries as a man 'who had seen a dale'; of what nature those sights or visions were was intimated by a mysterious look, and a solemn nod of the head.

In a little time Phadrig ran his little canoe aground on the sandy beach of Scattery, and, drawing her above high-water mark, proceeded to the humble dwelling of the gifted Sheep-shearer with feelings of profound fear and anxiety. He passed the lofty round tower – the ruined grave of St Senanus, in the centre of the little isle – the mouldering church, on which the eye of the poring antiquary may still discern the sculptured image of the two-headed monster, with which cottage tradition says the saint sustained so fierce a conflict on landing in the islet – and which the translator of Odranus has vividly described as 'a dragon, with his fore-part covered with huge bristles, standing on end like those of a boar; his mouth gaping wide open with a double row of crooked, sharp tusks, and with such openings that his entrails might be seen; his back like a round island, full of scales and shells; his legs short and hairy, with such steely talons, that the pebble-stones, as he ran along them, sparkled – parching the way wherever he went, and making the sea boil about him where he dived – such was his excessive fiery heat.' Phadrig's knees shook beneath him when he remembered this awful description – and thought of the legends of Lough Dhoola, on the summit of Mount Callon, to which the hideous animal was banished by the saint, to fast on a trout and a half per diem to the end of time; and where, to this day, the neighbouring fishermen declare that, in dragging the lake with their nets, they find the half trout as regularly divided in the centre as if it were done with a knife and scale.

While Phadrig remained with mouth and eyes almost as wide open as those of the sculptured image of the monster which had fascinated him to the spot, a sudden crash among the stones and dock-weed in an opposite corner of the ruin made him start and yell as if the original were about to quit Lough Dhoola on parole of honour, and use him as a relish after the trout and a half. The noise was occasioned by a little rotund personage, who had sprung from the mouldering wall, and now stood gazing fixedly on the terrified Phadrig, who continued returning that steady glance with a half-frightened, half-crying face – one hand fast clenched upon his breast, and the other extended, with an action of avoidance and deprecation. The person of the stranger was stout and short, rendered still more so by a stoop, which might almost have been taken for a hump – his arms hung forward from his shoulders, like those of a long-armed ape – his hair was grey and bushy, like that of a wanderoo – and his sullen grey eye seemed to be inflamed with ill-humour – his feet were bare and as broad as a camel's – and a leathern girdle buckling round his waist secured a tattered grey frieze riding-coat, and held an enormous pair of shears, which might have clipped off a man's head as readily, perhaps, as a lock of wool. This last article of costume afforded a sufficient indication to Phadrig that he stood in the presence of the awful object of his search.

'Well! an who are *you*?' growled the Sheep-shearer, after surveying Phadrig attentively for some moments.

The first gruff sound of his voice made the latter renew his start and roar for fright; after which, composing his terrors as well as he might, he replied, in the words of Autolycus, 'I am only a poor fellow, sir.'

'Well! an what's your business with me?'

'A cure, sir, I wanted for her. A cow o' mine that's very bad inwardly, an we can do nothen for her; an I thought may be you'd know what is it ail'ded her – an prevail on *them*' (this word was pronounced with an emphasis of deep meaning) 'to leave her to uz.'

'Huth!' the Sheep-shearer thundered out, in a tone that made poor Phadrig jump six feet backwards with a fresh yell, 'do you daare to spake of *them* before me. Go along! you villyan o' the airth, an wait for me outside the church, an I'll tell you all about it there; but, first – do you think I can get the *gentlemen* to do anything for me *gratish* – without offeren 'em a trate or a haip'-orth?'

'If their honours wouldn't think two tin-pennies and a fi'penny bit too little – It's all I'm worth in the wide world.'

'Well! we'll see what they'll say to it. Give it here to me. Go now – be off with yourself – if you don't want to have 'em all a-top o' you in a minnit.'

This last hint made our hero scamper over the stones like a startled fawn; nor did he think himself safe until he reached the spot where he had left his canoe, and where he expected the coming of the Sheep-shearer; conscience-struck by the breach of his promise to his dying Mauria, and in a state of agonizing anxiety with respect to the lowing patient in the cow-house.

He was soon after rejoined by Connor-of-the-Sheep.

'There is one way,' said he, 'of saving your cow – but you must lose one of your childer if you wish to save it.'

'O Heaven presarve uz, sir, how is that, if you plase?'

'You must go home,' said the Sheep-shearer, 'and say nothen to anybody, but fix in your mind which o' your three childer you'll give for the cow; an when you do that, look in his eyes, an he'll sneeze, an don't you bless him, for the world. Then look in his eyes again, an he'll sneeze again, an still don't think o' blessen him, be any mains. The third time you'll look in his eyes he'll sneeze a third time – an if you don't bless him the third time, he'll die – but your cow will live.'

'An this is the only cure you have to gi' me?' exclaimed Phadrig, his indignation at the moment overcoming his natural timidity.

'The only cure. It was by a dale to do I could prevail on them to let you make the choice itself.'

Phadrig declared stoutly against this decree, and even threw out some hints that he would try whether or no Shaun Lauther, or Strong John, a young rival of the sheep-shearing fairy doctor, might be able to make a better bargain for him with the 'gentlemen'.

'Shaun Lauther!' exclaimed Connor-of-the-Sheep, in high anger – 'Do you compare me to a man that never seen any more than yourself? – that never saw so much as the skirt of a dead man's shroud in the moonlight – or heard as much as the moanen of a sowlth[1] in an old graveyard? Do you know me? Ask them that do – an they'll tell you how often I'm called up in the night, and kep posten over bog an mountain, till I'm ready to drop down with the sleep – while few voices are heard, I'll be bail, at Shaun Lauther's windey – a little knollidge given him in his drames. It is then that I get mine. Didn't I say before the King o' France was beheaded that a blow would be struck wit an axe in that place, that the sound of it would be heard all over Europe? An wasn't it true? Didn't I hear the shots that were fired at Gibaralthur, an tell it over in Dooly's forge, that the place was relieved that day? – an didn't the news come afterwards in a month's time that I toult nothen but the truth?'

Phadrig had nothing to say in answer to this overwhelming list of interrogatories – but to apologize for his want of credulity, and to express himself perfectly satisfied.

With a heavy heart he put forth in his canoe upon the water and prepared to return. It was already twilight, and as he glided along the peaceful shores he ruminated mournfully within his mind on the course which he should pursue. The loss of the cow would be, he considered, almost equivalent to total ruin – and the loss of any one of his lovely children was a probability which he could hardly bear to dwell on for a moment. Still it behoved him to weigh the matter well.

[1] Bodiless spirit.

Which of them now – supposing it possible that he could think of sacrificing any – which of them would he select for the purpose? The choice was a hard one. There was little Mauria, a fair-haired, blue-eyed little girl – but he could not, for an instant, think of losing her, as she happened to be named after his first wife; her brother, little Shamus, was the least useful of the three, but he was the youngest – 'the child of his old age – a little one!' His heart bled at the idea; he would lose the cow, the pig along with it, before he would harm a hair of the darling infant's head. He thought of Patcy – and he shuddered and leaned heavier on his oars, as if to flee away from the horrible doubt which stole into his heart with that name. It must be one of the three, or the cow was lost for ever. The two first-mentioned he certainly would not lose – and Patcy; Again he bade the fiend begone, and trembling in every limb, made the canoe speed rapidly over the tide in the direction of his home.

He drew the little vessel ashore and proceeded towards his cabin. They had been waiting supper for him, and he learned with renewed anxiety that the object of his solicitude, the milch-cow, had rather fallen away than improved in her condition during his absence. He sat down in sorrowful silence with his wife and children to their humble supper of potatoes and thick milk.

He gazed intently on the features of each of the young innocents as they took their places on the suggan chairs that flanked the board. Little Mauria and her brother Shamus looked fresh, mirthful, and blooming from their noisy play in the adjoining paddock, while their elder brother, who had spent the day at school, wore – or seemed, to the distempered mind of his father, to wear a look of sullenness and chagrin. He was thinner, too, than most boys of his age – a circumstance which Phadrig had never remarked before. It might be the first indications of his poor mother's disease, consumption, that were beginning to declare themselves in his constitution; and if so, his doom was already sealed – and whether the cow died or not, Patcy was certain to be lost. Still the father could not bring his mind to resolve on any settled course, and their meal proceeded in silence.

Suddenly the latch of the door was lifted by some person outside, and a neighbour entered to inform Phadrig that the agent to his landlord had arrived in the adjacent village for the purpose of driving matters to extremity against all those tenants who remained in arrear. At the same moment, too, a low moan of anguish from the cow outside announced the access of a fresh paroxysm of her distemper, which it was very evident the poor animal could never come through in safety.

In an agony of distress and horror the distracted father laid his clenched fingers on the table, and looked fixedly in the eyes of the unsuspecting Patcy. The child sneezed, and Phadrig closed his lips hard, for fear a blessing might escape him. The child at the same time, he observed, looked paler than before.

Fearful lest the remorse which began to awake within his heart might oversway his resolution, and prevent the accomplishment of his unnatural design, he looked hurriedly a second time into the eyes of the little victim. Again the latter sneezed, and again the father, using a violent effort, restrained the blessing which was struggling at his heart. The poor child drooped his head upon his bosom, and letting the untasted food fall from his hand, looked so pale and mournful as to remind his murderer of the look which his mother wore in dying.

It was long – very long – before the heart-struck parent could prevail on himself to complete the sacrifice. The visitor departed; and the first beams of a full moon began to supplant the faint and lingering twilight which was fast fading in the west. The dead of the night drew on before the family rose from their silent and comfortless meal. The agonies of the devoted animal now drew rapidly to a close, and Phadrig still remained tortured by remorse on the one hand, and by selfish anxiety on the other.

A sudden sound of anguish from the cow-house made him start from his seat. A third time he fixed his eyes on those of his child – a third time the boy sneezed – but here the charm was broken.

Milly Rue, looking with surprise and tenderness on the fainting boy, said, 'Why, then, Heaven bless you, child! – It must be a cold you caught, you're sneezen so often.'

Immediately the cow sent forth a bellow of deep agony, and

expired; and at the same moment a low and plaintive voice outside the door was heard, exclaiming, 'And Heaven bless you, Milly! and the Almighty bless you, and spare you a long time over your children!'

Phadrig staggered back against the wall – his blood froze in his veins – his face grew white as death – his teeth chattered – his eyes stared – his hair moved upon his brow, and the chilling damp of terror exuded over all his frame. He recognized the voice of his first wife; and her pale, cold eye met his at that moment, as her shade flitted by the window in the thin moonlight, and darted on him a glance of mournful reproach. He covered his eyes with his hands, and sunk, senseless, into a chair, while the affrighted Milly and Patcy, who at once assumed his glowing health and vigour, hastened to his assistance. They had all heard the voice, but no one saw the shade nor recognized the tone excepting the conscience-smitten Phadrig.

# GEORGE MOORE

## Home Sickness

*George Moore (1852–1933) was from County Mayo. He was Anglo-Irish and one of the co-founders of Dublin's Abbey Theatre. He followed the realistic approach of Zola and Balzac and his best-known collection of short stories is* The Untilled Field. *Among his many novels,* Esther Waters *(1894) is his most famous but he also wrote* A Modern Lover *(1833) and his autobiography:* Hail and Farewell *(1911–14).*

HE told the doctor he was due in the bar-room at eight o'clock in the morning; the bar-room was in a slum in the Bowery; and he had only been able to keep himself in health by getting up at five o'clock and going for long walks in the Central Park.

'A sea-voyage is what you want,' said the doctor. 'Why not go to Ireland for two or three months? You will come back a new man.'

'I'd like to see Ireland again.'

And he began to wonder how the people at home were getting on. The doctor was right. He thanked him, and three weeks after he landed in Cork.

As he sat in the railway-carriage he recalled his native village, built among the rocks of the large headland stretching out into the winding lake. He could see the houses and the streets, and the fields of the tenants, and the Georgian mansion and the owners of it; he and they had been boys together before he went to America. He remembered the villagers going every morning to the big house to work in the stables, in the garden, in the fields – mowing, reaping, digging, and

Michael Malia building a wall; it was all as clear as if it were yesterday, yet he had been thirteen years in America; and when the train stopped at the station, the first thing he did was to look round for any changes that might have come into it. It was the same blue limestone station as it was thirteen years ago, with the same five long miles between it and Duncannon. He had once walked these miles gaily, in little over an hour, carrying a heavy bundle on a stick, but he did not feel strong enough for the walk today, though the evening tempted him to try it. A car was waiting at the station, and the boy, discerning from his accent and his dress that Bryden had come from America, plied him with questions, which Bryden answered rapidly, for he wanted to hear who were still living in the village, and if there was a house in which he could get a clean lodging. The best house in the village, he was told, was Mike Scully's, who had been away in a situation for many years, as a coachman in the King's County, but had come back and built a fine house with a concrete floor. The boy could recommend the loft, he had slept in it himself, and Mike would be glad to take in a lodger, he had no doubt. Bryden remembered that Mike had been in a situation at the big house. He had intended to be a jockey, but had suddenly shot up into a fine tall man, and had become a coachman instead; and Bryden tried to recall his face, but could only remember a straight nose and a somewhat dusky complexion.

So Mike had come back from King's County, and had built himself a house, had married – there were children for sure running about; while he, Bryden, had gone to America, but he had come back; perhaps he, too, would build a house in Duncannon, and – his reverie was suddenly interrupted by the carman.

'There's Mike Scully,' he said, pointing with his whip, and Bryden saw a tall, finely built, middle-aged man coming through the gates, who looked astonished when he was accosted, for he had forgotten Bryden even more completely than Bryden had forgotten him; and many aunts and uncles were mentioned before he began to understand.

'You've grown into a fine man, James,' he said, looking at Bryden's great width of chest. 'But you're thin in the cheeks, and you're very sallow in the cheeks too.'

'I haven't been very well lately – that is one of the reasons I've come back; but I want to see you all again.'

'And thousand welcome you are.'

Bryden paid the carman, and wished him 'God-speed'. They divided the luggage, Mike carrying the bag and Bryden the bundle, and they walked round the lake, for the townland was at the back of the domain; and while walking he remembered the woods thick and well forested; now they were wind-worn, the drains were choked, and the bridge leading across the lake inlet was falling away. Their way led between long fields where herds of cattle were grazing, the road was broken – Bryden wondered how the villagers drove their carts over it, and Mike told him that the landlord could not keep it in repair, and he would not allow it to be kept in repair out of the rates, for then it would be a public road, and he did not think there should be a public road through his property.

At the end of many fields they came to the village, and it looked a desolate place, even on this fine evening, and Bryden remarked that the county did not seem to be as much lived in as it used to be. It was at once strange and familiar to see the chickens in the kitchen; and, wishing to re-knit himself to the old customs, he begged of Mrs Scully not to drive them out, saying they reminded him of old times.

'And why wouldn't they?' Mike answered, 'he being one of ourselves bred and born in Duncannon, and his father before him.'

'Now, is it truth ye are telling me?' and she gave him her hand, after wiping it on her apron, saying he was heartily welcome, only she was afraid he wouldn't care to sleep in a loft.

'Why shouldn't I sleep in a loft, a dry loft! You're thinking a good deal of America over here,' he said, 'but I reckon it isn't all you think it. Here you work when you like and you sit down when you like; but when you've had a touch of blood-poisoning as I had, and when you have seen young people walking with a stick, you think that there is something to be said for old Ireland.'

'You'll take a sup of milk, won't you? You must be dry,' said Mrs Scully.

And when he had drunk the milk, Mike asked him if he would like to go inside or if he would like to go for a walk.

'Maybe resting you'd like to be.'

And they went into the cabin and started to talk about the wages a man could get in America, and the long hours of work.

And after Bryden had told Mike everything about America that he thought of interest, he asked Mike about Ireland. But Mike did not seem to be able to tell him much. They were all very poor – poorer, perhaps, then when he left them.

'I don't think anyone except myself has a five-pound note to his name.'

Bryden hoped he felt sufficiently sorry for Mike. But after all, Mike's life and prospects mattered little to him. He had come back in search of health, and he felt better already; the milk had done him good, and the bacon and the cabbage in the pot sent forth a savoury odour. The Scullys were very kind, they pressed him to make a good meal; a few weeks of country air and food, they said, would give him back the health he had lost in the Bowery; and when Bryden said he was longing for a smoke, Mike said there was no better sign than that. During his long illness he had never wanted to smoke, and he was a confirmed smoker.

It was comfortable to sit by the mild peat fire watching the smoke of their pipes drifting up the chimney, and all Bryden wanted was to be left alone; he did not want to hear of anyone's misfortunes, but about nine o'clock a number of villagers came in, and Bryden remembered one or two of them – he used to know them very well when he was a boy; their talk was as depressing as their appearance, and he could feel no interest whatever in them. He was not moved when he heard that Higgins the stonemason was dead; he was not affected when he heard that Mary Kelly, who used to go to do the laundry at the Big House, had married; he was only interested when he heard she had gone to America. No, he had not met her there; America is a big place. Then one of the peasants asked him if he remembered Patsy Carabine, who used to do the gardening at the Big House. Yes, he remembered Patsy well. He had not been able to do any work on account of his arm; his house had fallen in; he had given up his holding and gone into the poorhouse. All this was very sad, and to avoid hearing any further unpleasantness, Bryden began to tell them about America. And they sat round listening to him; but all the talking was on his side; he wearied of it; and looking round the group he recognized a ragged hunchback with grey hair; twenty years ago he was a young hunchback and, turning to him, Bryden asked him if he were doing well with his five acres.

'Ah, not much. This has been a poor season. The potatoes failed; they were watery – there is no diet in them.'

These peasants were all agreed that they could make nothing out of their farms. Their regret was that they had not gone to America when they were young; and after striving to take an interest in the fact that O'Connor had lost a mare and a foal worth forty pounds, Bryden began to wish himself back in the slum. And when they left the house he wondered if every evening would be like the present one. Mike piled fresh sods on the fire, and he hoped it would show enough light in the loft for Bryden to undress himself by.

The cackling of some geese in the street kept him awake, and he seemed to realize suddenly how lonely the country was, and he foresaw mile after mile of scanty fields stretching all round the lake with one little town in the far corner. A dog howled in the distance, and the fields and the boreens between him and the dog appeared as in a crystal. He could hear Michael breathing by his wife's side in the kitchen, and he could barely resist the impulse to run out of the house, and he might have yielded to it, but he wasn't sure that he mightn't awaken Mike as he came down the ladder. His terror increased, and he drew the blanket over his head. He fell asleep and awoke and fell asleep again, and lying on his back he dreamed of the men he had seen sitting round the fireside that evening, like spectres they seemed to him in his dream. He seemed to have been asleep only a few minutes when he heard Mike calling him. He had come half-way up the ladder, and was telling him that breakfast was ready.

'What kind of a breakfast will he give me?' Bryden asked himself as he pulled on his clothes. There were tea and hot griddle cakes for breakfast, and there were fresh eggs; there was sunlight in the kitchen, and he liked to hear Mike tell of the work he was going to be at in the farm – one of about fifteen acres, at least ten of it was grass; he grew an acre of potatoes, and some corn, and some turnips for his sheep. He had a nice bit of meadow, and he took down his scythe, and as he put the whetstone in his belt Bryden noticed a second scythe, and he asked Mike if he should go down with him and help him to finish the field.

'It's a long time since you've done any mowing, and it's heavier work than you think for. You'd better go for a walk by the lake.' Seeing that Bryden looked a little disappointed he added, 'If you like you can come up in the afternoon and help me to turn the grass over.' Bryden said he would, and the morning passed pleasantly by the lake shore – a delicious breeze rustled in the trees, and the reeds were talking together, and the ducks were talking in the reeds; a cloud blotted out the sunlight, and the cloud passed and the sun shone, and the reed cast its shadow again in the still water; there was a lapping always about the shingle; the magic of returning health was sufficient distraction for the convalescent; he lay with his eyes fixed upon the castles, dreaming of the men that had manned the battlements; whenever a peasant driving a cart or an ass or an old woman with a bundle of sticks on her back went by, Bryden kept them in chat, and he soon knew the village by heart. One day the landlord from the Georgian mansion set on the pleasant green hill came along, his retriever at his heels, and stopped, surprised at finding somebody whom he didn't know on his property. 'What, James Bryden!' he said. And the story was told again how ill health had overtaken him at last, and he had come home to Duncannon to recover. The two walked as far as the pine-wood, talking of the county, what it had been, the ruin it was slipping into, and as they parted Bryden asked for the loan of a boat.

'Of course, of course!' the landlord answered, and Bryden rowed about the islands every morning; and resting upon his oars looked at the old castles, remembering the prehistoric raiders that the landlord had told him about. He came across the stones to which the lake-dwellers had tied their boats, and these signs of ancient Ireland were pleasing to Bryden in his present mood.

As well as the great lake there was a smaller lake in the bog where the villagers cut their turf. This lake was famous for its pike, and the landlord allowed Bryden to fish there, and one evening when he was looking for a frog with which to bait his line he met Margaret Dirken driving home the cows for the milking. Margaret was the herdsman's daughter, and lived in a cottage near the Big House; but she came up to the village whenever there was a dance, and Bryden had found himself opposite to her in the reels. But until this evening he had had little opportunity of speaking to her, and he was glad to speak to someone, for the evening was lonely, and they stood talking together.

'You're getting your health again,' she said, 'and will be leaving us soon.'

'I'm in no hurry.'

'You're grand people over there; I hear a man is paid four dollars a day for his work.'

'And how much,' said James, 'has he to pay for his food and for his clothes?'

Her cheeks were bright and her teeth small, white and beautifully even; and a woman's soul looked at Bryden out of her soft Irish eyes. He was troubled and turned aside, and catching sight of a frog looking at him out of a tuft of grass, he said:

'I have been looking for a frog to put upon my pike line.'

The frog jumped right and left, and nearly escaped in some bushes, but he caught it and returned with it in his hand.

'It is just the kind of frog a pike will like,' he said. 'Look at its great white belly and its bright yellow back.'

And without more ado he pushed the wire to which the hook was fastened through the frog's fresh body, and dragging it through the mouth he passed the hooks through the hind-legs and tied the line to the end of the wire.

'I think,' said Margaret, 'I must be looking after my cows; it's time I got them home.'

'Won't you come down to the lake while I set my line?'

She thought for a moment and said:

'No, I'll see you from here.'

He went down to the reedy tarn, and at his approach several snipe got up, and they flew above his head uttering sharp cries. His fishing-rod was a long hazel-stick, and he threw the frog as far as he could in the lake. In doing this he roused some wild ducks; a mallard and two ducks got up, and they flew towards the larger lake in a line with an old castle; and they had not disappeared from view when Bryden came towards her, and he and she drove the cows home together that evening.

They had not met very often when she said: 'James, you had better not come here so often calling to me.'

'Don't you wish me to come?'

'Yes, I wish you to come well enough, but keeping company isn't the custom of the country, and I don't want to be talked about.'

'Are you afraid the priest would speak against us from the altar?'

'He has spoken against keeping company, but it is not so much what the priest says, for there is no harm in talking.'

'But if you're going to be married, there is no harm in walking out together.'

'Well, not so much, but marriages are made differently in these parts; there isn't much courting here.'

And next day it was known in the village that James was going to marry Margaret Dirken.

His desire to excel the boys in dancing had caused a stir of gaiety in the parish, and for some time past there had been dancing in every house where there was a floor fit to dance upon; and if the cottager had no money to pay for a barrel of beer, James Bryden, who had money, sent him a barrel, so that Margaret might get her dance. She told him that they sometimes crossed over into another parish where the priest was not so averse to dancing, and James wondered. And next morning at Mass he wondered at their simple fervour. Some of them held their hands above their head as they prayed, and all this was very new and very old to James Bryden. But the obedience of these people to their priest surprised him. When he was a lad they had not been so obedient, or he had forgotten their obedience; and he listened in mixed anger and wonderment to the priest, who was scolding his parishioners, speaking to them by name, saying that he had heard there was dancing going on in their homes. Worse than that, he said he had seen boys and girls loitering about the road, and the talk that went on was of one kind – love. He said that newspapers containing love stories were finding their way into the people's houses, stories about love, in which there was nothing elevating or ennobling. The people listened, accepting the priest's opinion without question. And their pathetic submission was the submission of a primitive people clinging to religious authority, and Bryden contrasted the weakness and incompetence of the people about him with the modern rest-lessness and cold energy of the people he left behind him.

One evening, as they were dancing, a knock came to the door, and the piper stopped playing, and the dancers whispered:

'Someone has told on us: it is the priest.'

And the awe-stricken villagers crowded round the cottage fire, afraid to open the door. But the priest said that if they didn't open the door he would put his shoulder to it and force it open. Bryden went towards the door, saying he would allow no one to threaten him, priest or no priest, but Margaret caught his arm and told him that if he said anything to the priest, the priest would speak against them from the altar, and they would be shunned by the neighbours.

'I've heard of your goings-on,' he said, 'of your beer-drinking and dancing. I'll not have it in my parish. If you want that sort of thing you'd had better go to America.'

'If that is intended for me, sir, I'll go back tomorrow. Margaret can follow.'

'It isn't the dancing, it's the drinking I'm opposed to,' said the priest, turning to Bryden.

'Well, no one has drunk too much, sir,' said Bryden.

'But you'll sit here drinking all night,' and the priest's eyes went to the corner where the women had gathered, and Bryden felt that the priest looked on the women as more dangerous than the porter. 'It's after midnight,' he said, taking out his watch.

By Bryden's watch it was only half past eleven, and while they were arguing about the time, Mrs Scully offered Bryden's umbrella to the priest, for in his hurry to stop the dancing the priest had gone out without his; and, as if to show Bryden that he bore him no ill will, the priest accepted the loan of the umbrella, for he was thinking of the big marriage fee that Bryden would pay him.

'I shall be badly off for the umbrella tomorrow,' Bryden said, as soon as the priest was out of the house. He was going with his father-in-law to a fair. His father-in-law was learning him how to buy and sell cattle. The country was mending, and a man might become rich in Ireland if he only had a little capital. Margaret had an uncle on the other side of the lake who would give twenty pounds, and her father would give another twenty pounds. Bryden had saved two hundred pounds. Never in the village of Duncannon had a young couple begun life with so much prospect of success, and some time after Christmas was spoken of as the best time for the marriage; James Bryden said that he would not be able to get his money out of America before the spring. The delay seemed to vex him, and he seemed anxious to be married, until one day he received a letter from America, from a man who had served in the bar with him. This friend wrote to ask Bryden if he were coming back. The letter was no more than a passing wish to see Bryden again. Yet Bryden stood looking at it, and everyone wondered what could be in the letter. It seemed momentous, and they hardly believed him when he said it was from a friend who wanted to know if his health were better. He tried to forget the letter, and he looked at the worn fields, divided by walls of loose stones, and a great longing came upon him.

The smell of the Bowery slum had come across the Atlantic, and had found him out in his western headland; and one night he awoke from a dream in which he was hurling some drunken customer through the open doors into the darkness. He had seen his friend in his white duck jacket throwing drink from glass into glass amid the din of voices and strange accents; he had heard the clang of money as it was swept into the till, and his sense sickened for the bar-room. But how should he tell Margaret Dirken that he could not marry her? She had built her life upon this marriage. He could not tell her that he would not marry her ... yet he must go. He felt as if he were being hunted; the thought that he must tell Margaret that he could not marry her hunted him day after day as a weasel hunts a rabbit. Again and again he went to meet her with the intention of telling her that he did not love her, that their lives were not for one another, that it had all been a mistake, and that happily he had found out it was a mistake soon enough. But Margaret, as if she guessed what he was about to speak of, threw her arms about him and begged him to say he loved her, and that they would be married at once. He agreed that he loved her, and that they would be married at once. But he had not left her many minutes before the feeling came upon him that he could not marry her – that he must go away. The smell of the bar-room hunted him down. Was it for the sake of the money that he might make there that he wished to go back? No, it was not the money. What then? His eyes fell on the bleak country, on the little fields divided by bleak walls; he remembered the pathetic ignorance of the people, and it was these things that he could not endure. It was the priest who came to forbid the dancing. Yes, it was the priest. As he stood looking at the line of the hills, the bar-room seemed by him. He heard the politicians, and the excitement of politics was in his blood again. He must go away from this place – he must get back to the bar-room. Looking up, he saw the scanty orchard, and he hated the spare road that led to the village, and he hated the little hill at the top of which the village began, and he hated more than all other places the house where he was to live with Margaret Dirken – if he married her. He could see it from where he stood – by the edge of the lake, with twenty acres of pasture land about it, for the landlord had given up part of his demesne land to them.

He caught sight of Margaret, and he called her to come through the stile.

'I have just had a letter from America.'

'About the money?'

'Yes, about the money. But I shall have to go over there.'

He stood looking at her, wondering what to say; and she guessed that he would tell her that he must go to America before they were married.

'Do you mean, James, you will have to go at once?'

'Yes,' he said 'at once. But I shall come back in time to be married in August. It will only mean delaying our marriage a month.'

They walked on a little way talking, and every step he took James felt that he was a step nearer the Bowery slum. And when they came to the gate Bryden said:

'I must walk on or I shall miss the train.'

'But,' she said, 'you are not going now – you are not going today?'

'Yes, this morning. It is seven miles. I shall have to hurry not to miss the train.'

And then she asked him if he would ever come back.

'Yes,' he said, 'I am coming back.'

'If you are coming back, James, why don't you let me go with you?'

'You couldn't walk fast enough. We should miss the train.'

'One moment, James. Don't make me suffer; tell me the truth. You are not coming back. Your clothes – where shall I send them?'

He hurried away, hoping he would come back. He tried to think that he liked the country he was leaving, that it would be better to have a farmhouse and live there with Margaret Dirken than to serve drinks behind a counter in the Bowery. He did not think he was telling her a lie when he said he was coming back. Her offer to forward his clothes touched his heart, and at the end of the road he stood and asked himself if he should go back to her. He would miss the train if he waited another minute, and he ran on. And he would have missed the train if he had not met a car. Once he was on the car he felt himself safe – the country was already behind him. The train and the boat at Cork were mere formulae; he was already in America.

And when the tall skyscraper stuck up beyond the harbour, he felt the thrill of home that he had not found in his native village and wondered how it was that the smell of the bar seemed more natural than the smell of fields, and the roar of crowds more welcome than the silence of the lake's edge. He entered into negotiations for the purchase of the bar-room. He took a wife, she bore him sons and daughters, the bar-room prospered, property came and went; he grew old, his wife died, he retired from business, and reached the age when a man begins to feel there are not many years in front of him, and that all he has had to do in life has been done. His children married, lonesomeness began to creep about him in the evening, and when he looked into the firelight, a vague tender reverie floated up, and Margaret's soft eyes and name vivified the dusk. His wife and children passed out of mind, and it seemed to him that a memory was the only real thing he possessed, and the desire to see Margaret again grew intense. But she was an old woman, she had married, maybe she was dead. Well, he would like to be buried in the village where he was born.

There is an unchanging, silent life within every man that none knows but himself, and his unchanging silent life was his memory of Margaret Dirken. The bar-room was forgotten and all that concerned it, and the things he saw most clearly were the green hillside, and the bog lake and the rushes about it, and the greater lake in the distance, and behind it the blue line of wandering hills.

# GEORGE MOORE

## Some Parishioners

### I

THE way before Father Maguire was plain enough, yet his uncle's
apathy and constitutional infirmity of purpose seemed at times to
thwart him. Only two or three days ago, he had come running down
from Kilmore with the news that a baby had been born out of
wedlock, and what do you think? Father Stafford had shown no desire
that his curate should denounce the girl from the altar.

'The greatest saints,' he said, 'have been kind, and have found
excuses for the sins of others.'

And a few days later, when he told his uncle that the Salvationists
had come to Kilmore, and that he had walked up the village street and
slit their drum with a carving-knife, his uncle had not approved of his
conduct, and what had especially annoyed Father Tom was that his
uncle seemed to deplore the slitting of the drum in the same way as he
deplored that the Kavanaghs had a barrel of porter in every Saturday,
as one of those regrettable excesses to which human nature is liable.
On being pressed, he agreed with his nephew that dancing and
drinking were no preparation for the Sabbath, but he would not agree
that evil could be suppressed by force. He even hinted that too strict a
rule brought about a revolt against the rule, and when Father Tom
expressed his disbelief at any revolt against the authority of the priest,
Father Stafford said:

'They may just leave you, they may just go to America.'

'Then you think that it is our condemnation of sin that is driving the people to America?'

'My dear Tom, you told me the other day that you met a boy and girl walking along the roadside, and drove them home. You told me you were sure they were talking about things they shouldn't talk about; you have no right to assume these things. You're asking of the people an abstinence you don't practise yourself. Sometimes your friends are women.'

'Yes. But –'

Father Tom's anger prevented him from finding an adequate argument, and Father Stafford pushed the tobacco-bowl towards his nephew.

'You're not smoking, Tom.'

'Your point is that a certain amount of vice is inherent in human nature, and that if we raise the standard of virtuous living our people will escape from us to New York or London.'

'The sexes mix freely everywhere in Western Europe; only in Ireland and Turkey is there any attempt made to separate them.'

Later in the evening Father Tom insisted that the measure of responsibility was always the same.

'I should be sorry,' said his uncle, 'to say that those who inherit drunkenness bear the same burden of responsibility as those who come of parents who are quite sane –'

'You cannot deny, uncle John, that free will and predestination –'

'My dear Tom, I really must go to bed. It is after midnight.'

And as he walked home, Father Maguire thought of the great change he perceived in his uncle. He liked an hour's small-talk after dinner, his pipe, his glass of grog, his bed at eleven o'clock, and Father Maguire thought with sorrow of their great disputations, sometimes prolonged till after three o'clock. The passionate scholiast of Maynooth seemed to him unrecognizable in the esurient Vicar-General, only occasionally interested in theology, at certain hours and when he felt particularly well. The first seemed incompatible with the second, his mind not being sufficiently acute to see that after all no one can discuss theology for more than five and twenty years without wearying of the subject.

The moon was shining among the hills and the mystery of the landscape seemed to aggravate his sensibility, and he asked himself if the guardians of the people should not fling themselves into the forefront of the battle. If men came to preach heresy in his parish was he not justified in slitting their drum?

He had recourse to prayer, and he prayed for strength and for guidance. He had accepted the Church, and in the Church he saw only apathy, neglect and bad administration on the part of his superiors ... He had read that great virtues are, like large sums of money, deposited in the bank, whereas humility is like the pence, always at hand, always current. Obedience to our superiors is the sure path. He could not persuade himself that it was right for him to allow the Kavanaghs to continue a dissolute life of drinking and dancing. They were the talk of the parish; and he would have spoken against them from the altar, but his uncle had advised him not to do so. Perhaps his uncle was right; he might be right regarding the Kavanaghs. In the main he disagreed with his uncle, but in this particular instance it might be well to wait and pray that matters might improve.

Father Tom believed Ned Kavanagh to be a good boy. Ned was going to marry Mary Byrne, and Father Tom had made up this marriage. The Byrnes did not care for the marriage – they were prejudiced against Ned on account of his family. But he was not going to allow them to break off the marriage. He was sure of Ned, but in order to make quite sure he would get him to take the pledge. Next morning, when the priest had done his breakfast, the servant opened the door, and told him that Ned Kavanagh was outside, and wanted to see him.

It was a pleasure to look at this nice clean boy, with his winning smile, and the priest thought that Mary could not wish for a better husband. The priest had done his breakfast, and was about to open his newspaper, but he wanted to see Ned Kavanagh, and he told his servant to let him in. Ned's smile seemed a little fainter than usual, and his face was paler; the priest wondered, and presently Ned told the priest that he had come to confession, and, going down on his knees, he told the priest that he had been drunk last Saturday night, and that he had come to take the pledge. He would never do any good while he was at home, and one of the reasons he gave for wishing to marry Mary Byrne was his desire to leave home. The priest asked him if matters were mending, and if his sister showed any signs of wishing to be married.

'Sorra sign,' said Ned.

'That's bad news you're bringing me,' said the priest, and he walked up and down the room, and they talked over Kate's wilful character.

'From the beginning she didn't like living at home,' said the priest.

'I wouldn't be caring about living at home,' said Ned.

'But for a different reason,' said the priest. 'You want to leave home to get married, and have a wife and children, if God is pleased to give you children.'

He sat thinking of the stories he had heard. He had heard that Kate had come back from her last situation in a cab, wrapped up in blankets, saying she was ill. On inquiry it was found that she had only been three or four days in her situation; three weeks had to be accounted for. He had questioned her himself regarding this interval, but had not been able to get any clear and definite answer from her.

'She and mother do be always quarrelling about Pat Connex.'

'It appears,' said the priest, 'that your mother went out with a jug of porter under her apron, and offered a sup of it to Pat, who was talking with Peter M'Shane, and now he is up at your cabin every Saturday.'

'That's so,' said Ned.

'Mrs Connex was here the other day, and I tell you that if Pat marries your sister he will find himself cut off with a shilling.'

'She's been agin us all the while,' said Ned. 'Her money has made her proud, but I wouldn't be blaming her. If I had the fine house she has, maybe I would be as proud as she.'

'Maybe you would,' said the priest. 'But what I'm thinking of is your sister Kate. She'll never get Pat Connex. Pat won't ever go against his mother.'

'Well, you see he comes up and plays the melodeon on Saturday night,' said Ned, 'and she can't stop him from doing that.'

'Then you think,' said the priest, 'that Pat will marry your sister?'

'I don't think she is thinking about him.'

'If she doesn't want to marry him, what's all this talk about?'

'She does like to be meeting Pat in the evenings and to be walking out with him, and him putting his arm round her waist and kiss her, saving your reverence's presence.'

'It is strange that you should be so unlike. You come here and ask me to speak to Mary Byrne's parents for you, and that I'll do, Ned, and it will be all right. You will make a good husband, and though you were drunk last night, you have taken the pledge to-day. And I will make a good marriage for Kate, too, if she'll listen to me.'

'And who may your reverence be thinking of?'

'I'm thinking of Peter M'Shane. He gets as much as six shillings a week and his keep on Murphy's farm, and his mother has got a bit of money, and they have a nice, clean cabin. Now listen to me. There is a poultry lecture at the schoolhouse to- night. Do you think you could bring your sister with you?'

'We did use to keep a great many hins at home, and Kate had the feeding of them, and now she's turned agin them, and she wants to live in town, and she even tells Pat Connex she would not marry a farmer, however much he was worth.'

'But if you tell her that Pat Connex will be at the lecture, will she come?'

'Yes, your reverence, if she believes me.'

'Then do as I bid you,' said the priest; 'you can tell her that Pat Connex will be there.'

## II

After leaving the priest Ned crossed over the road to avoid the public-house, and went for a walk on the hills. It was about five when he turned towards the village. On his way there he met his father, and Ned told him that he had been to see the priest, and that he was going to take Mary to the lecture.

'They're quarrelling at home.'

Michael was very tired, and he thought it was pretty hard to come home after a long day's work to find his wife and daughter quarrelling.

'I am sorry your dinner isn't ready, father,' said Kate, 'but it won't be long now. I'll cut the bacon.'

'I met Ned on the road,' her father answered. 'It's sorry I am that he has gone to fetch Mary. He's going to take her to the lecture on poultry-keeping at the schoolhouse.'

'Ah, he has been to the priest, has he?' said Kate, and her mother asked why she said that, and the wrangle began again.

Ned was the peacemaker; there was generally quiet in the cabin when he was there. And he dropped in as Michael was finishing his dinner, bringing with him Mary, a small, fair girl, who everybody said would keep his cabin tidy. His mother and sister were broad-shouldered women with blue-black hair and red cheeks, and it was said that he had said he would like to bring a little fair hair in the family.

'We've just looked in for a minute,' said Mary. 'Ned said that perhaps you'd be coming with us.'

'All the boys in the village will be there to-night,' said Ned. 'You had better come with us.' And pretending he wanted to get a coal of fire to light his pipe, Ned whispered to Kate as he passed her, 'Pat Connex will be there.'

She looked at the striped sunshade she had brought back from the dressmaker's – she had once been apprenticed to a dressmaker – but Ned said that a storm was blowing and she had better leave the sunshade behind.

The rain beat in their faces and the wind came sweeping down the mountain and made them stagger. Sometimes the road went straight on, sometimes it turned suddenly and went uphill. After walking for a mile they came to the schoolhouse. A number of men were waiting outside, and one of the boys told them that the priest had said they were to keep a look-out for the lecturer, and Ned said that he had better stay with them, that his lantern would be useful to show her the way. The women had collected into one corner, and the priest was walking up and down a long, smoky room, his hand thrust into the pockets of his overcoat. Now he stopped in his walk to scold two children who were trying to light a peat fire in a tumble-down grate.

'Don't be tired, go on blowing,' he said. 'You are the laziest child I have seen this long while.'

Ned came in and blew out his lantern, but the lady he had mistaken for the lecturer was a lady who had come to live in the neighbourhood lately, and the priest said:

'You must be very much interested in poultry, ma'am, to come out on such a night as this.'

The lady stood shaking her waterproof.

'Now, then, Lizzie, run to your mother and get the lady a chair.'

And when the child came back with the chair, and the lady was seated by the fire, he said:

'I'm thinking there will be no lecturer here tonight, and that it would be kind of you if you were to give the lecture yourself. You have read some books about poultry, I am sure?'

'Well, a little – but –'

'Oh, that doesn't matter,' said the priest. 'I'm sure the book you have read is full of instruction.'

He walked up the room towards a group of men and told them they must cease talking, and coming back to the young woman he said:

'We shall be much obliged if you will say a few words about poultry. Just say what you have in your mind about the different breeds.'

The young woman again protested, but the priest said:

'You will do it very nicely.' And he spoke like one who is not accustomed to being disobeyed. 'We will give the lecturer five minutes more.'

'Is there no farmer's wife who could speak?' the young lady asked in a fluttering voice. 'She'd know much more than I. I see Biddy M'Hale there. She has done very well with her poultry.'

'I dare say she has,' said the priest. 'but the people would pay no attention to her. She is one of themselves. It would be no amusement to them to hear her.'

The young lady asked if she might have five minutes to scribble a few notes. The priest said he would wait a few minutes, but it did not matter much what she said.

'But couldn't someone dance or sing?' said the young lady.

'Dancing and singing!' said the priest. 'No!'

And the young lady hurriedly scribbled a few notes about fowls for laying, fowls for fattening, regular feeding, warm houses, and something about a percentage of mineral matter. She had not half finished when the priest said:

'Now will you stand over there near the harmonium. Whom shall I announce?'

The young woman told him her name, and he led her to the harmonium and left her talking, addressing most of her instruction to Biddy M'Hale, a long, thin, pale-faced woman, with wistful eyes.

'This won't do,' said the priest, interrupting the lecturer – 'I'm not speaking to you, miss, but to my people. I don't see one of you taking notes, not even you, Biddy M'Hale, though you have made a fortune out of your hins. Didn't I tell you from the pulpit that you were to bring pencil and paper and write down all you heard? If you had known years ago all this young lady is going to tell you, you would be rolling in your carriages to-day.'

Then the priest asked the lecturer to go on, and the lady explained that to get hens to lay about Christmas time, when eggs fetched the best price, you must bring on your pullets early.

'You must,' she said, 'set your eggs in January.'

'You hear that,' said the priest. 'Is there anyone who has got anything to say about that? Why is it that you don't set your eggs in January?'

No one answered, and the lecturer went on to tell of the advantages that would come to the poultry keeper whose eggs were hatched in December.

As she said this, the priest's eyes fell upon Biddy M'Hale, and, seeing that she was smiling, he asked her if there was any reason why eggs could not be hatched in the beginning of January.

'Now, Biddy, you must know all about this, and I insist on your telling us. We are here to learn.'

Biddy did not answer.

'Then what were you smiling at?'

'I wasn't smiling, your reverence.'

'Yes; I saw you smiling. Is it because you think there isn't a brooding hin in January?'

It had not occurred to the lecturer that hens might not be brooding so early in the year, and she waited anxiously. At last Biddy said:

'Well, your reverence, it isn't because there are no hins brooding. You'll get brooding hins at every time in the year; but, you see, you couldn't be rearing chickens earlier than March. The end of February is the earliest ever I saw. But, sure, if you could be rearing them in January, all that the young lady said would be quite right. I have nothing to say agin it. I have no fault to find with anything she says, your reverence.'

'Only that it can't be done,' said the priest. 'Well, you ought to know, Biddy.'

The villagers were laughing.

'That will do,' said the priest. 'I don't mind your having a bit of amusement, but you're here to learn.'

And as he looked round the room, quieting the villagers into silence, his eyes fell on Kate. He looked for the others, and spied Pat Connex and Peter M'Shane near the door. 'They're here, too,' he thought. 'When the lecture is over I will see them and bring them all together. Kate Kavanagh won't go home until she promises to marry Peter. I have had enough of her goings on in my parish.'

But Kate had caught sight of Peter. She would get no walk home with Pat that night, and she suspected her brother of having done this for a purpose and got up to go.

'I don't want anyone to leave this room,' said the priest. 'Kate Kavanagh, why are you going? Sit down till the lecture is over.'

And as Kate had not the strength to defy the priest, she sat down, and the lecturer continued for a little while longer. The priest could see that the lecturer had said nearly all she had to say, and he had begun to wonder how the evening's amusement was to be prolonged. It would not do to let the people go home until Michael Dunne had closed his public-house, and the priest looked round the audience thinking which one he might call upon to say a few words on the subject of poultry-keeping.

From one of the back rows a voice was heard: 'What about the pump, your reverence?'

'Well, indeed, you may ask,' said the priest.

And immediately he began to speak of the wrong they had suffered by not having a pump in the village. The fact that Almighty God had endowed Kilmore with a hundred mountain streams did not release the authorities from the obligation of supplying the village with a pump. Had not the authorities put up one in the neighbouring village?

'You should come out,' he said, 'and fight for your rights. You should take off your coats like men, and if you do I'll see that you get your rights,' and he looked round for someone to speak.

There was a landlord among the audience, and as he was a Catholic the priest called upon him to speak. He said that he agreed with the priest in the main. They should have their pump, if they wanted a pump; if they didn't, he would suggest that they asked for something else. Farmer Byrne said he did not want a pump, and then everyone spoke his mind, and things got mixed. The Catholic landlord regretted that Father Maguire was against allowing a poultry-yard to the patients in the lunatic asylum. If, instead of supplying a pump, the Government would sell them eggs for hatching at a low price, something might be gained. If the Government would not do this, the Government might be induced to supply books on poultry free of charge. It took the Catholic landlord half an hour to express his ideas regarding the asylum, the pump, and the duties of the Government, and in this way the priest succeeded in delaying the departure of the audience till after closing time. 'However fast they walk,' he said to himself, 'they won't get to Michael Dunne's public-house in ten minutes, and he will be shut by then.' It devolved upon him to bring the evening's amusement to a close with a few remarks, and he said:

'Now, the last words I have to say to you I'll address to the women.

Now listen to me. If you pay more attention to your poultry you'll never be short of half a sovereign to lend your husbands, your sons, or your brothers.'

These last words produced an approving shuffling of feet in one corner of the room, and seeing that nothing more was going to happen the villagers got up and they went out very slowly, the women curtseying and the men lifting their caps to the priest as they passed him.

He had signed to Ned and Mary that he wished to speak to them, and after he had spoken to Ned he called Kate and reminded her that he had not seen her at confession lately.

'Pat Connex and Peter M'Shane, now don't you be going. I will have a word with you presently.'

And while Kate tried to find an excuse to account for her absence from confession, the priest called to Ned and Mary, who were talking at a little distance. He told them he would be waiting for them in church to-morrow, and he said he had never made a marriage that gave him more pleasure. He alluded to the fact that they had come to him. He was responsible for this match, and he accepted the responsibility gladly. His uncle, the Vicar-General, had delegated all the work of the parish to him.

'Father Stafford,' he said abruptly, 'will be very glad to hear of your marriage, Kate Kavanagh.'

'My marriage,' said Kate . . . . 'I don't think I shall ever be married.'

'Now, why do you say that?' said the priest.

Kate did not know why she had said that she would never be married. However, she had to give some reason, and she said:

'I don't think, your reverence, anyone would have me.'

'You are not speaking your mind,' said the priest, a little sternly. 'It is said that you don't want to be married, that you like courting better.'

'I'd like to be married well enough.'

'Those who wish to make safe, reliable marriages consult their parents and they consult the priest. I have made your brother's marriage for him. Why don't you come to me and ask me to make up a marriage for you?'

'I think a girl should make her own marriage, your reverence.'

'And what way do you go about making up a marriage? Walking about the roads in the evening, and turning into public-houses, and leaving your situations. It seems to me, Kate Kavanagh, you have been a long time making up this marriage.'

'Now, Pat Connex, I've got a word with you. You're a good boy, and I know you don't mean any harm by it; but I have been hearing tales about you. You've been up to Dublin with Kate Kavanagh. Your mother came up to speak to me about this matter yesterday, and she said: "Not a penny of my money will he ever get if he marries her," meaning the girl before you. Your mother said: "I've got nothing to say against her, but I've got a right to choose my own daughter-in-law." Those are your mother's very words, Pat, so you had better listen to reason. Do you hear me, Kate?'

'I hear your reverence.'

'And if you hear me, what have you got to say to that?'

'He's free to go after the girl he chooses, your reverence,' said Kate.

'There's been courting enough,' the priest said. 'If you aren't going to be married you must give up keeping company. I see Paddy Boyle outside the door. Go home with him. Do you hear what I'm saying, Pat? Go straight home, and no stopping about the roads. Just do as I bid you; go straight home to your mother.'

Pat did not move at the bidding of the priest. He stood watching Kate as if he were waiting for a sign from her, but Kate did not look at him.

'Do you hear what I'm saying to you?' said the priest.

'Yes, I hear,' said Pat.

'And aren't you going?' said the priest.

Everyone was afraid Pat would raise his hand against the priest, and they looked such strong men, both of them, that everyone wondered which would get the better of the other.

'You won't go home when I tell you to do so. We will see if I can't put you out of the door then.'

'If you weren't a priest,' said Pat, 'the divil a bit of you would put me out of the door.'

'If I weren't a priest I would break every bone in your body for talking to me like that. Now out you go,' he said, taking him by the collar, and he put him out.

'And now, Kate Kavanagh,' said the priest, coming back from the door, 'you said you didn't marry because no man would have you. Peter has been waiting for you ever since you were a girl of sixteen years old, and I may say it for him, since he doesn't say much himself, that you have nearly broken his heart.'

'I'm sure I never meant it. I like Pether.'

'You acted out of recklessness without knowing what you were doing.'

A continual smile floated round Peter's moustache, and he looked like a man to whom rebuffs made no difference. His eyes were patient and docile; and whether it was the presence of this great and true love by her side, or whether it was the presence of the priest, Kate did not know, but a great change came over her, and she said:

'I know that Pether has been very good, that he has a liking for me .... If he wishes to put the ring on me –'

When Kate gave him her hand there was a mist in his eyes, and he stood trembling before her.

# CANON SHEEHAN

## A Spoiled Priest[1]

*Canon Patrick, Augustine, Sheehan (1852–1913) was highly prized as a short story writer in Catholic Ireland and, though sometimes religiose, is perspicacious about the moral problems facing the priesthood. He was born in Cork where he was ordained in 1875. His first novel,* Geoffrey Austin, Student *(1895) and its sequel,* The Triumph of Failure *(1898) dealt with the problems of Catholic youth. Among his other books are* Glenanaar *(1905),* Luke Delmege *(1905) and* Lisheen *(1907).*

HE kept his school in a large town in county Waterford. His range of attainments was limited; but what he knew he knew well, and could impart it to his pupils. He did his duty conscientiously by constant, unremitting care, and he emphasized his teachings by frequent appeals to the ferule.

However, on one day in midsummer it would be clearly seen that all hostilities were suspended and a truce proclaimed. This one day in each year was eagerly looked forward to by the boys. The master would come in, dressed in his Sunday suit, with a white rose in his button-hole, and on his lips a smile – a deep, broad, benevolent smile – which, to preserve his dignity, he would vainly try to conceal. No

[1] This is the term used in some parts of the country to express the failure of a student who has just put his foot within the precincts of the sanctuary, and been rejected. Up to quite a recent period such an ill-fated youth was regarded by the peasantry with a certain amount of scorn, not unmingled with superstition. Happily, larger ideas are being developed even on this subject; and not many now believe that no good fortune can ever be the lot of him who has made the gravest initial mistake of his life. (Author's footnote)

implement of torture was visible on that day; and the lessons were repeated, not with the usual rigid formalism but in a perfunctory manner, *ad tempus terendum*. Twelve o'clock would strike, the master would smite the desk and cry:

'Donovan, take the wheelbarrow and bring down Master Kevin's portmanteau from the station.'

Then there was anarchy. Forms were upset, desks overturned, caps flung high as the rafters, and a yell, such as might be given by Comanches around the stake, broke from three hundred boys as they rushed pell-mell from the school. The master would make a feeble effort at restoring order, but his pride in his boy, coming home from Maynooth, stifled the habitual tyranny which brooked no dis- obedience or disorder. In two long lines the boys, under the com- mand of some natural leader, would be drawn up in front of the school. In half-an-hour the wheelbarrow and trunk would be rolled up the gravelled walk; then the expected hero would appear. One tremendous salvo of cheers, and then a glorious holiday!

There was, however, amongst these young lads, one to whom the home-coming of the Maynooth student was of special interest. He was a fair-haired, delicate boy, with large, wistful blue eyes, that looked at you as if they saw something behind and beyond you. He was a bit of a dreamer, too; and when the other lads were shouting at play, he went alone to some copse of thicket, and with a book, or more often without one, would sit and think, and look dreamily at floating clouds or running stream, and then, with a sigh, go back to the weary desk again. Now, he had one idol enshrined in the most sacred recesses of his heart, and that was Kevin O'Donnell. It is quite probable his worship commenced when he heard his sisters at home discussing the merits of this young student in that shy, half-affec- tionate, half-reverential manner in which Irish girls are wont to speak of candidates for the priesthood. And when he heard, around the winter fireside, stories of the intellectual prowess of his hero, in that exaggerated fashion which the imagination of the Irish people so much affects, he worshipped in secret this 'Star of the South', and made desperate vows on sleepless nights to emulate and imitate him. What, then, was his delight when, on one of these glorious summer holidays, the tall, pale-faced student, 'lean' like Dante, 'from much thought', came and invited all his friends to the tea and music that were dispensed at the school-house on Sunday evenings; and when he turned round and, placing his hand on the flaxen curls of the boy, said:

'And this little man must come too; I insist on it.'

Oh! those glorious summer evenings, when the long yellow streamers of the sun lit up the dingy school-house, and the master, no longer the Rhadamanthus of the ruler and rattan, but the magician and conjurer, drew the sweetest sounds from the old violin, and the girls, in their Sunday dresses, swept round in dizzy circles; when the tea and lemonade, and such fairy cakes went round; and the hero, in his long black coat, came over and asked the child how he enjoyed himself, and the boy thought it was heaven, or at least the vestibule and atrium thereof. But even this fairy-land was nothing to the home-coming, when the great tall student lifted the sleepy boy on his shoulders, and wrapped him round against the night air with the folds of his great Maynooth cloak, that was clasped with brass chains that ran through lions' heads, and took him out under the stars, and the warm summer air played around them; and in a delicious half-dream they went home, and the child dreamt of fairy princesses and celestial music, and all was incense and adulation before his idol and prodigy. Ah! the dreams of childhood. What a heaven they would make this world, if only children could speak, and if only their elders would listen!

So two or three years sped by, and then came a rude shock. For one day in the early summer, the day on which the students were expected home, and the boys were on the tiptoe of expectation for their glorious holiday, a quiet, almost inaudible whisper went round that there was something wrong. The master came into school in his ordinary dress; there was no rose in his button-hole; he was quiet, painfully, pitifully quiet; he looked aged, and there were a few wrinkles round his mouth never seen before. A feeling of awe crept over the faces of the boys. They feared to speak. The sight of the old

man going around listlessly, without a trace of the old fury, touched
them deeply. They would have preferred one of his furious explosions
of passion. Once in the morning he lifted the rattan to a turbulent
young ruffian, but, after swishing it in the air, he let it fall, like one
paralysed, to the ground, and then he broke the stick across his knees,
and flung the fragments from the window. The boys could have cried
for him. He dismissed them at twelve o'clock, and they dispersed
without a cheer.

'What was it all? Was Kevin dead?

By-and-by, in whispers around the hearth, he heard that Kevin was
coming home no more. Some one whispered: 'He was expelled;' but
this supposition was rejected angrily. 'He would never be priested,'
said another.

'Why?'

'No one knows. The professors won't tell.'

And some said they expected it all along. 'These great stars fall
sometimes; he was too proud and stuck-up, he wouldn't spake to the
common people – the ould neighbours.' But in most hearts there was
genuine regret, and the truest sympathy for the poor father and
mother, to whom this calamity meant the deepest disgrace. They
would never lift their heads again. Often, for hours together, Kevin's
mother would linger around the fireside, receiving such sympathy as
only Irish hearts can give. Her moans sank deep into the soul of the
listening child.

'Sure I thought that next Sunday I would see my poor boy in
vestments at the altar of God, and then I could die happy. Oh, wirra,
wirra! O Kevin! Kevin! what did you do? what did you do at all, at all?
When he was a little weeshy fellow he used to be playing at saying
Mass – "Dominus vobiscum," and his little sisters used to be serving.
Once his father beat him because he thought it wasn't right. And I
said: "Let the boy alone, James; sure you don't know what God has in
store for him. Who knows what God has in store for him. Who knows
but one day we'll be getting his blessing." Oh, my God, Thy will be
done!'

'How do you know yet?' the friends would say; 'perhaps he's only gone to Dublin, and may be home to-morrow.'

'Thank you kindly, ma'am, but no. Sure his father read the letter for me. "Good-bye, father," it said; "good-bye, mother; you'll never see me again. But I've done nothing to disgrace ye. Would father let me see his face once more? I'll be passing by on the mail to-morrow on my way to America."'

'And did he go to see him?'

'Oh no! he wouldn't. His heart was that black against his son he swore he should never see his face again.'

'Wisha, then,' the women would say, 'how proud he is! What did the poor boy do? I suppose he never made a mistake himself, indeed!'

But the young girls kept silent. They had mutely taken down the idol from their shrine, or rather drawn the dark veil of pitying forgetfulness over it. A student refused Orders was something too terrible. The star had fallen in the sea.

His little friend, however, was loyal to the heart's core. He knew that his hero had done no wrong. He was content to wait and see him justified. He would have given anything to have been able to say a parting word. If he had known Kevin was passing by, shrouded in shame, he would have made his way to the station and braved even the hissing engine, that was always such a terror to him, to touch the hand of his friend once more and assure him of his loyalty. He thought with tears in his eyes of the lonely figure crossing the dread Atlantic; and his nurse was sure he was in for a fit of illness, for the boy moaned in his sleep, and there were tears on his cheeks at midnight.

But from that day his son's name never passed the father's lips. He had uttered in his own mind the cold, iron sentence: 'Non ragioniam di lor.'

The years sped on relentlessly. Never a word came from the exiled student. In a few months the heart-broken mother died. The great school passed into the hands of monks; and the master, in his old age, had to open a little school in the suburbs of the town. Families had been broken up and dispersed, and event after event had obliterated

every vestige of the little tragedy, even to the names of the chief actors
or sufferers. But in the heart of the little boy, Kevin O'Donnell's name
was written in letters of fire and gold. His grateful memory held fast its
hero. Then he, too, had to go to college – and for the priesthood. On
his very entrance into his Diocesan Seminary he was asked his name
and birthplace. When he mentioned the latter, a professor exclaimed:

'Why, Kevin O'Donnell was from there!'

The boy nearly choked. A few weeks after, his heart in his mouth,
he timidly approached the Professor, and asked:

'Did you know Kevin O'Donnell?'

'Why, of course,' said the priest, 'he was a class-fellow of mine.'

'What was – was – thought of him in Maynooth?'

'Why, that he was the cleverest, ablest, jolliest, dearest fellow that
ever lived. You couldn't help loving him. He swept the two soluses in
his logic year, led his class up to the second year's divinity, then fell
away, but again came to the front easily in his fourth. We used to say
that he "thought in Greek".'

'And why did he leave? Why wasn't he ordained?'

'Ah! there's the mystery, and it's a clever man that could answer it.
No one knows.'

They became great friends by reason of this common love for the
disgraced student, and one evening in the early summer the Professor
told the boy all he knew. He had an attentive listener. The conversation came around in this way. Something in the air, or the glance
of the sun, or some faint perfume of hyacinth or early rose, awoke
remembrances in the mind of the boy, and he said, as they sat under
some dwarfed elms:

'This reminds me of Kevin and his holidays at home. The same
summer evening, the same sunlight – only a little faded to me – the
old school-room lighted up by the sunset, the little musical parties, the
young ladies in their white dresses, my head swimming round as they
danced by in polka and schottische –'

'Ha!' said the professor. But, recovering himself, he said hastily:

'Well, go on!'

'Oh, nothing more!' said the boy, 'but my homeward rides on

Kevin's shoulders, and the long folds of his cloak wrapped around me, and – and – how I worshipped him!'

There was a pause, the Professor looking very solemn and thoughtful.

'But, father,' said the boy, 'you never told me. How did it all happen?'

'This way,' said the Professor, shaking himself from his reverie. 'You must know, at least you will know some time, that there is in Maynooth one day – a day of general judgment, a 'Dies iræ, dies illa' – before which the terrors of Jehoshaphat, far away as they are, pale into utter insignificance. It is the day of the 'Order list' – or, in plainer language, it is the dread morning when those who are deemed worthy are called to Orders, and those who are deemed unworthy are rejected. It is a serious ordeal to all. Even the young logician, who is going to be called to tonsure only, looks with fearful uncertainty to his chances. It is always a stinging disgrace to be set aside – or, in college slang, 'to be clipped'. But for the fourth year's divine who is finishing his course, it is the last chance, and woe to him if he fails! He goes out into the world with the brand of shame upon him, and men augur no good of his future. Now, our friend Kevin had been unmercifully 'clipped' up to the last day. Why, we could not ascertain. He was clever; too clever. He had no great faults of character; he was a little careful, perhaps foppish, in his dress; he affected a good deal of culture and politeness; but, so far as we could see, and students are the best judges, there was nothing in his conduct or character to unfit him for the sacred office. But we don't know. There are no mistakes made in that matter. Students who are unfit sometimes steal into the sanctuary, but really fit and worthy students are never rejected. There may be mistakes in selection; there are none in rejection. Well, the fateful morning came. We were all praying for poor Kevin. The most impenetrable silence is kept by the Professors on this matter. Neither by word nor sign could we guess what chances he had; and this added to our dread interest in him. In fact, nothing else was talked of but Kevin's chances; and I remember how many and how diverse were the opinions entertained about them. The bell rang, and we all

trooped into the Senior Prayer Hall. We faced the altar, three hundred
and fifty anxious students, if I except the deacons and subdeacons,
who, with their books – that is, their breviaries – under their arms,
looked jaunty enough. I was one of them, for I was ordained Deacon
the previous year, and I was certain of my call to Priesthood; but my
heart was like lead. Kevin walked in with me.

' "Cheer up, old man," I said; "I tell you it will be all right. Come,
sit near me." His face was ashen, his hands cold and trembling. He
picked up the end of his soutane, and began to open and close the
buttons nervously. The superiors – four Deans, the Vice-President,
and President – came in and took their places in the gallery behind us,
and at the end of the hall. An awful silence filled the place. Then the
President began, after a brief formula, to call out rapidly in Latin the
names of those who were selected "ad primam tonsuram". He passed
on to the Porters, the Lectors, the Acolytes, the Exorcists. Then came
the higher Orders, and hearts beat anxiously. But this was rapidly over.
Then came the solemn words, "Ad Presbyteratum". Poor Kevin
dropped his soutane, and closed his hands tightly. My name was read
out first in alphabetical order. Kevin's name should come in between
the names O'Connor and Quinn. The President read rapidly down
the list, called:

> Gulielmus O'Connor, Dunensis;
> Matthæus Quinn, Midensis;

and thus sentence was passed.

Kevin was rejected. I heard him start, and draw in his breath rapidly
two or three times. I was afraid to look at him. The list was closed. The
Superiors departed, apparently heedless of the dread desolation they
had caused; for nothing is so remarkable in our colleges as the apparent
utter indifference of Professor and Superiors to the feelings or interests
of the students. I said "apparent" because, as a matter of fact, the
keenest interest is felt in every student from his entrance to his
departure. His is not only constantly under surveillance, but he is
spoken of, canvassed, his character, talents, habits passed under survey
by those grave, solemn men, who preserve, in their intercourse with

the students, a sphinx-like silence and indifference, which to many is painful and inexplicable.

'Well, the ordeal was over; and we rose to depart. Then Kevin turned round and looked at me. He smiled in a ghastly way, and said: "This little tragedy is over."

'I said nothing. Words would have been mockery under such a stunning blow. Nothing else was talked of in the house for the remaining days. There was infinite sympathy for poor Kevin, and even the Superiors dropped the veil of reserve, and spoke kindly to him. It is customary to ask some one of the Superiors the cause of rejection. To keep away from them savours of pride. Kevin went to the Vice-President, a kindly old man, and asked why he was deemed unfit for Orders. The old priest placed his hands on Kevin's shoulders and said, through his tears:

' "Nothing in particular, my dear; but some general want of the ecclesiastical manner and spirit."

' "I haven't been a hypocrite," replied Kevin, "I wore my heart on my sleeve. Perhaps if –' he said no more.

'The examinations were over. The day for the distribution of prizes came on. The Bishops assembled in the Prayer Hall. The list of prize-men was called. Kevin was first in Theology, first in Scripture, second in Ecclesiastical History, first in Hebrew. It was a ghastly farce. Kevin, of course, was not there. Later in the day a deputation of the students of the diocese waited on their Bishop. It was a most unusual pro-ceeding. They asked the Bishop to ordain Kevin, in spite of the adverse decision of the College authorities. They met under the President's apartments. The Bishop, grave and dignified, listened with sympathy, and when their representations had been made, he said he would consult the President.

'It was a faint gleam of hope. They waited, Kevin in their midst, for three-quarters of an hour, hoping, despairing, anxious. The Bishop came down. With infinite pity he looked at Kevin, and said: "I am sorry, Mr O'Donnell, I can do nothing for you. I cannot contravene the will of the Superiors." Then the last hope fled. Next day Kevin was on his way to America. That is all. You'll understand it better when you go to Maynooth.'

He did go in due time, and he understood the story better. Like a careful dramatist, he went over scene after scene in the College life of Kevin. He found his desk, his cell; he sought out every tradition in the College concerning him; and that College, completely sequestered from the outer world as it is, is very rich in traditions, and tenacious of them. He stood in the wide porch under the President's apartments and pictured the scene of Kevin's final dismissal from the sacred ministry. And the first time he sat in the Prayer Hall, at the calling of the Order list, although he himself was concerned, he forgot everything but the picture of his hero, unnerved, despairing, and saw his ghastly smile, and heard: 'This little tragedy is over.'

Once or twice he ventured to ask one of the deans whether he had ever heard of Kevin O'Donnell, and what was the secret of his rejection.

'Ah! yes, he knew him well. Clever, ambitious, rather worldly-minded. Why was he finally thought unfit for Orders? Well, there were various opinions. But no one knew.'

It happened that one of the old men-servants knew Kevin well.

'Mr O'Donnell, of C—? A real gintleman. Wouldn't ask you to clane his boots without giving you half-a-crown. Heard he was a doctor, doing well; was married, and had a large family.'

'You heard a lie,' said the student, the strongest expression he had ever used. But the thing rankled in his heart. Was his hero dethroned? or was the drapery of the veil drawn across the shrine? No; but he had seen the feet of clay under the beautiful statue. The Irish instinct cannot understand a married hero – at least in the sense in which this youth worshipped Kevin O'Donnell as a hero.

The years rolled by. Ah, those years, leaden-footed to the hot wishes of youth, how swiftly, with all their clouds and shadows, and all their misty, nimble radiances, they roll by and break and dissolve into airy nothings against the azure of eternity!

Our little hero-worshipper was a priest, and, after some years, was

appointed temporarily to a curacy in his native parish. I am afraid he
was sentimental, for he loved every stone and tree and bush in the
neighbourhood. He lived in the past. Here was the wall against which
he had played ball – the identical smooth stone, which he had to be so
careful to pick out; here was the rough crease, where they had played
cricket; here the little valleys where they had rolled their marbles; here
the tiny trout-stream, where they had fished. How small it seems now!
What a broad, terrible river it was to the child of thirty years ago! But
he loved to linger most of all around the old school-house, to sit
amongst the trees again, and to call up all the radiant dreams that float
through the 'moonlight of memory'. Alas! all, or nearly all, the
companions of his childhood had fallen or fled. The few that remained
he interrogated often about the past. This, too, with them, was fading
into a soft dream. Their children were around their knees, and life was
terribly real to them.

One night, again in the soft summer, he was suddenly called to the
sick-bed of a dying woman. He hastily dressed and went. The doctor
was before him, but reverently made way.

'It will be slow, sir,' he said, 'and I must wait.'

The young priest performed his sacred duties to the dying woman,
and then, out of sheer sympathy, he remained sitting by the fire,
chatting with the husband of the patient.

It appeared that the dispensary doctor was away on another call, and
they had taken the liberty to call in this strange doctor, who had been
only a few months in the country, and had taken Rock Cottage for a
few years. He was a tall, angular man, his face almost concealed under
a long, black beard, streaked with white. He was a silent man, it
appeared, but very clever. The 'head doctors' in Cork couldn't hold a
candle to him. He would take no money. He was very good to the
poor. His name was Dr Everard.

The young priest had seen him from time to time, but had never
spoken to him. Perhaps his curiosity was piqued to know a little more
of him. Perhaps he liked him for his kindness to the poor. At any rate
he would remain and walk home with him. Late in the summer night,
or rather, early in the summer dawn, the doctor came out from the

sick-room and asked for water to wash his hands. He started at the
young priest waiting; and the latter passed in to the sick woman, who,
now relieved, looked pleased and thankful. He said a few kind words
and came out quickly. The doctor was just swinging on his broad
shoulders a heavy military cloak; and the priest, lifting his eyes, saw the
same old lions' heads and the brass chain-clasps that he remembered so
well in Kevin's cloak so many years ago.

'Our roads lead in the same direction,' said the priest. 'May I
accompany you?'

'Certainly,' said the doctor.

It was a lovely summer morning, dawn just breaking roseate and
clear, preluding a warm day. The birds were up and alert, trying to get
out all the day's programme of song and anthem before the dread heat
should drive them to shelter and silence. The river rolled sluggishly
along, thin and slow and underfed, for the mountains were dry and
barren, and the fruitful clouds were afar. No men were stirring. The
shops were closely shuttered; but here and there a lamp, left lighted,
looked sickly in the clear dawnlight. Their footsteps rang hollow with
echoes along the street, and one or two dogs barked in muffled anger
as the steps smote on their ears. They had been talking about many
things, and the young priest had mentioned casually that this was his
native place.

'And there's the very house I was born in.' The doctor stopped, and
looked curiously at the shuttered house, as if recalling some memories.
But he said nothing.

At last they left the town; and the priest, rambling on about his
reminiscences, and the other listening attentively, they came at last
opposite the old school-house, and by some spontaneous impulse they
rested their arms on a rude gate and gazed towards it. Then the young
priest broke out into his old rhapsody about the summer twilights, and
the violin, and the merry dances of the girls, and all those things round
which, commonplace though they may be, memory flings a nimbus of
light that spiritualizes and beautifies them. And then his own secret
hero-worship for the great Kevin, and the ride on his shoulders home

from the dance and the supper, and the great cloak that enveloped him –

'Just like yours, with the same brass clasps and chains, that jingled, oh! such music in my memory.'

The doctor listened gravely and attentively. Then he asked:

'And what became of this wonderful Kevin?'

And he was told his history. And how the heart of one faithful friend yearned after him in his shame, and believed in him, and knew, by a secret but infallible instinct, that he was true and good and faithful, although thrust from the Sanctuary in shame.

'We may meet yet,' continued the young priest. 'Of course he could not remember me. But it was all sad, pitifully sad; and I am sure he had grave trials and difficulties to overcome. You know it is in moments of depression, rather than of exultation, that the great temptations come.'

'Good night, or rather good morning,' said the doctor. 'What did you say your hero's name was? Kevin – I think –'

'Yes, Kevin O'Donnell,' said the priest.

A few weeks after the doctor disappeared, and Rock Cottage was closed again. Twelve months later the young priest was dining with his Bishop, and the latter asked him:

'Did you ever hear of a Kevin O'Donnell, from your town?'

'Yes, of course, my Lord. He was a Maynooth student many years ago.'

'Well, here is a letter from him, from Florence, demanding his *exeat*, in order that he may be ordained priest.'

A rush of tumultuous delight flushed the cheeks of the young priest, but he only said: 'I knew 'twould come all right in the end.'

He went home. There was a letter on his desk. Florence was the post-mark. With trembling fingers he read: –

'CERTOSA, FIRENZE,

*July 12, 187–.*

'FRIEND AND CHILD, – You have saved a soul! And it is the soul of your early friend, Kevin. Embittered and disappointed, I left Ireland many years ago. Not one kindly word nor friendly grasp was with me in my farewell. I came back to Ireland, successful as to worldly affairs, but bitter and angry towards God and man. I had but one faith left – to do good in a world where I had received naught but evil. Your faith in me has revived my faith in God. I see now that we are in His hands. If a little child could retain the memory of small kindnesses for thirty years, can we think that the great All-Father has forgotten? You are puzzled; you do not know me. Well, I am the doctor with the great cloak, who accompanied you from a sick-call some months ago. I did not know you. I had forgotten your name. But while you spoke, and showed me how great was your fidelity and love, my heart thawed out towards God and man. I left hurriedly and hastened here. I am, thank God, a professed Carthusian, and the Orders denied me in Maynooth Prayer Hall thirty years ago I shall receive in a few days.

'Farewell, and thank God for a gentle heart. You never know where its dews may fall, and bring to life the withered grass or the faded flower – Yours in Christ,

'KEVIN O'DONNELL (late Dr Everard.)'

# SOMERVILLE AND ROSS

## The Holy Island

*E. Œ Somerville (1858–1949) and 'Martin Ross' (1862–1950), the pen name of her cousin Violet Florence Martin, wrote humorous novels of the Irish gentry which include* The Real Charlotte, In Mr Knox's Country *and* Some Experiences of an Irish R M *from which this story is taken (An R M is a Resident Magistrate.)*

FOR three days of November a white fog stood motionless over the country. All day and all night smothered booms and bangs away to the south-west told that the Fastnet gun was hard at work, and the sirens of the American liners uplifted their monstrous female voices as they felt their way along the coast of Cork. On the third afternoon the wind began to whine about the windows of Shreelane, and the barometer fell like a stone. At 11 p.m. the storm rushed upon us with the roar and the suddenness of a train; the chimneys bellowed, the tall old house quivered, and the yelling wind drove against it, as a man puts his shoulder against a door to burst it in.

We none of us got much sleep, and if Mrs Cadogan is to be believed – which experience assured me she is not – she spent the night in devotional exercises, and in ministering to the panic-stricken kitchen-maid by the light of a Blessed candle. All that day the storm screamed on, dry-eyed; at nightfall the rain began, and next morning, which happened to be Sunday, every servant in the house was a messenger of Job, laden with tales of leakages, floods, and fallen trees, and inflated with the ill-concealed glory of their kind in evil tidings. To Peter

Cadogan, who had been to early Mass, was reserved the crowning satisfaction of reporting that a big vessel had gone on the rocks at Yokahn Point the evening before, and was breaking up fast; it was rumoured that the crew had got ashore, but this feature, being favourable and uninteresting, was kept as much as possible in the background. Mrs Cadogan, who had been to America in an ocean liner, became at once the latest authority on shipwrecks, and was of opinion that 'whoever would be dhrownded, it wouldn't be thim lads o' sailors. Sure wasn't there the greatest storm ever was in it the time meself was on the say, and what'd thim fellows do but to put us below entirely in the ship, and close down the doors on us, the way their-selves'd leg it when we'd be dhrownding!'

This view of the position was so startlingly novel that Philippa withdrew suddenly from the task of ordering dinner, and fell up the kitchen stairs in unsuitable laughter. Philippa has not the most rudi-mentary capacity for keeping her countenance.

That afternoon I was wrapped in the slumber, balmiest and most profound, that follows on a wet Sunday luncheon, when Murray, our DI of police, drove up in uniform, and came into the house on the top of a gust that set every door banging and every picture dancing on the walls. He looked as if his eyes had been blown out of his head, and he wanted something to eat very badly.

'I've been down at the wreck since ten o'clock this morning,' he said, 'waiting for her to break up, and once she does there'll be trouble. She's an American ship, and she's full up with rum, and bacon, and butter, and all sorts. Bosanquet is there with all his coastguards, and there are five hundred country people on the strand at this moment, waiting for the fun to begin. I've got ten of my fellows there, and I wish I had as many more. You'd better come back with me, Yeates, we may want the Riot Act before all's done!'

The heavy rain had ceased, but it seemed as if it had fed the wind instead of calming it, and when Murray and I drove out of Shreelane, the whole dirty sky was moving, full sailed, in from the south-west, and the telegraph wires were hanging in a loop from the post outside the gate. Nothing except a Skebawn car-horse would have faced the whooping charges of the wind that came at us across Corran Lake; stimulated mysteriously by whistles from the driver, Murray's yellow hireling pounded woodenly along against the blast, till the smell of the torn sea-weed was borne upon it, and we saw the Atlantic waves come towering into the bay of Tralagough.

The ship was, or had been, a three-masted barque; two of her masts were gone, and her bows stood high out of water on the reef that forms one of the shark-like jaws of the bay. The long strand was crowded with black groups of people, from the bank of heavy shingle that had been hurled over on to the road, down to the slope where the waves pitched themselves and climbed and fought and tore the gravel back with them, as though they had dug their fingers in. The people were nearly all men, dressed solemnly and hideously in their Sunday clothes; most of them had come straight from Mass without any dinner, true to that Irish instinct that places its fun before its food. That the wreck was regarded as a spree of the largest kind was sufficiently obvious. Our car pulled up at a public-house that stood askew between the road and the shingle; it was humming with those whom Irish publicans are pleased to call 'Bonâ feeds', and sundry of the same class were clustered round the door. Under the wall on the leeside was seated a bagpiper, droning out 'The Irish Washerwoman' with nodding head and tapping heel, and a young man was cutting a few steps of a jig for the delectation of a group of girls.

So far Murray's constabulary had done nothing but exhibit their imposing chest measurements and spotless uniforms to the Atlantic, and Bosanquet's coastguards had only salvaged some spars, the debris of a boat, and a dead sheep, but their time was coming. As we stumbled down over the shingle, battered by the wind and pelted by clots of foam, some one beside me shouted, 'She's gone!' A hill of water had smothered the wreck, and when it fell from her again nothing was left but the bows, with the bowsprit hanging from them in a tangle of rigging. The clouds, bronzed by an unseen sunset, hung low over her; in that greedy pack of waves, with the remorseless rocks above and below her, she seemed the most lonely and tormented of creatures.

About half-an-hour afterwards the cargo began to come ashore on
the top of the rising tide. Barrels were plunging and diving in the
trough of the waves, like a school of porpoises; they were pitched up
the beach in waist-deep rushes of foam; they rolled down again, and
were swung up and shouldered by the next wave, playing a kind of
Tom Tiddler's ground with the coastguards. Some of the barrels were
big and dangerous, some were small and nimble like young pigs, and
the bluejackets were up to their middles as their prey dodged and
ducked, and the police lined out along the beach to keep back the
people. Ten men of the RIC can do a great deal, but they cannot be in
more than twenty or thirty places at the same instant; therefore they
could hardly cope with a scattered and extremely active mob of four
or five hundred, many of whom had taken advantage of their privi-
leges as 'bona-fide travellers', and all of whom were determined on
getting at the rum.

As the dusk fell the thing got more and more out of hand; the
people had found out that the big puncheons held the rum, and had
succeeded in capturing one. In the twinkling of an eye it was
broached, and fifty backs were shoving round it like a football
scrummage. I have heard many rows in my time: I have seen two Irish
regiments – one of them Militia – at each other's throats in Fermoy
barracks; I have heard Philippa's water spaniel and two fox-terriers
hunting a strange cat round the dairy; but never have I known such
untrammelled bedlam as that which yelled round the rum-casks on
Tralagough strand. For it was soon not a question of one broached
cask, or even of two. The barrels were coming in fast, so fast that it was
impossible for the representatives of law and order to keep on any sort
of terms with them. The people, shouting with laughter, stove in the
casks, and drank rum at 34° above proof, out of their hands, out of
their hats, out of their boots. Women came fluttering over the hillsides
through the twilight, carrying jugs, milk-pails, anything that would
hold the liquor; I saw one of them, roaring with laughter, tilt a filthy
zinc bucket to an old man's lips.

With the darkness came anarchy. The rising tide brought more and
yet more booty: great spars came lunging in on the lap of the waves,

mixed up with cabin furniture, seamen's chests, and the black and slippery barrels, and the country people continued to flock in, and the drinking became more and more unbridled. Murray sent for more men and a doctor, and we slaved on hopelessly in the dark; collaring half-drunken men, shoving pig-headed casks up hills of shingle, hustling in among groups of roaring drinkers – we rescued perhaps one barrel in half-a-dozen. I began to know that there were men there who were not drunk and were not idle; I was also aware, as the strenuous hours of darkness passed, of an occasional rumble of cart wheels on the road. It was evident that the casks which were broached were the least part of the looting, but even they were beyond our control. The most that Bosanquet, Murray, and I could do was to concentrate our forces on the casks that had been secured, and to organize charges upon the swilling crowds in order to upset the casks that they had broached. Already men and boys were lying about, limp as leeches, motionless as the dead.

'They'll kill themselves before morning, at this rate!' shouted Murray to me. 'They're drinking it by the quart! Here's another barrel; come on!'

We rallied our small forces, and after a brief but furious struggle succeeded in capsizing it. It poured away in a flood over the stones, over the prostrate figures that sprawled on them, and a howl of reproach followed.

'If ye pour away any more o' that, Major,' said an unctuous voice in my ear, 'ye'll intoxicate the stones and they'll be getting up and knocking us down!'

I had been aware of a fat shoulder next to mine in the throng as we heaved the puncheon over, and I now recognized the ponderous wit and Falstaffian figure of Mr James Canty, a noted member of the Skebawn Board of Guardians, and the owner of a large farm near at hand.

'I never saw worse work on this strand,' he went on. 'I considher these debaucheries a disgrace to the counthry.'

Mr Canty was famous as an orator, and I presume that it was from long practice among his fellow PLG's that he was able, without apparent exertion, to out-shout the storm.

At this juncture the long-awaited reinforcements arrived, and along with them came Dr Jerome Hickey, armed with a black bag. Having mentioned that the bag contained a pump – not one of the common or garden variety – and that no pump on board a foundering ship had more arduous labours to perform, I prefer to pass to other themes. The wreck, which had at first appeared to be as inexhaustible and as variously stocked as that in the *Swiss Family Robinson*, was beginning to fail in its supply. The crowd were by this time for the most part incapable from drink, and the fresh contingent of police tackled their work with some prospect of success by the light of a tar barrel, contributed by the owner of the public-house. At about the same time I began to be aware that I was aching with fatigue, that my clothes hung heavy and soaked upon me, that my face was stiff with the salt spray and the bitter wind, and that it was two hours past dinner-time. The possibility of fried salt herrings and hot whisky and water at the public-house rose dazzlingly before my mind, when Mr Canty again crossed my path.

'In my opinion ye have the whole cargo under conthrol now, Major,' he said, 'and the police and the sailors should be able to account for it all now by the help of the light. Wasn't I the finished fool that I didn't think to send up to my house for a tar barrel before now! Well – we're all foolish sometimes! But indeed it's time for us to give over, and that's what I'm after saying to the Captain and Mr Murray. You're exhausted now the three of ye, and if I might make so bold, I'd suggest that ye'd come up to my little place and have what'd warm ye before ye'd go home. It's only a few perches up the road.'

The tide had turned, the rain had begun again, and the tar barrel illumined the fact that Dr Hickey's dreadful duties alone were pressing. We held a council and finally followed Mr Canty, picking our way through wreckage of all kinds, including the human variety. Near the public-house I stumbled over something that was soft and had a squeak in it; it was the piper, with his head and shoulders in an overturned rum-barrel, and the bagpipes still under his arm.

I knew the outward appearance of Mr Canty's house very well. It was a typical southern farmhouse, with dirty whitewashed walls, a slated roof, and small, hermetically-sealed windows staring at the morass of manure which constituted the yard. We followed Mr Canty up the filthy lane that led to it, picked our way round vague and squelching spurs of the manure heap, and were finally led through the kitchen into a stifling best parlour. Mrs Canty, a vast and slatternly matron, had evidently made preparations for us; there was a newly-lighted fire pouring flame up the chimney from layers of bogwood, there were whisky and brandy on the table, and a plateful of biscuits sugared in white and pink. Upon our hostess was a black silk dress which indifferently concealed the fact that she was short of boot-laces, and that the boots themselves had made many excursions to the yard and none to the blacking-bottle. Her manners, however, were admirable, and while I live I shall not forget her potato cakes. They came in hot and hot from a pot-oven, they were speckled with car-away seeds, they swam in salt butter, and we ate them shamelessly and greasily, and washed them down with hot whisky and water; I knew to a nicety how ill I should be next day, and heeded not.

'Well, gentlemen,' remarked Mr Canty later on, in his best Board of Guardians' manner, 'I've seen many wrecks between this and the Mizen Head, but I never witnessed a scene of more disgraceful excess than what was in it tonight.'

'Hear, hear!' murmured Bosanquet with unseemly levity.

'I should say,' went on Mr Canty, 'there was at one time to-night upwards of one hundhred men dead dhrunk on the strand, or anyway so dhrunk that if they'd attempt to spake they'd foam at the mouth.'

'The craytures!' interjected Mrs Canty sympathetically.

'But if they're dhrunk to-day,' continued our host, 'it's nothing at all to what they'll be to-morrow and afther to-morrow, and it won't be on the strand they'll be dhrinkin' it.'

'Why, where will it be?' said Bosanquet, with his disconcerting English way of asking a point-blank question.

Mr Canty passed his hand over his red cheeks.

'There'll be plenty asking that before all's said and done, Captain,'

he said, with a compassionate smile, 'and there'll be plenty that could
give the answer if they'll like, but by dam I don't think ye'll be apt to
get much out of the Yokahn boys!'

'The Lord save us, 'twould be better to keep out from the likes o'
thim!' put in Mrs Canty, sliding a fresh avalanche of potato cakes on to
the dish; 'didn't they pull the clothes off the gauger and pour potheen
down his throath till he ran screeching through the streets o' Skebawn!'

James Canty chuckled.

'I remember there was a wreck here one time, and the undher-
writers put me in charge of the cargo. Brandy it was – cases of the best
Frinch brandy. The people had a song about it, what's this the first
verse was –

> One night to the rocks of Yokahn
> Came the barque *Isabella* so dandy,
> To pieces she went before dawn,
> Herself and her cargo of brandy.
> And all met a wathery grave
> Excepting the vessel's car*pen*ther,
> Poor fellow, so far from his home.

Mr Canty chanted these touching lines in a tuneful if wheezy tenor.
'Well, gentlemen, we'll all friends here,' he continued, 'and it's no
harm to mention that this man below at the public-house came askin'
me would I let him have some of it for a consideration. "Sullivan,"
says I to him, "if ye ran down gold in a cup in place of the brandy, I
wouldn't give it to you. Of coorse," says I, "I'm not sayin' but that if a
bottle was to get a crack of a stick, and it to be broken, and a man to
drink a glass out of it, that would be no more than an accident."
"That's no good to me," says he, "but if I had twelve gallons of that
brandy in Cork," says he, "by the Holy German!" says he, saying an
awful curse, "I'd sell twenty-five out of it!" Well, indeed, it was true
for him; it was grand stuff. As the saying is, it would make a horse out
of a cow!'

'It appears to be a handy sort of place for keeping a pub,' said Bosanquet.

'Shut to the door, Margaret,' said Mr Canty with elaborate caution. 'It'd be a queer place that wouldn't be handy for Sullivan!'

A further tale of great length was in progress when Dr Hickey's Mephistophelian nose was poked into the best parlour.

'Hullo, Hickey! Pumped out? eh?' said Murray.

'If I am, there's plenty more like me,' replied the Doctor enigmatically, 'and some of them three times over! James, did these gentlemen leave you a drop of anything that you'd offer me?'

'Maybe ye'd like a glass of rum, Doctor?' said Mr Canty with a wink at his other guests.

Dr Hickey shuddered.

I had next morning precisely the kind of mouth that I had anticipated, and it being my duty to spend the better part of the day administering justice in Skebawn, I received from Mr Flurry Knox and other of my brother magistrates precisely the class of condolences on my 'Monday head' that I found least amusing. It was unavailing to point out the resemblance between hot potato cakes and molten lead, or to dilate on their equal power of solidifying; the collective wisdom of the Bench decided that I was suffering from contraband rum, and rejoiced over me accordingly.

During the next three weeks Murray and Bosanquet put in a time only to be equalled by that of the heroes in detective romances. They began by acting on the hint offered by Mr Canty, and were rewarded by finding eight barrels of bacon and three casks of rum in the heart of Mr Sullivan's turf rick, placed there, so Mr Sullivan explained with much detail, by enemies, with the object of getting his licence taken away. They stabbed potato gardens with crowbars to find the buried barrels, they explored the chimneys, they raided the cow-houses; and in every possible and impossible place they found some of the cargo of the late barque *John D. Williams*, and, as the sympathetic Mr Canty said, 'For as much as they found, they left five times as much afther them!'

It was a wet, lingering autumn, but towards the end of November the rain dried up, the weather stiffened, and a week of light frosts and blue skies was offered as a tardy apology. Philippa possesses, in common with many of her sex, an inappeasable passion for picnics, and her ingenuity for devising occasions for them is only equalled by her gift for enduring their rigours. I have seen her tackle a moist chicken pie with a splinter of slate and my stylograph pen. I have known her to take the tea-basket to an auction, and make tea in a four-wheeled inside car, regardless of the fact that it was coming under the hammer in ten minutes, and that the kettle took twenty minutes to boil. It will therefore be readily understood that the rare occasions when I was free to go out with a gun were not allowed to pass uncelebrated by the tea-basket.

'You'd much better shoot Corran Lake tomorrow,' my wife said to me one brilliant afternoon. 'We could send the punt over, and I could meet you on Holy Island with –'

The rest of the sentence was concerned with ways, means, and the tea-basket, and need not be recorded.

I had taken the shooting of a long snipe bog that trailed from Corran Lake almost to the sea at Tralagough, and it was my custom to begin to shoot from the seaward end of it, and finally to work round the lake after duck.

Tomorrow proved a heavenly morning, touched with frost, gilt with sun. I started early, and the mists were still smoking up from the calm, all-reflecting lake, as the Quaker stepped out along the level road, smashing the thin ice on the puddles with his big feet. Behind the calves of my legs sat Maria, Philippa's brown Irish water-spaniel, assiduously licking the barrels of my gun, as was her custom when the ecstasy of going out shooting was hers. Maria had been given to Philippa as a wedding-present, and since then it had been my wife's ambition that she should conform to the Beth Gelert standard of being 'a lamb at home, a lion in the chase'. Maria did pretty well as a lion: she hunted all dogs unmistakably smaller than herself, and whenever it was reasonably possible to do so she devoured the spoils of the chase, notably jack snipe. It was as a lamb that she failed; objectionable as I have no doubt a lamb would be as a domestic pet, it at least would not

snatch the cold beef from the luncheon-table, nor yet, if banished for
its crimes, would it spend the night in scratching the paint off the hall
door. Maria bit beggars (who valued their disgusting limbs at five
shillings the square inch), she bullied the servants, she concealed
ducks' claws and fishes' backbones behind the sofa cushions, and yet,
when she laid her brown snoud upon my knee, and rolled her
blackguard amber eyes upon me, and smote me with her feathered
paw, it was impossible to remember her iniquities against her. On
shooting mornings Maria ceased to be a buccaneer, a glutton, and a
hypocrite. From the moment when I put my gun together her
breakfast stood untouched until it suffered the final degradation of
being eaten by the cats, and now in the trap she was shivering with
excitement, and agonizing in her soul lest she should even yet be left
behind.

Slipper met me at the cross roads from which I had sent back the
trap; Slipper, redder in the nose than anything I had ever seen off the
stage, very husky as to the voice, and going rather tender on both feet.
He informed me that I should have a grand day's shooting, the head-
poacher of the locality having, in a most gentlemanlike manner,
refrained from exercising his sporting rights the day before, on hearing
that I was coming. I understood that this was to be considered as a
mark of high personal esteem, and I set to work at the bog with
suitable gratitude.

In spite of Mr O'Driscoll's magnanimity, I had not a very good
morning. The snipe was there, but in the perfect stillness of the
weather it was impossible to get near them, and five times out of six
they were up, flickering and dodging, before I was within shot. Maria
became possessed of seven devils and broke away from heel the first
time I let off my gun, ranging far and wide in search of the bird I had
missed, and putting up every live thing for half a mile round, as she
went splashing and steeple-chasing through the bog. Slipper expressed
his opinion of her behaviour in language more appallingly picturesque
and resourceful than any I have heard, even in the Skebawn Court-
house; I admit that at the time I thought he spoke every suitably.
Before she was recaptured every remaining snipe within earshot was

lifted out of it by Slipper's steam-engine whistles and my own infuriated bellows; it was fortunate that the bog was spacious and that there was still a long tract of it ahead, where beyond these voices there was peace.

I worked my way on, jumping treacle-dark drains, floundering through the rustling yellow rushes, circumnavigating the bog-holes, and taking every possible and impossible chance of a shot; by the time I had reached Corran Lake I had got two-and-a-half brace, retrieved by Maria with a perfection that showed what her powers were when the sinuous adroitness of Slipper's woodbine stick was fresh in her mind. But with Maria it was always the unexpected that happened. My last snipe, a jack, fell in the lake, and Maria, bursting through the reeds with kangaroo bounds, and cleaving the water like a torpedo-boat, was a model of all the virtues of her kind. She picked up the bird with a snake-like dart of her head, clambered with it on to a tussock, and there, well out of reach of the arm of the law, before our indignant eyes crunched it twice and bolted it.

'Well,' said Slipper complacently, some ten minutes afterwards, 'divil such a bating ever I gave a dog since the day Prince kill owld Mrs Knox's paycock! Prince was a lump of a brown tarrier I had one time, and faith I kicked the toes out o' me owld boots on him before I had the owld lady composed!'

However composing Slipper's methods may have been to Mrs Knox, they had quite the contrary effect upon a family party of duck that had been lying in the reeds. With horrified outcries they broke into flight, and now were far away on the ethereal mirror of the lake, among strings of their fellows that were floating and quacking in preoccupied indifference to my presence.

A promenade along the lake-shore demonstrated the fact that without a boat there was no more shooting for me; I looked across to the island where, some time ago, I had seen Philippa and her punt arrive. The boat was tied to an overhanging tree, but my wife was nowhere to be seen. I was opening my mouth to give a hail, when I saw her emerge precipitately from among the trees and jump into the boat; Philippa had not in vain spent many summers on the Thames,

she was under way in a twinkling, sculled a score of strokes at the rate
of a finish, then stopped and stared at the peaceful island. I called to
her, and in a minute or two the punt had crackled through the reeds,
and shoved its blunt nose ashore at the spot where I was standing.

'Sinclair,' said Philippa in awe-struck tones, 'there's something on
the island!'

'I hope there's something to eat there,' said I.

'I tell you there *is* something there, alive,' said my wife with her
eyes as large as saucers; 'it's making an awful sound like snoring.'

'That's the fairies, ma'am,' said Slipper with complete certainty;
'sure I know them that seen fairies in that island as thick as the grass,
and every one o' them with little caps on them.'

Philippa's wide gaze wandered to Slipper's hideous pug face and
back to me.

'It was not a human being, Sinclair!' she said combatively, though I
had not uttered a word.

Maria had already, after the manner of dogs, leaped, dripping, into
the boat: I prepared to follow her example.

'Major,' said Slipper, in a tragic whisper, 'there was a man was a
night on that island one time, watching duck, and Thim People cot
him, and dhragged him through Hell and through Death, and threw
him in the tide –'

'Shove off the boat,' I said, too hungry for argument.

Slipper obeyed, throwing his knee over the gunwale as he did so,
and tumbling into the bow; we could have done without him very
comfortably, but his devotion was touching.

Holy Island was perhaps a hundred yards long, and about half as
many broad; it was covered with trees and a dense growth of rhododendrons; somewhere in the jungle was a ruined fragment of a
chapel, smothered in ivy and briars, and in a little glade in the heart of
the island there was a holy well. We landed, and it was obviously a
sore humiliation to Philippa that not a sound was to be heard in the
spellbound silence of the island, save the cough of a heron on a tree-
top.

'It *was* there,' she said, with an unconvinced glance at the surrounding thickets.

'Sure, I'll give a thrawl through the island, ma'am,' volunteered Slipper with unexpected gallantry, 'an' if it's the divil himself is in it, I'll rattle him into the lake!'

He went swaggering on his search, shouting, 'Hi, cock!' and whacking the rhododendrons with his stick, and after an interval returned and assured us that the island was uninhabited. Being provided with refreshments he again withdrew, and Philippa and Maria and I fed variously and at great length, and washed the plates with water from the holy well. I was smoking a cigarette when we heard Slipper addressing the solitudes at the farther end of the island, and ending with one of his whisky-throated crows of laughter.

He presently came lurching towards us through the bushes, and a glance sufficed to show even Philippa – who was as incompetent a judge of such matters as many of her sex – that he was undeniably screwed.

'Major Yeates!' he began, 'and Mrs Major Yeates, with respex to ye, I'm bastely dhrunk! Me head is light since the 'fluenzy, and the doctor told me I should carry a little bottle-een o' sperrits –'

'Look here,' I said to Philippa, 'I'll take him across, and bring the boat back for you.'

'Sinclair,' responded my wife with concentrated emotion, 'I would rather die than stay on this island alone!'

Slipper was getting drunker every moment, but I managed to stow him on his back in the bows of the punt, in which position he at once began to uplift husky and wandering strains of melody. To this accompaniment we, as Tennyson says,

> moved from the brink like some full-breasted swan,
> That, fluting a wild carol ere her death,
> Ruffles her pure cold plume, and takes the flood
> With swarthy web.

Slipper would certainly have been none the worse for taking the flood, and, as the burden of 'Lannigan's Ball' strengthened and spread along the tranquil lake, and the duck once more fled in justifiable consternation, I felt much inclined to make him do so.

We made for the end of the lake that was nearest Shreelane, and, as we rounded the point of the island, another boat presented itself to our view. It contained my late entertainer, Mrs Canty, seated bulkily in the stern, while a small boy bowed himself between the two heavy oars.

'It's a lovely evening, Major Yeates,' she called out. 'I'm just going to the island to get some water from the holy well for me daughter that has an impression on her chest. Indeed, I thought 'twas yourself was singing a song for Mrs Yeates when I heard you coming, but sure Slipper is a great warrant himself for singing.'

'May the divil crack the two legs undher ye!' bawled Slipper in acknowledgment of the compliment.

Mrs Canty laughed genially, and her boat lumbered away.

I shoved Slipper ashore at the nearest point. Philippa and I paddled to the end of the lake, and abandoning the duck as a bad business, walked home.

A few days afterwards it happened that it was incumbent upon me to attend the funeral of the Roman Catholic Bishop of the diocese. It was what is called in France *um bel enterrement*, with inky flocks of tall-hatted priests, and countless yards of white scarves, and a repast of monumental solidity at the Bishop's residence. The actual interment was to take place in Cork, and we moved in long and imposing procession to the railway station, where a special train awaited the cortège. My friend Mr James Canty was among the mourners: an important and active personage, exchanging condolences with the priests, giving directions to porters, and blowing his nose with a trumpeting mournfulness that penetrated all the other noises of the platform. He was condescending enough to notice my presence, and found time to tell me that he had given Mr Murray 'a sure word' with regard to some of 'the wreckage' – this with deep significance, and a wink of an inflamed and tearful eye. I saw him depart in a first-class carriage, and the odour of sanctity; seeing that he was accompanied by seven priests, and that both windows were shut, the latter must have been considerable.

Afterwards, in the town, I met Murray, looking more pleased with himself than I had seen him since he had taken up the unprofitable task of smuggler-hunting.

'Come along and have some lunch,' he said, 'I've got a real good thing on this time! That chap Canty came to me late last night, and told me he knew for a fact that the island on Corran Lake was just stiff with barrels of bacon and rum, and that I'd better send every man I could spare today to get them into the town. I sent the men out at eight o'clock this morning; I think I've gone one better than Bosanquet this time!'

I began to realize that Philippa was going to score heavily on the subject of the fairies that she had heard snoring on the island, and I imparted to Murray the leading features of our picnic there.

'Oh, Slipper's been up to his chin in that rum from the first,' said Murray. 'I'd like to know who is sleeping partner was!'

It was beginning to get dark before the loaded carts of the salvage party came lumbering past Murray's windows and into the yard of the police-barrack. We followed them, and in so doing picked up Flurry Knox, who was sauntering in the same direction. It was a good haul, five big casks of rum, and at least a dozen smaller barrels of bacon and butter, and Murray and his Chief Constable smiled seraphically on one another as the spoil was unloaded and stowed in a shed.

'Wouldn't it be as well to see how the butter is keeping?' remarked Flurry, who had been looking on silently, with, as I had noticed, a still and amused eye. 'The rim of that small keg there looks as if it had been shifted lately.'

The sergeant looked hard at Flurry; he knew as well as most people that a hint from Mr Knox was usually worth taking. He turned to Murray.

'Will I open it, sir?'

'Oh! open it if Mr Knox wishes,' said Murray, who was not famous for appreciating other people's suggestions.

The keg was opened.

'Funny butter,' said Flurry.

The sergeant said nothing. The keg was full of black bog-mould. Another was opened, and another, all with the same result.

'Damnation!' said Murray, suddenly losing his temper. 'What's the use of going on with those? Try one of the rum casks.'

A few moments passed in total silence while a tap and a spigot were sent for and applied to the barrel. The sergeant drew off a mugful and put his nose to it with the deliberation of a connoisseur.

'Water, sir,' he pronounced, 'dirty water, with a small indication of sperrits.'

A junior constable tittered explosively, met the light blue glare of Murray's eye, and withered away.

'Perhaps it's holy water!' said I, with a wavering voice.

Murray's glance pinned me like an assegaii, and I also faded into the background.

'Well,' said Flurry in dulcet tones, 'if you want to know where the stuff is that was in those barrels, I can tell you, for I was told it myself half-an-hour ago. It's gone to Cork with the Bishop by special train!'

Mr Canty was undoubtedly a man of resource. Mrs Canty had mistakenly credited me with an intelligence equal to her own, and on receiving from Slipper a highly colourful account of how audibly Mr Canty had slept off his potations, had regarded the secret of Holy Island as having been given away. That night and the two succeeding ones were spent in the transfer of the rum to bottles, and the bottles and the butter to fish boxes; these were, by means of a slight lubrication of the railway underlings loaded into a truck as 'Fresh Fish, Urgent', and attached to the Bishop's funeral train, while the police, decoyed far from the scene of action, were breaking their backs over barrels of bog-water. 'I suppose,' continued Flurry pleasantly, 'you don't know the pub that Canty's brother has in Cork. Well, I do. I'm going to buy some rum there next week, cheap.'

'I shall proceed against Canty!' said Murray, with fateful calm.

'You won't proceed far,' said Flurry; 'you'll not get as much evidence out of the whole country as'd hang a cat.'

'Who was your informant?' demanded Murray.

Flurry laughed. 'Well, by the time the train was in Cork, yourself and the Major were the only two men in the town that weren't talking about it.'

# W. B. YEATS

## The Twisting of the Rope

*William Butler Yeats (1865–1939), in addition to his poetry and plays, also wrote one novel and three volumes of short stories. 'The Twisting of the Rope' is from* Tales of Red Hanrahan.

HANRAHAN was walking the roads one time near Kinvara at the fall of day, and he heard the sound of a fiddle from a house a little way off the roadside. He turned up the path to it, for he never had the habit of passing by any place where there was music or dancing or good company, without going in. The man of the house was standing at the door, and when Hanrahan came near he knew him and he said: 'A welcome before you, Hanrahan, you have been lost to us this long time.' But the woman of the house came to the door and she said to her husband: 'I would be as well pleased for Hanrahan not to come in to-night, for he has no good name now among the priests, or with women that mind themselves, and I wouldn't wonder from his walk if he has a drop of drink taken.' But the man said, 'I will never turn away Hanrahan of the poets from my door,' and with that he bade him enter.

There were a good many neighbours gathered in the house, and some of them remembered Hanrahan; but some of the little lads that were in the corners had only heard of him, and they stood up to have a view of him, and one of them said: 'Is not that Hanrahan that had the school, and that was brought away by Them?' But his mother put her hand over his mouth and bade him be quiet, and not be saying things like that. 'For Hanrahan is apt to grow wicked,' she said, 'if he hears talk of that story, or if any one goes questioning him.' One or another called out then, asking him for a song, before he had rested himself; and he gave him whiskey in a glass, and Hanrahan thanked him and wished him good health and drank it off.

The fiddler was tuning his fiddle for another dance, and the man of the house said to the young men, they would all know what dancing was like when they saw Hanrahan dance, for the like of it had never been seen since he was there before. Hanrahan said he would not dance, he had better use for his feet now, travelling as he was through the five provinces of Ireland. Just as he said that, there came in at the half-door Oona, the daughter of the house, having a few bits of bog deal from Connemara in her arms for the fire. She threw them on the hearth and the flame rose up, and showed her to be very comely and smiling, and two or three of the young men rose up and asked for a dance. But Hanrahan crossed the floor and brushed the others away, and said it was with him she must dance, after the long road he had travelled before he came to her. And it is likely he said some soft word in her ear, for she said nothing against it, and stood out with him, and there were little blushes in her cheeks. Then other couples stood up, but when the dance was going to begin, Hanrahan chanced to look down, and he took notice of his boots that were worn and broken, and the ragged grey socks showing through them; and he said angrily it was a bad floor, and the music no great things, and he sat down in the dark place beside the hearth. But if he did, the girl sat down there with him.

The dancing went on, and when that dance was over another was called for, and no one took much notice of Oona and Red Hanrahan for a while, in the corner where they were. But the mother grew to be uneasy, and she called to Oona to come and help her to set the table in the inner room. But Oona, that had never refused her before, said she would come soon, but not yet, for she was listening to whatever he was saying in her ear. The mother grew yet more uneasy then, and she would come nearer them, and let on to be stirring the fire or sweeping the hearth, and she would listen for a minute to hear what the poet was saying to her child. And one time she heard him telling about white-handed Deirdre, and how she brought the sons of Usnach to their death; and how the blush in her cheeks was not so red as the blood of kings' sons that was shed for her, and her sorrows had never gone out of mind; and he said it was maybe the memory of her that made the cry of the plover on the bog as sorrowful in the ear of the poets as the keening of young men for a comrade. And there would never have been that memory of her, he said, if it was not for the poets that had put her beauty in their songs. And the next time she did not well understand what he was saying, but as far as she could hear it had the sound of poetry though it was not rhymed, and this is what she heard him say: 'The sun and the moon are the man and the girl, they are my life and your life, they are travelling and ever travelling through the skies as if under the one hood. It was God made them for one another. He made your life and my life before the beginning of the world, he made them that they might go through the world, up and down, like the two best dancers that go on with the dance up and down the long floor of the barn, fresh and laughing, when all the rest are tired out and leaning against the wall.'

The old woman went then to where her husband was playing cards, but he would take no notice of her, and then she went to a woman of the neighbours and said: 'Is there no way we can get them from one another?' and without waiting for an answer she said to some young men that were talking together: 'What good are you when you cannot make the best girl in the house come out and dance with you? And go now the whole of you,' she said, 'and see can you bring her away from the poet's talk.' But Oona would not listen to any of them, but only moved her hand as if to send them away. Then they called to Hanrahan and said he had best dance with the girl himself or let her dance with one of them. When Hanrahan heard what they were saying he said: 'That is so, I will dance with her; there is no man in the house must dance with her but myself.'

He stood up with her then, and led her out by the hand, and some of the young men were vexed, and some began mocking at his ragged coat and his broken boots. But he took no notice, and Oona took no notice, but they looked at one another as if all the world belonged to themselves alone. But another couple that had been sitting together like lovers stood out on the floor at the same time, holding one another's hands and moving their feet to keep time with the music. But Hanrahan turned his back on them as if angry, and in place of dancing he began to sing, and as he sang he held her hand, and his voice grew louder, and the mocking of the young men stopped, and the fiddle stopped, and there was nothing heard but his voice that had in it the sound of the wind. And what he sang was a song he had heard or had made one time in his wanderings on Slieve Echtge, and the words of it as they can be put into English were like this:

> O Death's old bony finger
> Will never find us there
> In the high hollow townland
> Where's love to give and to spare;
> Where boughs have fruit and blossom
> At all times of the year;
> Where rivers are running over
> With red beer and brown beer.
> An old man plays the bagpipes
> In a gold and silver wood;
> Queens, their eyes blue like the ice,
> Are dancing in a crowd.

And while he was singing it Oona moved nearer to him, and the colour had gone from her cheek, and her eyes were not blue now, but grey with the tears that were in them, and any one that saw her would have thought she was ready to follow him there and then from the west to the east of the world.

But one of the young men called out: 'Where is that country he is singing about? Mind yourself, Oona, it is a long way off, you might be a long time on the road before you would reach to it.' And another said: 'It is not the Country of the Young you will be going if you go with him, but to Mayo of the bogs.' Oona looked at him then as if she would question him, but he raised her head in his hand, and called out between singing and shouting: 'It is very near us that country is, it is on every side; it may be on the bare hill behind it is, or it may be in the heart of the wood.' And he said out very loud and clear: 'In the heart of the wood; oh, death will never find us in the heart of the wood. And will you come with me there, Oona?' he said.

But while he was saying this the two old women had gone outside the door, and Oona's mother was crying, and she said: 'He has put an enchantment on Oona. Can we not get the men to put him out of the house?'

'That is a thing you cannot do,' said the other woman, 'for he is a poet of the Gael, and you know well if you would put a poet of the Gael out of the house, he would put a curse on you that would wither the corn in the fields and dry up the milk of the cows, if it had to hang in the air seven years.'

'God help us,' said the mother, 'and why did I ever let him into the house at all, and the wild name he has!'

'It would have been no harm at all to have kept him outside, but there would great harm come upon you if you put him out by force. But listen to the plan I have to get him out of the house by his own doing, without any one putting him from it at all.'

It was not long after that the two women came in again, each of them having a bundle of hay in her apron. Hanrahan was not singing now, but he was talking to Oona very fast and soft, and he was saying: 'The house is narrow but the world is wide, and there is no true lover that need be afraid of night or morning or sun or stars or shadows of evening, or any earthly thing.' 'Hanrahan,' said the mother then, striking him on the shoulder, 'will you give me a hand here for a minute?' 'Do that, Hanrahan,' said the woman of her neighbours, 'and help us to make this hay into a rope, for you are ready with your hands, and a blast of wind has loosened the thatch on the haystick.'

'I will do that for you,' said he, and he took the little stick in his hands, and the mother began giving out the hay, and he twisting it, but he was hurrying to have done with it, and to be free again. The women went on talking and giving out the hay, and encouraging him, and saying what a good twister of a rope he was, better than their own neighbours or than any one they had ever seen. And Hanrahan saw that Oona was watching him, and he began to twist very quick and with his head high, and to boast of the readiness of his hands, and the learning he had in his head, and the strength in his arms. And as he was boasting, he went backward, twisting the rope always till he came to the door that was open behind him, and without thinking he passed the threshold and was out on the road. And no sooner was he there than the mother made a sudden rush, and threw out the rope after him, and she shut the door and the half-door and put a bolt upon them.

She was well pleased when she had done that, and laughed out loud, and the neighbours laughed and praised her. But they heard him beating at the door, and saying words of cursing outside it, and the mother had but time to stop Oona that had her hand upon the bolt to open it. She made a sign to the fiddler then, and he began a reel, and one of the young men asked no leave but caught hold of Oona and brought her into the thick of the dance. And when it was over and the fiddle had stopped, there was no sound at all of anything outside, but the road was as quiet as before.

As to Hanrahan, when he knew he was shut out and that there was neither shelter nor drink nor a girl's ear for him that night, the anger and the courage went out of him, and he went on to where the waves were beating on the strand.

He sat down on a big stone, and he began swinging his right arm and singing slowly to himself, the way he did always to hearten himself when every other thing failed him. And whether it was that time or another time he made the song that is called to this day 'The Twisting of the Rope', and that begins, 'What was the dead cat that put me in this place,' is not known.

But after he had been singing a while, mist and shadows seemed to gather about him, sometimes coming out of the sea, and sometimes moving upon it. It seemed to him that one of the shadows was the queen-woman he had seen in her sleep at Slieve Echtge; not in her sleep now, but mocking, and calling out to them that were behind her: 'He was weak, he was weak, he had no courage.' And he felt the strands of the rope in his hand yet, and went on twisting it, but it seemed to him as he twisted that it had all the sorrows of the world in it. And then it seemed to him as if the rope had changed in his dream into a great water-worm that came out of the sea, and that twisted itself about him, and held him closer and closer, and grew from big to bigger till the whole of the earth and skies were wound up in it, and the stars themselves were but the shining of the ridges of its skin. And then he got free of it, and went on, shaking and unsteady, along the edge of the strand, and the grey shapes were flying here and there around him. And this is what they were saying, 'It is a pity for him that refuses the call of the daughters of the Sidhe, for he will find no comfort in the love of the women of the earth to the end of life and time, and the cold of the grave is in his heart for ever. It is death he has chosen; let him die, let him die, let him die.'

# FRANK MATHEW

## The Reverend Peter Flannery

*Frank Mathew (1865–1924) evoked Irish life in many stories. This one is from his best book* At the Rising of the Moon.

MY friend the Reverend Peter Flannery is the sternest-looking and the gentlest of men. To look at him you would fancy he had spent a fierce life; but the truth is that he has lived in a wilderness and that in his broad parish of Moher there is not a mouse afraid of him.

I first met him in an hotel at Lisdoonvarna. One night there was singing, and a big, truculent old priest sang in his turn:

> When we went a-gipsying,
> A long time ago

He was very serious and hoarse. With his grim face and white hair he looked the last man in the world to 'go a-gipsying'. Afterwards I came to know Peter, and spent many evenings with him in the little house where he lives with an old housekeeper of singular ugliness and a turbulent small boy known as Patrick Flannery. I found him absurdly simple, a man knowing nothing of the world and troubling himself little about anything beyond the borders of Moher; but though he is so unpretending he has deep respect for his dignity as a parish priest. On one of those evenings in his naked little parlour he told me the story of the only adventure of his life.

A small island with a ruined house on it lies near the shore of the most desolate part of the parish; at high tide it is ringed with white jumping waves, but at ebb it is set in a black rim of rocks. A miser was strangled there for his money by his daughter, seventy years ago, so the house is known for miles around as the 'House of the Murder'. Then it was a headland, but afterwards the encroaching sea cut it off from the coast. The Moher folk say the island is haunted by the ghost of an old man with a choked face and with purple foam on his lips, and is given up to the Evil Spirits.

One stormy winter's night, nearly twelve years ago now, Peter Flannery was riding back from visiting a dying woman near Liscannor. It was raining, the wind was dead against him; he had seldom been out on such a night though his life-work took him on many a wild lonely ride. As he reached the Liscannor Cross-roads his horse stopped, and a heart-broken voice came from under the trees.

'Remember the Dark Man! For God's sake remember the Dark Man!' He knew that it was Andy Lonergan, the 'Dark Man' – that is, the blind man – who haunted that place day and night.

'Is that yourself, Andy?' said he.

''Tis so, your reverence, but 'tis the black night to be abroad, sure the Banshee is keenin' on th' island.'

'The Banshee, is it? I know, I know, and manny's the time I've heard that same, Andy. There's never a rough night without her.'

'Is it the wind ye mane, father? I know the wind's cry if annyone, but 'twasn't only that on th' island to-night; 'twas a woman's voice, sometimes 'twas like a child's. There'll be sore hearts in Moher the morn.'

'Ah well, Andy! manny's the queer thing ye've heard in your time,' said Peter, and he rode homewards, but Andy's words kept in his head. Now, the blind man was half crazed, yet dared not lie about the Banshee; perhaps there was some poor soul out on the island. At last he turned his horse; as he rode back past the Cross-roads he called out, 'Are ye there, Andy?' but no answer came. The horse seemed to have strong objections to going seaward, and Peter himself had misgivings; he is a Clare man, the son of a Ballyvaughan fisherman, and though of course he does not believe in the Banshee, yet would rather not have gone where there was any chance of meeting her. Then he thought – suppose Andy was fooling him! He could fancy the blind man sitting hidden and grinning at him as he rode back pass the Cross-roads. It would be a fine joke in Moher; he flushed at such irreverence.

Then he reached the shore, and dismounting fastened his horse to a wall, and walked down across the slipping shingle, crunching it under foot; he was tripped by tangles of seaweed, and stumbled over a fishing coracle, could see scarcely a yard in front of him. ''Tis a blind man's holiday,' he thought. 'Faith, Dark Andy could see as much as I can, and why couldn't McCaura leave his coracle in a sensible place?' He went to the water's edge, the foam splashed over him, he could see nothing but the white flashes of breakers and was deafened by the noise. A few minutes of this was enough; he turned back with a smile at the absurdity of his going out there at that time of night. 'There's no fool like an old one,' he said; then stopped to listen again, and in a pause (when the wind seemed to be taking breath for a howl) heard a child's cry from the island. How could a baby be on the island in a hurricane, when there was not a soul for miles around would go there for love or money at any time? His misgivings rushed back with uncanny legends of lost souls bound on the winds or imprisoned in the waves that always keep racing towards the land yet always break before reaching it. This might be some Devil's trap. True, he could exorcise the Devil, but would rather not.

He waited during the new howl of the wind – it seemed endless – then in the next pause heard the child's voice again; it was an unmistakably human squall. ''Tis a child, sure enough,' he said, 'an' a strong one at that.' The question for him was not how did the baby get on the island, but how was he to get it off? McCaura's cabin was a mile away across the bog, and on such a night no one would be out except Dark Andy, who would be worse than useless. The only thing was to go out to the island himself, so he groped his way to the coracle.

Now a coracle is a sort of punt, a shallow frame covered with tarpaulin, a ticklish craft, but it can live in the wildest sea, though as

Peter said – "'Tis always on the look-out for a chance to drown ye.' He shouldered it as one to the manner born. Many a day and night had he spent afloat in the time when he was a fisher-boy; he thought how often since then he had longed to put out to sea, only his mighty dignity as a parish priest forbade it. His old bones were stiff, but he was as strong as ever.

Well, to cut a long story short, he launched that coracle and reached the island, not without risky and hard work. Dragging the coracle ashore, he made his way to the ruined house; the roof had fallen in, the windows were gone, only the walls were left. He could see nothing, but the child's cry guided him, and then in a corner he found a woman lying huddled on a heap of fallen plaster and laths; her face was to the wall, her left arm clutched a tiny baby. He knelt down by her and touched her forehead – she was dead. By her dress he knew she came from the Arran Islands. Perhaps she had been brought to the 'House of the Murder' to keep the birth secret; or perhaps the fishers bringing her to the mainland had been caught by the gale, and could place her in no better shelter in the time of her trouble. Now the Arran folk were familiar to him, many were of his kindred; he must have known this woman from her babyhood, and as a slip of a girl running barefoot on the hills. He turned her face to him, but could only see it dimly; it was much changed too, and half hidden by wet hair. Then the thought came that he had no right to pry into her secret; he laid her head back reverently. She lay there with her face to the wall as if she had died in shame.

He took the baby and chafed it, wrapping his woollen comforter round it; he thought it was dying – his knowledge of babies was small – so he decided to baptize it at once. There was no lack of water, for the rain was still falling in torrents, so he filled a cup that was lying with some untasted food by the mother, and baptized that whining infant as reverently and solemnly as if he had been in a great cathedral.

It must have been a strange scene in the 'House of the Murder' – the gaunt old man dripping from the rain and the sea, holding the baby tenderly and awkwardly, with the body of the mother lying beside them. He gave the baby the name Patrick, the first that came to him, '*Pathricius, ego te baptizo,*' and so forth in his queer Latin brogue, and the small new Christian howled dismally, and the gale answering howled outside. Then he unbuttoned the breast of his greatcoat and fastened the baby inside – so that only its ridiculous red face could be seen – and started for home. Crossing more easily this time, he found his old horse huddled in dumb resignation under the lee of the wall, and rode home through the storm at a good pace with a light heart. Every now and then the child cried to show that the life was in it, and then he tried to quiet it tenderly with 'Be hushed now, *vick machree*, son of my heart! Ah! Be sthill, Pathrick. Be aisy, ye cantakerous little cur!'

There was great work that night in the little house, when the old priest and his housekeeper welcomed their guest. And when the baby was cosily asleep, Peter got into his big arm-chair and mixed himself a steaming tumbler of punch – for no man values punch more, though of course in strict moderation – and he felt he deserved it to-night. 'An' would ye believe it?' and at this point of his story his voice shook with pathos – 'would ye believe it, and th' instant when I was putting it to me lips the clock shtruck twelve, and so I couldn't taste a dhrop, not a single dhrop!' For if he had tasted it after midnight he could not have said Mass. This was a lame ending to his one adventurous night. The baby was kept in the priest's house, and, when the gale went down, the mother's body was brought from the island and buried; I think Father Peter found afterwards who she was, though her name never passed his lips.

For nearly twelve years 'Pathrick' has ruled the priest's house, thriving under the rough tenderness of Peter Flannery. Meanwhile Peter has led always the same life, rising in the early morning to say Mass in the cold chapel before a scanty congregation of women; many of them pray aloud with shut eyes and entire disregard of their neighbours, and Patrick now serves him as clerk, looking very serious in his little white surplice, like a Cupid in a monk's cowl.

Then he rides on his sick-calls, miles and miles away through the bogs and over the hills, for he goes at any hour of the day or night to any one who chooses to summon him; or he walks down to the

school – where he usually finds Patrick standing in the corner with his
face to the wall, in disgrace – or he goes his rounds through the Village
of Moher. Many a time have I seen him striding down the Village 'like
an executioner' and the dirty little ragged children running to meet
him and snuggling their smeared faces against his long coat. The first
time babies see him they yell as if he was the Devil; but the next time
they would yell louder still if he forgot to fondle them. Many a time
have I seen him standing in the street, beleaguered by a cluster of
women, scowling nervously over them and looking to see if there is
any chance of rescue; while they all talk at once, quarrelling among
themselves:

'Ah! Peggy Lonergan, dacint woman, be whisht, can't ye?'

'Mary Ronan, I take shame o' ye to be throublin' the holy priest so.
Won't ye be lettin' me have a single word wid him?'

And now in the evenings he has something to dream about, and
when he sits alone by the fire in his naked parlour, smoking his old
pipe – with his tumbler of punch smoking too, to keep him company
– he dreams of the great future of Patrick Flannery. He sees that urchin
grow up as a model, go to Maynooth and win prizes there, rise rapidly
in the Church, and even become a Bishop. It is true Pat will have to
change greatly before them, for it is a queer Bishop he would make
now; but time works wonders and Pat has a good heart.

Peter hears him preaching the great sermons himself has never
preached to the great congregations he has never seen. And he thinks
that 'His Lordship Docthor Flannery' has a pleasing sound, that Bishop
Flannery will be loved by all, that blessings will go with him; it is he
that will have an eye for true worth and never let a plain man spend his
life in a wilderness while smoother-tongued men have all they want.
But at this point, the dream breaks, for he knows in his heart that he
would be sorry to leave his wilderness; so when the clock strikes nine
he slowly finishes his punch, knocks out the ashes from his pipe and
goes up the steep stairs to his bedroom, quavering in his hoarse voice,

> When we went a-gipsying,
> A long time ago.

# AGNES CASTLE

## Rosanna

*Mrs Agnes Castle was the author, with her husband Egerton Castle, of 'costume'
romances of old England in the manner of Sir Walter Scott. She was also capable of
writing excellent short stories set in Ireland, of which this is an example.*

SITTING by the fire we were, smoking our bits of pipes, just him and
me together, when, of a sudden, he turns on me an' he says: 'Da,' he
says, 'it's about time I was thinking of taking a wife,' says he.

'An' is that way wid ye?' I says. 'Troth, an' I'm thinking as much
meself this long time. Sure it's scandalizing discomfirture we're living
in.' I says, 'ever since poor auld Maria went and died on us, – the Lord
be merciful to her soul! Your poor mother, – the Lord be merciful to
her! – she'd like to tear the eyes out of them sluts of girls this minute, –
the blessed saint in Heaven, that she is! Thrue for ye, me boy, it's a
wife we want, and who'd be the wan to look out but yourself, since
it's the auld fellow I'm getting, entirely. And who'll it be?' says I, that
innicent, niver suspecting he'd be so undutiful as to be making his
choice unbeknownst to me – let alone that same grand choice!
'Who'll be it?' I axes him. 'What would ye say to Miss Condren at the
Cross Roads? It's thrue she's a long nose of her own; but what's that?
She's the rale auld family.'

'What 'ud I say to Miss Condren?' cries he. 'It's making game o' me
ye are, I think. What 'ud I say to Judy Condren?' says he, grinning at

me wid all his white teeth an' thim clinched over his pipe. 'Sure, if I
saw that long nose of hers poking about here – "Take your snipe's
beak out of this house," that's what I'd say to her.'

'Then it's one of them thriftless Roches ye've got in your mind,'
says I; 'not but what auld Roche is a dacent feller, an' the girls has fine
figures of their own, I'm not denying. But it's not much fortune
they'd be bringing a boy.'

'Is it I,' he cried, "d take up wid one of them? Bedad, I'm surprised
at ye for mintioning them at all! What would I be doing with such
flithereens, streeling about wid their ribbins an' their feathers an' the
impident airs of them?'

'Then it'll be Mary Cassidy, I'll be bound,' says I.

'No such thing,' says he; 'she's been walking wid Jim Nolan this
month past.'

'Will it be Miss O'Donnell?' says I.

'It will not,' says he; 'I'd rather go single all me days.'

'Well, in the name of God,' says I, 'who is it to be, thin? May be it's
a town-girl ye're set on after all. There's Miss Hinnegan at the hotel, –
it's not the family connection I'd choose for ye, Johnny, the
O'Moores have never wedded wid trade yet – but they do be sayin'
it's rolling in gold she'll be when auld Hinnegan dies. She'll not say no
to ye, Johnny. Troth, and I was noticing them were quare looks she
was giving ye last Saturday after the pig-fair.'

'An' what sort of looks would ye have her give anny wan wid them
crass eyes of hers,' says me young man, an' he takes his pipe out of his
mouth an' bursts out laughing. 'Sure, God help her, she can't look one
way widout lookin' the other. She'd be the right sort to put things
straight for us.'

At that I bid him lave off his moidering thricks, for I knew it was
humbugging me, he was, an' not a bit of marrying on him. An' he
never answered me back a word, but was spacheless, playing a chune
on the stem of his pipe wid his fingers, an' puffing at it, an' it black out.
An' thin he says: 'It's not money we want wid a wife; ye're a warm
man, father – an' its not beholden to a slip of a girl we'd be – you an'
me.'

'It's aisy talking that-a-way,' says I, 'but it 'ud be no use at all, at all, for a fine young feller like yourself to go taking up wid a body that hadn't enough to keep herself. It 'ud not be respectable,' says I, 'not what your father's son was rared up to.'

'An' as for family,' says he, kind of dreamy, as if he had not heard me, 'isn't it the rale auld stock we are ourselves? O'Moores of Moorestown, discindints of Rory O'Moore, – king's blood,' says he, 'an' what's Roches, an' Condrens, an' O'Donnells to that? It's no sort of use to try and ally ourselves wid thim as'll match us,' says he; 'an' why? Because they're not to be found – that's why. We'll mate to plaze ourselves,' he says, as bould as brass; 'an' what we want is a little young crathur wid a heart full of love; a little weeshy, dawshy, coaxing bit of a thing wid eyes the colour of violets, that would swally ye'r heart alive and niver let it out again; an' a head full of curls that would drive a boy wild just to look at!'

'What sort of blasphemious talk is that out of ye?' cries I, interrupting him. 'It's meself ye'll have wild in a minute or two,' for I didn't fancy the looks of him, wid his head on one side an' a kind of silly smile on him. 'What in the whole wide worrld's upon ye?' says I. 'Spake out, man, or I'll drag the tongue out of ye jaws an' make you tell the thrut that-a-way.'

He turns upon me wid his hands on his knees, an' his face the colour of the peeonies in the garden beyant. 'Da,' he says, an' rasps his throat; 'Father,' he says an' thin out he bursts. 'You've no right,' he says, 'to be casting up at her thim rogues and vagabonds of parints of hers! Shure her mother isn't her mother at all, on'y her stepmother; an' as for her father – bad scran to him – he's the greatest bla'guard between this and Dublin. However, it's not fair,' says he, 'to be goin' on this way, for sure it's niver themselves they are, at all, but blind drunk every day of the week, an' Sundays into the bargain. But as for herself, it's the purty little crathur she is, like an angel from heaven, her that's niver seen nothing but hell's wickedness since the day she was born. She doesn't rightly know how to set about anything yit, an' if she is a Protestant it's on'y because she know no betther. She learnt no

wickedness off anny of thim, an' troth it's a Catholic she'll be the
minute she's told how.'

'Tare an' ages,' says I. 'ye murthering villain, hold yer tongue! Hold
yer tongue, you spawn of hell, an' tell me the name of her widout
another word!'

He was white now from red he was before, but his impidence was
beyond everything. 'It's Rosanna Moriarty,' he says.

'Well, I let out a screech – I have a quick kind of temper, not a bad
one, mind ye, but hasty-like. My poor mother – God be merciful to
her! – manny's the time she'd tell us of the day I nearly murthered her
wid the pitaty knife, an' I but seven years of age; an' the day I had me
little sisther – God be merciful to her, that's poor auld Maria, I mean –
strangled wid her apron-strings for letting me little pet rabbits run
away. Blue in the face she was, an' I pulling at the strings as hard as I
could! We used to be kilt wid the laughing, talking of it. But I was
always the rale good Catholic, an' sure me blood was up entirely. I was
like to kill him dead that minute, break his head open on him, an'
small blame to me. But I controlled meself. Wid a moighty effort I
kep' calm. 'Johnny O'Moore,' I says, 'ye black, onfilial, heathen
scrawn of a bla'guard scamp, mintion that name in my hearing again
an' I'll have your life, as sure as you stand there.'

Wid that he says no more, an' I says no more, nor was the subject as
much as remarked upon between us till the next time he had impidence enough to dare, an' that was the very week after.

What did that owdacious rogue of a Moriarty go for to do, but die
on us all of a suddent in the Delirious Trimmings, as the Docthur
called it – a real roaring fit of drunkenness – an' his limb of a wife, she
takes to her heels an' off wid her out of the place, sorra a one knew
where, an' the little schemer of a Rosanna left behind on our hands
together wid the corpse an' a power of debts.

It was auld Jim Roche first gave us the news; an' says he: 'It's rale
bad Rosanna is, the crathur! Sure they can't get her away from the
poor fella' at all, an' neither bite nor sup has crossed her lips this blessed
day. It 'ud break your heart to see her, with them purty red curls of

hers hanging every way, and them big black eyes of hers swollen up wid the crying. An' him the bitther bad father!'

An' then I see me fine young man start up from his corner an' off wid him widout a word.

Sure I knew the way it 'ud be. Some one would be offering to take in the girl out of charity, an' me fella' would have to be keeping up them sperrits of hers and' consoling of her an' wiping away all them tears – him as cute as a pet fox from the day he was weaned! But there's two of us can be cute, thinks I, an' out of the place she goes, or my name's not Larry O'Moore. There's the workhouse for her, an' the likes of her, beyant in the town. She'll be fed, an' warmed, an' clothed dacenter there than ever she's been in her life, an' my money helping to do it into the bargain. But I'll not have her left here to be bringing disgrace into my family. So I just says a word to Jim Roche, an' then I took a bit of a stroll, an' wint here and there, an' dropt into this wan an' that, an' be jabers I gave them all the hint. There isn't wan but 'ud be afeard to fall out wid me for they, most of them, owes me a bit an' I've been a good friend to them in the bad times. An', to tell the thrut, I'm plisanter as a friend than as an enemy.

Av course not a boy of them let on he understood what I was dhriving at: they wouldn't be that onpolite, an' I wouldn't have misdemeaned meself by speaking too plain. But, lonnies, it's aisy to say a good deal when you're saying nothin' at all, and when I came home, sure, I knew I had settled the young gintleman's nonsense for him, for as grand as he thought himself.

The auld cuckoo-clock had gone twelve (an' it's twenty minutes late regular) before Johnny came back that night. A rale warm spring night it was, black and moist, an' all his curls were plastered down his cheeks wid the way he'd been stravaguing round.

I was sitting waiting for him, smoking me pipe wid a peaceful soul, for it was a good stroke of work I had done the day, an' so I kep' telling meself, when in he burst like a wild fella.

'Father,' says he, 'I've tauld ye I wanted to marry Rosanna Moriarty; an' I mean to marry her,' he says.

'Och, listen to him,' says I, scornful; 'sure it's wandering in his speech, he is!'

'Father,' he says, rale earnest and eager, 'I've always been a good son to you. I've never been drunk nor contradictious, an' when other young men would have gone off an' seen the world, I've kep' at home an' worked an' helped you. In the name of God,' says he, pitiful-like, 'do not drive me to be undutiful now! Oh, father, it is a poor little innocent thing she is, an' it's alone and desolate she is, an' by Heaven,' he cries, 'this is a hard cruel worrld! There's not one of them'll give her a shelter or a crust this blessed night; an' on'y for auld Kitty who's sittin' and wakin' the corpse, the poor crathur 'ud be alone wid the dead this minute – enough to drive her distracted entirely! But give your consent to our wedding,' he cries, 'an' then it's who'll have her, I'll be bound. The cauld-hearted scoundrels as could shut their doors on her that way – why, it's fighting for her they'll be then! But I'll be even wid them yet, the whole lot of them, whatever black curse of cruelty has come over them, at all, at all.'

I was puffing away at my pipe, an' for the life of me I could not but give an agreeable smile to meself, thinking it was the rale proper kind of respect I was held in all over the place; not but that I knew there was not one of them as 'ud dare to go agin me.

When he sees me smile, he stops suddent and gives me a quare look. 'Father,' says he, 'I see what you have been after. God forgive you,' he says, 'but it's a wicked man you are.'

'Whisht, now, don't be goin' on,' says I; 'you will live to thank me yet.'

'An' what is to become of that poor young crathur?' says he, quite quiet; 'have ye thought of that? She cannot live alone in that auld tumble-down place, an' her that purty an' little, an' black Mac (divel take him!) wid his eye on her this many a day. What is to become of her, father?'

'Let her go to the workhouse,' says I; 'she need not fear black Mac there, for they keep them away from each other fast enough, the young boys an' the young girls too. They will be coming, no doubt, to bury the father from the Union to-morrow; let them take the daughter too; it's the right place for her.'

Wid that, he lets the awfullest oath ever ye heard. 'She'll not go there,' he says, 'so long as I'm alive.'

'May I ax what you intend to do, then?' says I, very polite.

'I have tauld you already,' says he; 'I intend to marry her.'

'An' may I inquire what yez are going to live on then? For I warn ye fair,' says I, in a white rage – for I seen by the obstinate look of him that he was set on his wickedness – 'I warn ye,' says I, 'that across this thrashle ye will niver step once ye take up wid that Protestant slut of Moriarty's; nor a penny of me money ye will never see, neither now nor when I am gone.'

'Is that your last word?' says he, an' stands up.

'It's me last word,' says I. 'as I'm a living man.'

'Then, good-bye, father,' says he.

'Good-bye,' says I, 'an' me curse upon you,' says I. 'My father's curse on the two of yez!'

Well, out he stamps widout as much as another word, an' I sits by the fire thinking it's home again he'll be before I can turn round. Sure an' I never thought he'd have thrown me over that-a-way, an' him an' me always together from the time he was a babby. But the turf itself burnt white under my eyes, an' the dawn broke that cauld an' desolate into the room, but sorra a bit of him come back to me. An' for three days I heard no news of him, an' sure I was that dark an' down in meself not wan dared to speak to me. The fellers was afraid to tell me the thrut, an' to be plain wid ye, I was not, so to say, encouraging to conversation. Bedad, I would not let them think I cared a halfpenny what that scoundrel of a boy was up to, when he chose to go against his father that rate.

He niver came home to me, an' I axed no questions of nobody. But on the Thursday it was, Mrs Malony (his Rivirence's housekeeper, a contrary fidget of an auld woman she is) stops me just as I was passing the door. 'Oh, Mr O'Moore,' she cries, in that mincing way of hers, 'what is this I hear about Johnny?' she says. 'Father O'Hara will be fit to be tied,' she says, 'when he comes back from visiting His Holiness at Rome.'

'What may ye have heard, ma'am?' says I. 'For it's little I know or want to know about him.'

'Oh,' she says, throwing up her eyes like an auld hen in a fit, 'oh, Mr O'Moore, sir, do not ax me; I couldn't defile my tongue by speaking of it.'

'Well, an' that happens to come right,' says I, 'for I don't want to hear. Though if you can reconcile it to your conscience to be keeping the thrut from his own father, it is surprised at ye I am, Mrs Malony, an' that's all I have got to say.'

Sure, it was just itching the auld girl was to tell me the bad news. 'Is it possible you don't know, Mr O'Moore?' she says. 'Oh dear, how can I bring meself to discourse of such a scandal! It is the real saint we all thought Mr Johnny, an' him so good in the choir, an' so regular at the Stations. Och, the shame of it!' she says. 'Father O'Hara will be leppin' mad, he will! But there's little shame about either of them,' she says, 'going about that brazen, an' buying things together – set up house they have as bold as man an' wife – the like was niver seen hereabouts before. Set up house in that ruinacious auld cabin of Moriarty's, an' him not a week dead yet. And she, the dirthy Protestant. Now if she'd been a Catholic itself – Och, it's a terrible visitation to the place, an' the remarks of the folks, an' the illusions, an' the jokes, – it's shocking altogether! Could not ye speak to your son, now?'

'Mrs Malony,' says I, an' I niver turned a hair, 'he is no longer anny son of mine, an' I will thank ye to remember it. I have cast him off,' I says; 'he is no O'Moore, at all, at all, to be bringing disgrace upon the name of them that has been kings in the land. An' as for that other,' says I, 'I'm wondering how ye have the face to mintion her to me!' Wid that I made her an iligant bow an' left her.

Well, that was the cruel, hard time for me. And, as if they'd given each other the word, sure every one in the place had something to say to me about them, wonst it was out that I knew their goings on. This boy told me wan thing, an' that boy would tell another, till it is distracted I was. An' sure did not one up to me an' says he: 'Ye'd better let them be married off at wonst,' says he, 'an' save the shame of it.' I struck him prostrate for that same, for as auld as I am. 'I will let them go to hell together,' says I.

If only Father O'Hara had been back home, but it's visiting His Holiness in Rome he was, an' not expected for another week.

Sunday was the rale disgraceful day. On my entry into the chapel, before I could as much as kneel down, I hears a kind of stir in the place behind me, an' I sees all them rows of Roche girls nudging each other and tossing their heads. An' there was a kind of titter among the boys, an' auld Biddy Flannagan, the crathur, who always kneels in the middle just before the rails, where she can have a good view of his Rivirence an' plenty of room to be rocking herself about, looks over her shoulder, an' snorts like an auld say-pig, an' rolls her eyes that wild-like I thought she was struck wid an apple-complex. An' then what should I see but my young gentleman marching up the chapel, an' Miss Moriarty, if ye plaze, alongside of him in a bran new black gown, an' a white sun-bonnet – he looking neither to right nor left, an' she watching him with them saucer eyes, that had done all the mischief. An' when he salutes the altar, she gives a little dip beside him, the heathen! He kneels down at the end of the bench an' she inside. An' in a minute or two out comes little Father Jo, the curate from town beyant, who says Mass of a Sunday when Father O'Hara is away; an' glad I was to see him, for the cheeks was burning off of me. When he done the Gospel, an' he had off wid his vestment, an' come to the altar-steps to read out the notices an' everyone was quiet listening to what he was going to say, if the first things he lets out is not the banns of marriage between John O'Connell O'Moore of Moorestown in this parish an' Rosanna Moriarty of Mount Pleasant in the same! Begorrah, the whole place was swimming round wid me. Spacheless I was, an' all I could do was just to look at them, thinking it 'ud be a wonder if the auld flags would not open and swalley them up.

Himself was sitting like a lamb, niver stirring hand nor foot, his eyes fixed rale pious on the alther, as if butther would not melt in his mouth. An' she, wid her sun-bonnet tumbled off them red curls of hers, as rosy over the impident face of her as ye plaze, wid a kind of dimple coming an' going on one side of her cheek that was just bursting wid smiles as anny one could see. At the sight of them I don't know what came over me, bit I gives a kind of bawl, and ups on me feet. 'Your Rivirence,' says I, 'I forbid them banns.'

An' Father Jo, who was rambling on quite aisy, stops as if he had been shot. 'What's that?' says he, very sharp — you could have heard a pin drop. But my blood was up, an' the whole place looking at me. 'I forbid them banns,' I says; 'an' if your Rivirence wants to know about the impidiment, sure there she is, an' sorra a bit of spiritual relation either, but a real orange heretic, an' not a bit of shame on her, the dirthy streel, shamming prayer beside the poor boy she had deluded entirely — an' her breaking all the Commandments this minute. She'll not wed him, I'll have her know it.'

'This is very onseemly,' says Father Jo, as pink as a babby to the roots of his hair; 'I cannot have this disturbance in the chapel,' he says.

'But your Rivirence,' says I, 'didn't ye give it out this minute? "If any one is aware," says you, and sure —'

'Whisht!' says he; 'this is scandalizing behaviour.'

'An' it is that same, yer Rivirence,' says I, 'but that's no fault of mine.'

'Sit down,' says he; 'I'll see ye after Mass in the vestry.'

An' Johnny niver a word out of him, but sitting there like a statue. I sees her crudle up to him like a child, an' now an' agin she shoots a look at me out of her eyes that was swalleying up her face — too big was they entirely. And what wid one thing an' another, I felt that mad, that it's not a prayer I said that day.

Well, I gives Father Jo a bit o' me mind in the vestry; but not a ha'-porth of good could I get out of him. 'Ye must speak to Father O'Hara,' says he, 'for I cannot interfere.'

An' when I got out of the chapel, och, to hear them all talking! 'What's the meaning of her coming to chapel wid him, and her a Protestant?' says one. 'Why it's converting her he is,' says another, and wid that they were all fit to die wid laughing. An' didn't that scrawn of hell, black Mac, catch up the pair of them on the road, an' out with

some of his impidence, an' did not Johnny an' he have the grandest
set-to that ever was seen in these parts, an' did not Johnny give him
such a pair of black eyes that the folks do be talking about it still? The
finest shindy ever they saw, they tell me: but sure, I could not be
taking pleasure out of anything wid the shame of the world upon me.

Well, on Tuesday evening, as I was sitting down to me bit of a
supper, on the stroke of ten o'clock, who should come tearing in upon
me but Father O'Hara himself. It is the holy show he was with grime
an' the smuts of the railway on the pale face of him, an' his long white
hair hanging wild-like over his eyes. 'What is this I hear,' he says,
widout as much as reaching me his hand, 'what is this I hear about
Johnny?' I was right glad to tell him the story, but when I had finished
I thought he was going to murther me entirely. Rale wicked, he was,
an' I as innicent as the babe unborn.

'You onnatural man,' says he, 'an' can ye sit there and tell me in
cold blood that you have drove these unfort'nit children into sin?
Och, God help us all,' he cries, 'that I should have to come home to
this! I have been among yez forty years come Christmas an' I have had
the grief of the world over yez all, God knows,' he says. 'An' manny
an' manny a time I have seen yez break our Divine Master's holy
commandments; manny a time, my poor flock, I have had to weep
over yez and for yez. I have seen yez fighting, an' injuring, an'
cheating each other, an' seen yez in jail an' in throuble, an' known in
me sorrowful soul that the sentence of the law was just. When we had
that terrible murther here,' he went on, ''tis fifteen year ago now, on'y
for the grace of God an' His powerful consolation an' the sight of the
poor sinner's beautiful penitence, sure I must have died of the agony
in me heart, for it is the heart of a father I have to yez all. But niver,' he
says, 'niver before in all the days I have been among yez have anny of
my children fell into such sin as this. An' to think it should be the child
of me predelection, little Johnny,' he cries, his voice breaking with
sorrow, 'him that was my pride an' my joy, him that your sainted wife,
Laurence O'Moore, laid in me arms wid her last dying effort! Oh,
man,' he goes on, turning on me again, 'I hold you responsible before

the throne of God for all the guilt that lies on the souls of that poor boy an' girl to-night.'

An' not bit of reason wud he hear from me. Priests an' women is that-a-way where the young folks is concerned: they do be forgetting the Fourth Commandment altogether. I could not pacify him at all, at all. 'Come wid me,' he says, 'come this minute, an' let us seek these childer. Not another night will I consent to let them stray without the Fold. Come, Laurence,' he says, 'in the name of your God, I command you; come and repair in so far as His mercy will permit the cruel wrong you have done!'

Nothing would serve him but I must set out wid him into the night beyant that very instant. An' on'y that I was afeared for his sake, on account of the state he was in, an' him such an auld man an' so frail, sure I had niver have demeaned meself by going a step.

But out he runs me, an' down the lane, an' across the village – thanks to goodness there was none about – an' up the bit of bog to the shanty, where Johnny had set up wid his light-of-love. The moon burst out of the clouds; there was a soft wind blowing round us, an' his Rivirence's face shone as pale as death wid all the white locks round it, an' him skimming along like a hare, so that I was hard set to keep up wid him. Well, we soon come in sight of Mount Pleasant. There it stood in the moonlight, wid the thatch falling off the roof, an' the mud of the walls crumbling away, the miserablest, most God-forsake hole of a place I ever see. An' as I thought of my on'y son disgracing himself by coming down to such a residence, I could not help it, but I let a curse on the pair of them.

His Rivirence whisks round an' lifts his hand, an' then he clutches me with one hand by the arm, an' points wid the other. 'See yonder!' he says, wid a kind of strangled whisper. 'See yonder, you sinful man!' An' he pointed to a black heap lying in the shade of the hovel across the door; an' then he motioned me back, so stern I durst not disobey him, an' himself went forward up to it.

'Johnny, my poor child,' he says – his voice was like a cooing dove's – 'Johnny, my poor child, what are ye lying out there for?'

An' Johnny, for Johnny it was, sleeping like a tramp on the bare turf, he up like a shot, an' rubbed his eyes, an' stared at Father O'Hara like wan daft. 'Oh, your Rivirence,' says he, reproachful like, 'sure you not have me lying widin wid the poor little girl, an' the holy words not spoken over us yet!' An' his Rivirence he beat his hands together, and fell upon the fella's neck and sobbed aloud. 'I thank God,' he cries, 'I thank God!'

'Father O'Hara, is it you?' cries Johnny, that surprised and as if he had just waked out of a dream. 'Oh, father, we have wanted ye sore, an' it's the cruel time we have had! An' it's the cruel things that people have said of us, an' she as innicent as the flowers of the field. Sure she does not know what they do be meaning. My heart's been fit to break,' he says.

An' then his Rivirence let a shout for me. 'Come here,' he says, 'Laurence O'Moore, an' bless your good son, an' give praise to the Father above that kep' him and his bride from sin, when his earthly father would have driven them into it. Come here an' tell him that ye have seen the hardness of your heart, an' repented. Tell him that he an' the good little girl he has chosen for his wife will be welcome to your hearth. An' in the meantime,' he says, 'Rosanna shall come to my house; an' Johnny, me boy, it's meself will give the wedding-feast.' An' after that what could I do?

# SHAN F. BULLOCK

## They That Mourn

*Shan Bullock (1865–1935) was born in County Fermanagh and is best known for his collection of short stories,* Ring O'Rushes *(1896), from which this story is taken. He published other short stories,* The Awkward Squad *(1893) and* By Thrasna River *(1895),* The Squireen *(1903) and* Dan the Dollar *(1905), a series of novels about Fermanagh life.*

BUNN market was over, its hurry and haggle. In corners and quiet spots of the big market-yard, you saw men and women carefully counting their little stores of silver, testing the coins with their teeth, knotting them firmly in red pocket-handkerchiefs, finally stowing them away in their long wide pockets as cautiously as though every sixpence were a diamond. In the streets, people were leisurely moving towards the shops, where tills were rattling, and counters teeming, and trade, for a few hours, mightily flourishing after its whole six days of blissful stagnation.

A cart laden with butter, chiefly in firkins, issued from the market-yard gate, a man between the shafts, one at either wheel, two pulling behind, all noisily endeavouring to keep the cart from running amuck downhill into the river. Close behind, like chief mourners after a hearse, one might fancy, came Tim Kerin and Nan his wife; a battered, slow-footed couple, heavily burdened with the big load of their years, white haired both of them, and lean as greyhounds. Heavily they shuffled along in their clumsy boots; the man with one arm across

his back, the other swinging limply; the woman holding up her skirt
with one hand, and gripping with the other the handle of an empty
basket; both looking fixedly over the tail-board of the cart at the few
pounds of butter for which they had slaved hard for weeks, and for
which, after hours of haggling, they had just received a few most
precious shillings. Fixedly they watched it, and mournfully almost, as
though they were bidding it a last farewell.

They passed through the gate, straggled across the footpath, and
silently watched the cart zigzag down the street, run presently against
the kerb, and, amid great shouting, discharge its contents into the
packing-house.

'Faith,' said Tim, across his shoulder, ''twas cliverly done. I wonder,
some day, they don't break their necks.' He wagged his head
dubiously; Nan tucked up her skirt; the two turned their faces uphill,
and set out to share their profits with the shops. The butter was gone,
and sorrow go with it: 'twas a heartbreak.

Tim Kerin's share of the profits was a shining sixpence, reluctantly
tendered to him by Nan his wife, who now walked a couple of steps
behind him, with eighteenpence shut tight in her hand, and the
remainder of the butter-money (only a shilling or two) tied fast in a
cotton bag and safely stowed away in the neck of her linsey-woolsey
dress. Threepence of Tim's sixpence was to buy tobacco, a penny
might go in the purchase of a weekly newspaper, a penny would buy a
pair of whangs (leather laces) for his boots; the penny remaining, when
all those luxuries had been honestly paid for, would buy a whole
tumblerful of frothing porter. A whole tumblerful! At sight of it, with
his mind's eye, Tim's lips dried and his feet went quicker over the
cobble stones.

Nan's lips were tight, her brow wrinkled. She was figuring. It
would take her to be powerful 'cute to fill her basket with the value of
eighteenpence. Och, the lot o' things she wanted: tea, sugar, bacon, a
herring for the Sunday's dinner, a bit o' white bread – and – and
supposing there were a penny or two left over (with knowing bar-
gaining there might be), was it likely, now, that Mr Murphy, the
draper, would let her have cheap a yard of narrow soiled lace to go

round the border of her nightcaps? Twopence might do, threepence would be sure to – Aw, glory be to goodness, did anybody ever hear of such romancin', such extravagance? Sure it was runnin' wild her wits were! Threepence for lace indeed!

A friend stepped from behind a cart and caught Nan by the arm. What! was it pass a neighbour like that Mrs Kerin would do? Pass her ouldest friend, Mrs Brady, as if she were a milestone, and never pass the time of day, or tell how she sold her butter, or how the world was using herself? 'Och, och, Mrs Kerin,' moaned Mrs Brady, 'what have I done to ye at all, at all?'

Nan stopped and put out her hand; then volubly began explaining: sure, sorrow the sight of Mrs Brady she had seen; sure, she never passed a neighbour without speaking; sure, 'twas walking along romancin' she was, figuring in her head, seeing how far she could make the few shillings go. 'An' how are you, ma'am?' asked Nan, when full pardon for her oversight had been generously given and gratefully received. 'How are you an' all your care?'

Swiftly the two old heads bobbed together; ceaselessly the tongues began to wag; freely the full tide of their softly drawling speech flowed gurgling round the little nothings of their little world.

Meanwhile, Tim, his sixpence hot in his palm, had taken a turn through the throng of the streets; had questioned his neighbours about sales and prices (just as though his pockets bulged with bank-notes); had spelt out the time on the big market-house clock as he stood by the town pump listening to the hoarse drone of a ballad singer; and now, on the sidewalk of Main Street, stood dreamily looking through a shop window at a pile of newspapers which stood precariously among an array of tobacco pipes and sweet bottles. If he brought a paper, Tim was thinking, he would have a whole week's diversion o' nights; if he didn't buy it, he would save the price of another tumblerful o' – A heavy hand fell on his shoulder.

'Hello, Tim,' said his neighbour, Shan Grogan; 'havin' a wee squint at the sugar-sticks is it, ye are?'

'Aw ay,' answered Tim, turning; 'aw ay! I was just lookin' at the papers there, an' wonderin' what an ojus lot o' news they give us nowadays for a penny. Enough to keep one goin' for a week. Powerful it is.'

'Yis,' said Shan; 'it's a wonderful world. But aisy, Tim; ha' ye been to the Post lately?'

'Naw,' said Tim.

'Well, look in there if you're passin', me son. The lassie that sells the stamps asked me to tell ye. Away quick; mebbe she'll give ye news for nothin'.'

'Now, now,' answered Tim. 'I'm obliged to ye, Shan; I'm obliged to ye. Now, now,' he repeated to himself, as he shuffled off along the pavement; 'now, now. Is Shan havin' a wee joke, I wonder?' he said; and coming to the post-office doubtfully sidled in.

'Me name is Kerin, Miss,' he said to the clerk, very humbly as to one of the representatives of mighty Government itself, 'Tim for Christian; an' they tell me ye'd mebbe be havin' somethin' for me?'

The girl handed him a letter bearing the Chicago postmark, stamped in one of the bottom corners, and carrying its address thence right up to the top of the envelope. Tim bore it tenderly to the door and carefully inspected it; then took it back to the counter.

'Whose countersign might that be, Miss, if ye please?' he asked, and placed his thumb over the postmark. Humbly he asked; curtly he was answered.

'Chicago?' said Tim. 'Ay, ay! I'm obliged to ye, Miss; I'm obliged to ye. May the Lord be good to ye, an' send ye a duke for a husband. Good-day to ye, Miss,' said he; then, with his hand deep in his pocket and the letter in his hand, stepped out into the street and went off in search of Nan.

It's from Padeen, he kept thinking to himself, as he walked joyfully along, his feet clattering loosely on the pavement, his old face turning here and there, watching for his wife; it's from Padeen, sure as ever was. Aw! but he was glad. Aw! but Nan would be glad. So long it was, ages and ages ago, since they heard from him. 'Twasn't Padeen's handwrite – naw! but sure it might have altered; everything altered in the Big Country. Ay! 'twas only poor ould Ireland that kept the same – never any worse, never any better. But where was Nan? Sure she ought to be in the shops. He was dying to find her. Up and down he went; at last found her still bobbing heads at the top of Bridge Street with her friend Mrs Brady.

'Aw, it's here ye are, Nan?' said he, coming up. 'An' me huntin' the town for ye. It's yourself is well, Mrs Brady, I'm hopin'? That's right, that's right.'

His voice came strangely broken and shrill; his eyes danced like a child's; still his hand gripped the letter in his pocket.

'What's the matter, Tim?' whispered Nan. 'Is it news ye have?'

'Ay, ay,' he answered. 'Come away till I tell ye; come away.'

He turned and, with Nan at his heels, set off almost at a run downhill towards the river. Aw! but his heart was thumpin'.

'Aisy, Tim,' cried Nan behind him; 'aisy, man, or me breath – me breath –'

Without answering, or slackening his pace, Tim went on, turned through the butter-market gate, crossed the empty yard, came to the furthermost corner of one of the long low sheds, and there halted, with his face to the wall. Aw! but his heart was thumpin'. Presently, Nan came to him, panting and flurried.

'What is it, Tim?' she asked; 'what is it?'

Slowly Tim brought out his letter, and, holding it by both hands, let his wife look at it.

'It's – it's from Padeen!' cried she; 'it's from Padeen!'

'Yis,' said Tim; 'yis. It's not his hand-write; but – but it must be from him.'

'Aw, glory be to God!' cried Nan. 'Glory be to God! Sure it's ages since we heard from the boy, ages!'

She put down her basket, and, with her head between Tim's shoulder and the wall, looked fixedly at the envelope. Aw! but she was glad to see it. Such a time it was since they had heard from Padeen! A whole two years it was, come Christmas, since the last letter came, with that money order in it, an' the beautiful picture of Padeen himself, dressed out in his grand clothes, with a gold chain across his waistcoat, and a big gold ring on his finger. A whole two years almost. And now maybe –

'Aw, Tim, open it quick,' she panted; 'open it quick!'

'Mebbe,' said Tim, 'we'd better wait till we get home. The light's bad, an' –'

'No – no, Tim! No – no; it'd kill me to wait.'

'Ay?' said Tim; then slowly drew his knife from his pocket and tenderly cut open the top of the envelope. His fingers trembled greatly as he fumbled with the enclosure. Nan's hand went quick to her heart.

'Aw, quick, Tim!' she cried. 'Quick, quick!'

'Don't – don't flooster me, woman,' said Tim; 'I can't – can't –' The next moment his shaking old fingers held a sheet of notepaper, and a black-edged card on which, in large letters, beneath a long silvern cross, were the words: PATRICK KERIN.

Nan fell back with a step; her fingers clutched at her dress over her heart. Tim's knife clattered upon the stones, and the envelope fluttered down. For a while they stood there silent, dread-stricken. At last Nan spoke. 'Read, Tim,' she said. 'Read!'

'I – I can't.'

'Ye must, Tim; it's better, Let us know the worst, for God's sake! Read, Tim.'

'I – I –' Tim began; then quickly opened the sheet. 'It's – it's too dark here,' he mumbled; 'I – I want me specs.'

'Read what ye can, Tim – an' quick, for God's sake!'

So Tim, still with his face to the wall, raised the letter to catch the light, and began to read:

CHICAGO CITY, U.S.A.

DEAR – DEAR MISTER KERIN, – *It is my – my sad duty to in-form you that your son Patrick died* ('Aw, Padeen, Padeen!') *of ty – typhus here on the 2nd of this month at twelve o'clock a.m.* ('God's mercy!' cried Nan). *As his oldest friend, I was with him at the end. He died in peace. He was buried at his request in — Cemetery. I – I send you something to – to keep . . . .*

'Aw, I can read no more,' said Tim, with a groan; 'it's too dark. I can read no more. Me poor auld Padeen!'

Nan turned and looked vacantly across at the busy street, dry-eyed and grey-faced. Ah! her poor Padeen, dead and buried away among the strangers, dead and buried, and never, never would she see him again, never hear his voice, never grip his hand! Dead, dead! her big, handsome, noble son ....

She turned to Tim and caught him by the sleeve.

'Come away home, Tim,' she said. 'Come away wi' me.' Tim looked at her.

'Ah! Nan, Nan,' he said, as the big tears sprang to his eyes. 'Nan, me girl, but's it's hard!'

'Ah yis,' said she, and lifted her basket; 'but come away, Tim, come away. Home's the best place for us.'

'Yis,' said Tim, wiping his eyes with his hand. 'Yis, Nan.' Then, Nan leading the way and Tim shuffling after, the two old people (mourners now in real earnest) crossed the yard; and at the gate Nan halted.

'I think,' said she, as Tim came up, 'I think we can manage this week wi'out the bits o' groceries. Sure they're only luxuries anyway. I'll go an' see if Mr Murphy can find me a bit o' crape for me bonnet. Yis.'

'Do,' said Tim. 'Do, Nan; an' when you're about it,' he said, taking his sixpence from his pocket and handing it to her, 'ye may as well get me a bit for me hat. Ay! sure I can do wi'out me tabaccy for one week. Aw yis! Away quick, Nan; an' hurry back, me girl, hurry back.'

So Nan turned up towards the market-house; but Tim went downhill towards the bridge; and when, presently, Nan came to him, carrying her little packet of crape in her big basket, Tim's head was bowed over the parapet and he was mumbling tearfully:

'Aw, me poor Padeen, me poor Padeen!'

Nan plucked at his sleeve.

'Come away home, Tim,' she said; 'come away.' And at the word Tim raised his head, dried his eyes, and set off slowly after Nan up the long, dusty road that wearily led towards home.

# SEAMAS MACMANUS

## The Bewitched Fiddle

*Seamas MacManus (1869–1960) was born in County Donegal. He wrote many tales of old Ireland and the Irish peasantry in particular. 'The Bewitched Fiddle' is based on a story told him in his boyhood and is full of humour. In his time, he was a writer highly popular in the United States where he lived for some time, dying in New York.*

FAIX, it's a good long wheen of years since it happened now. It was ould Jimmy Higgerty, that was uncle to Mickey acrass there, reharsed the passage to me. An' it was ould Jimmy himself, more betoken, that was the cause of the whole affair – for Jimmy, ye know, was what we call a canny man, very knowin' intirely, an' up to all sorts of saicrets that you nor me nor one belonging to us, thanks be to Providence, knows nothin' at all, at all about. Jimmy was right-han' man with the fairies; an' if ye'd believe all the stories ye hear goin' he come through some quare things, too, in his day – used to be out, they say, as reg'lar as the sunset, an' away ridin' aist an' waist with the good people, an' gettin' insight into their ways of workin'; an' sure it's meself that rec'le'ts if there was only a bit of a year-oul' calve sick from one end of the barony to the other, it was nothin' but post haste for Jimmy Higgerty to cure it – an', sure enough, when Jimmy put the charm on it, it either lived or died afther; there was no middle coorse.

Well, howsomiver, in Jimmy's day there was in Doorin a one Solomon Casshidy; an' the same Solomon in his young days was a thrifle wild – the fact is (to kill the hare at a blow), Solomon was the completest rascal ivir run on two feet, an' was a parable for the counthry. Christenin', weddin', wake, funeral, patthern, fair, or market nivir wint off complete without Solomon Casshidy; dance, raffle, or spree of any sort, shape, or patthern nivir missed Solomon Casshidy, who, by the way, was the very life an' sowl of the gatherin's; an' people would as soon think of doin' without the fiddler at one of these merry-makin's as without Solomon Casshidy. An' that just put me in mind that Solomon was the dandy hand at the fiddle; the bate of him wasn't to be got between cock-crow an' candlelight the longest day in June. He would charm the heart of a whin-bush; arrah, good luck to your wit, man, he'd actually make the fiddle spake! They say it was as good as a sarcus to hear how he'd handle it.

But poor Solomon, good luck to him, soon came to the end of his tether, an', afther takin' all the fun he could out of the worl', he, as himself said, turned over a new laif an' begun to look at the other side of the picther. An' I'm thinkin' whatsomiver he seen on the other side of it must have been deuced onpleasant, for the rollickin', singin', laughin', fiddlin', reckless, ne'er-do-well Solomon pulled a face on him the length of a tailyer's lapboord, an' if any of his ould comrades attempted to make him convarsible on the fun that was goin' in any quarther of the counthry, Solomon would dhrop his jaws, an' fetch a groan would frighten a corp'; an' 'My fren',' he would say, 'this is all vanity, vanity! Life is hollow, an' these frivolities are only snares spread in our paths by the divil.'

Anyhow, Solomon was an althered man, an' where he would go formerly to honour the Sabbath by a rousin' game of *caman* with the good boys, he was now seen makin' his way to the meetin'-house with a Bible anondher his arm the size of a salt-box, an' as many hime-books as would set up a hawker in a daicent way of thradin', an' he obsarvin' naither to the right nor to the left, but away a thousand miles ahead of him, as if he was always thryin' to make out the way to heaven somewhere in the skies foreninst him; an' where he would of another time be makin' his way across the counthry, maybe to the shouldher of Srual mountain for a spree, with the fiddle anondher his coat, ye might now meet him in the dusk of the evenin', still with the fiddle ondher the coat, but on a far betther errand – goin' to some prayer-meetin' at Inver, or Killymard, or Ballywell, or the divil only knows where; he wouldn't go within an ass's roar of a raffle-house; an' if you tould him there was to be a dance or any other wee divarshin in sich and sich a place he'd strive to put the breadth of a townlan' betwixt him an' it, for he said the divil was chained to the back-stone of any house that there was a hornpipe played in.

Well, one evenin', it was in October, an' jist about night-fallin', Solomon was makin' his way for Billy Knox's of the head of the Glibe, where a great and very pious man, one Bartholomew Binjamin Rankin, was to hold a prayer-meetin' for the benefit of all the well-disposed sinners in that stretch of counthry; an' throth, it seems to me that, onless the Glibe's changed mortially within the last jinnyration, there must have been a daicent quantity of sinners in them same parts. But, as I was sayin', Solomon was this evenin' on the good arrand, with his fiddle peepin' out from ondher his coat – for ye see, Solomon's ould practice whin he was a sinner come in handy now that he was a saint, an' no prayer-meetin' could be held without Solomon's fiddle to steady the voices, when they joined to sing the himes. She was a splendid piece of a fiddle, an' Solomon, when he turned over the new laif, was goin' out to brak her neck across the nixt ditch, when he remembered how she might come in handy this way, so he said to himself (as he tould afther), that 'he'd make the occasion of his sins a steppin'-stone to new vartues, an' cause her that was hairtofore jiggin' him down to the place below, now fiddle him into heaven'.

He thought to himself this evenin' that he'd jist light the pipe to keep him company as he jogged on, so where do ye think he'd dhrop into, on purpose to light it, but ould Jimmy Higgerty's, the fairyman's, that I reharsed to yet about before. On layin' 'Pagganinny', as he called the fiddle, down on a stool, whilst he was puttin' a screed of coal to the pipe, Jimmy Higgerty lifted her, an' dhrawin' the bow acrass her, he took a bar of a lively tune out of her, when Solomon jumped up as if he was sthruck.

'Higgerty, me good man,' he says, 'you have shocked me. Thim vain airs,' siz he, 'has been long unknown to that fiddle, an' I trusted that she would nivir more be an insthrument that the divil would gamble for sowls on. Paice, paice, and dhraw not the bow in idle vanity again!'

'Arrah, good morra to ye,' siz Jimmy, that way back to him, 'but it's delicate yer narves must have got intirely, lately. Throth, Misther Casshidy, I seen the time this wouldn't frighted ye one bit'; an' all at oncet he sthruck up, 'Go to the divil an' shake yerself,' while poor Solomon stood thrimblin' in the middle of the flure like a man with the aguey. While Jimmy finished up with a flourish that would have delighted Solomon the days he was at himself (for, be the same token, Solomon was no miss at handlin' the bow naither), he cut some quare figures with his left han' three times over the fiddle, an' handin' it to Solomon, he says, 'May ye nivir have more raison to be frightened than by a jig from the same fiddle – *that's all I say!*'

Poor Solomon didn't know the hidden mainin' of them words, or it would have made him look crooked; nor he didn't know naither that Jimmy had put *pisherogues* on the fiddle; but all the same he took it from him with a glum look enough, and afther praichin' an edifyin' sarmon on frivolities, an' death an' jedgment, to Jimmy Higgerty, he betook him on the road again.

There was a wonderful congregation of the sinners an' saints of the Glibe – but the sinners had the best of it anyhow, in regards to numbers – in Bill Knox's that night. An' Bartholomew Binjamin Rankin was there, an' it was as good as a sarmin in itself just to get one glance at his face. There was as much holiness an' piety in it, ye'd a'most think, as would save the sowls of a whole barony., Solomon, who now got all sorts an' sizes of respect, as bein' a reformed sinner, an' was looked up to with ten times as much honour and rivirence as was paid to them that was saints all their life, got a salt, as was usual, beside the praicher. An' it's himself that was proud, an' he'd look down on the common crowd below with a most pityin' look on his face. An' the well-disposed ones in the congregation would look up at Solomon an' then give a groan that ye might hear at Srual; an' Solomon would look down on the sinners an' give another groan that ye might hear him at Barnesmore; an' then both Solomon an' the sinners would look up at the rafthers, an' give a groan that ye might hear at Muckish. Afther some time, when they had got faistin' their sowls fairly well on Solomon, a hime was called out, a very solemn one. 'An',' says the praicher, lookin' at Solomon, 'our saintly brother here, of whom aich and ivery heart in this gatherin' feels proud, an' whose pious ways are the glorification, admiration, an' edifycation of every true Christian since he gave up his ungodly life, an' turned onto the path of righteousness – brother Solomon will give us the keynote, an' lend us the aid of his unmusical box, throughout.'

Brother Solomon, be me socks, dhrew a face on him the length of his own fiddle, as if he was thinkin' of his own unworthiness, poor man, an' says:

'If affords me a pious pleasure to dhraw my bow ondher the circumstances – that bow which so often snared me into the divil's sarvice; but I thank God with my heart that I have long since departed from my wicked, wicked, unspaikably vile an' sinful ways; an' this han' has long since forgotten them vain and ungodly airs that at one time occupied every spare moment of my then onChristian life – long since, I say, have I buried deep in obliveen every remimbrance of thim wicked tunes, an' the cunnin' of my han' is now only used for a far loftier an' betther purpose. Bretherin, I shall begin.'

And Solomon dhraws the bow across the fiddle, an' of all the himes tunes which was prented, what do ye think does he sthrike up? 'Go to the divil an' shake yerself!' Och, it's as thrue as I'm telling it to ye. But, *ochón*, if there wasn't consternation in that house, I'm a gintleman! Solomon himself stopped suddent, for all the world lookin' like a stuck pig; an' he looked at the praicher, an' the praicher looked at him, and the congregation looked at both of them, and then Solomon prayed from his heart as he nivir prayed afore, that the Lord in His marcy might make the flure open and swallow him. The flure, though, as I suppose ye have guessed, did not open, but Bartholomew Binjamin's mouth did, an' he sayed, siz he:

'Bretherin! bretherin! this is a sad fallin' away! Alas ! alas! Who should have thought that Brother Solomon, the deformed sinner, would have returned to his ould godless coorses! The rulin' passion, my dear bretherin, is so sthrong in him – waxin' sthrong with new strength – that he has onvoluntarily bethrayed the divil that has again got hould on him. Bretherin, let us pray for him!'

An' in a jiffey the thunderstruck congregation were on their knees prayin' like Trojans for the delivery of poor Solomon from the divil. Solomon, of course, for appairance' sake, had to take to his knees, too, but between you an' me, it's meself's afeard that all the prayers he said would not fetch him very far on the way to the first milestone that leads to heaven. I'll wager whoivir heerd him, that his prayers were sweet ones, that the divil might saize ould Jimmy Higgerty an' carry him off body an' bones, an' give him a toastin' on a special griddle down below. When they thought they had prayed long enough, an' that the divil was gone out of Solomon, they got up to their feet again, and they turned up the whites of their eyes till Bartholomew Binjamin announced that they would oncest more put Brother Solomon's faith to the test, to see if he had profited by the few minutes' sperritial recreation that they had indulged in. Solomon lifted the bow, an' afore he started he turned up the whites of his eyes in the usual fashion, as if he was lookin' for guidance, but in his heart he was only callin' down another black curse on Jimmy Higgerty.

'Bretherin!' siz he, as solemn as a judge – 'Bretherin! The temper' (by which he meant the divil of coorse) 'possessed the fiddle, and not my humble self; in witness whereof just attind to the solemn an' addyfyin' air I will now produce for ye.' An' down comes the bow on the fiddle, an' up starts that beautiful jig tune, 'The Siege of Carrick'!

Och, tarnation to me waistcoat, but there was sich a scene in two minnits as would charm a dancin' masther! When Solomon played the first bar of it, he could as soon comb his head with his toes as he could stop it. But that wasn't the best of it. Bartholomew Binjamin, instead of goin' into a cowld dead faint, as one would expect, begun to shuffle his feet in a suspicious way, an' afore ye'd say 'thrapsticks' he was weltin' the flure like the broth of a boy, tearin' away at the jig like the ould Nick! An' in the squintin' of yer eye there wasn't a sowl anondher the roof, man, woman, or child, saint or sinner, that wasn't whackin' away at it like the forties, iviry man of them leatherin' the flure like a thrasher, jumpin' up till their heads would a'most sthrike the rafters, an' yellin' like red Injins, whilst me brave Solomon played like a black, put new life into the fiddle at ivery squeak, an' gave the jiggers whativer wee encouragement that he could spare time from the fiddle for:

'Come, boys, yez haven't fair play to foot it properly here. Yez is the finest set at a jig that I have faisted me eyes on since I give up me ungodly ways, an' it would be a pity for not to give yez ivery privilege – it's a fine clear moonlight, an' we'll go outside where we'll have room an' fair play at it. Come along, me mirry, mirry lads!' An' Solomon fiddled away out of the dure, an' the whole congregation leapt an' flung an' jigged it out in all possible an' onpossible shapes afther him. Och, they say it was a sight for sore eyes to see the capers that the party cut; ivery man jack of them tryin' to see who could be crazier than his naybour; an' out they got that way on the road, like a lunatic asylum turned loose for a holiday; an' Solomon headed down the road in the direction of Donegal, while the whole countryside turned out when they heard the yellin' an' fiddlin' an' prancin', an' seein' Solomon headin' them with the fiddle, an' Bartholomew Binjamin fillin' the front rank in company with his two feet, an' he jiggin' it away at the rate of a christenin'! The people were first inclined to laugh, but be the powdhers the nixt thing they done was join in themselves, an' foot it way afther the fiddle ninety-nine times crazier than the congregation. An' hot foot they kept it goin', up hill an' down dale, over height an' hollow, with fresh batches joinin' in at ivery lane an' turn, an' Solomon, the boy, layin' into the fiddle at a rate as if he was gettin' a salary for it; an', be the boots, by the time they raiched the foot of the road, you niver seen in all your born days a harvest fair or a Repale meetin' as big as it was!

Here Solomon turned to the left, with the purcession still jiggin' it afther him, an' he nixt got onto the lane that leads up to the Killymard ould graveyard, an' over the stile, in among the graves with the mirry company brakin' their necks over, afther him; an' when they got in here, Solomon made thracks for a nate dandy bit of a tombstone in the centre of the yard, an' upon it he h'isted himself, with Bartholomew Binjamin up beside him, whilst the remainder of the party reshumed their attitudes all roun' about, an' they fightin' like wild cats to see who would get pursession of the tombstones, for they say they were as good as barn-doors for dancin' on. An' throgs, there might be purty good dancers there, but divil resave the one of them that Solomon and Bartholomew Binjamin couldn't take the shine out of. They had a bran' new tombstone, the pick an' choice of all in the yard, an' if they didn't do it in royal style, an' cut a copy to the crowd, call me a cuckoo!

But what would ye have of it, but the nixt man lands on the scene was Sandy Montgomery, the Recthor. He was passin' the road, an' seein' the fun in the graveyard, he come up in a t'undherin' passion to horsewhip iviry mother's sowl of them. But, sweet good luck to ye, if he didn't jump up on the fiddler's tombstone, an' catchin' Bartholomew Binjamin by the han', foot it away, likewise.

An' it would have gone on to daylight in the mornin', if ould Jimmy Higgerty, the rascal, who followed the fun the whole way from the Glibe, for the purpose of tastifyin' to it – if he hadn't come behin' Solomon an' tould him to kick up his right heel, dhraw his left thumb three times over the sthrings of the fiddle, an' look over his left shouldher at the moon, an' then see what music he'd take out of it. No sooner sayed nor done; an' all at once the tune changed to a hime tune, all mournful, an' iviry heel in the graveyard was paralyzed. Ivery sowl of them looked at one another like they wor wakenin' out of a dhraim.

Solomon himself dhrew up, an' he gave a bewildhered look all roun' him, an' then looked at Sandy Montgomery, who was standin' forenenst him on the stone, an' he as pale as a sheet. Ivery man of the three on the tombstone gave themselves up as lost men, ruinated intirely, out an' out, afther making' such spectacles of themselves for the counthry. The Recthor lost conthrol of himself completely, an' puttin' his fist anondher Solomon's nose, he says:

'Ye common scoundhril, ye; ye've made me disgrace my cloth, ye cut-throat villain –'

But afore he could get another word, Solomon, who had some of the spunk of his early days in him still, and was a thrifle hasty, besides that his dandher was riz in regards to the purty pickle he was in – Solomon ups with the fiddle, an' dhrawin' it roun' his head with a swing, he takes the Recthor across the noddle an' knocked him a'most into kingdom come, away off the tombstone. But, my hearty, in swingin' the fiddle, doesn't he catch Bartholomew Binjamin, who was standin' behind him, a nate little bit of a knock on the skull. So, now turnin' round to apologize to him, Bartholomew Binjamin ups with his fist an' plants it undher Solomon's nose, too, for he was just commencin' a norration.

'Ye mane, onprincipled, ungodly bla'guard!'

But Solomon couldn't stand this neither. He says to himself he might as well be hung for a sheep as a lamb, and that when he knocked down a Recthor, he might with an asier conscience knock down a praicher. So he took the praicher a wallop with the fiddle that left him sprawlin' in the Recthor's lap with his heels uppermost, and Solomon leapt from the tombstone, an' off through the crowd for the bare life, wallopin' them right an' left. They all slunk home afther a while with their tails between their legs, but poor Solomon was the worst of all. He made 'Pagganinny' into smithereens – what remained of her. An' he didn't lift his head for twelve months afther.

# DANIEL CORKERY

## The Breath of Life

*Daniel Corkery (1878–1964) was Professor of English at University College, Cork from 1931–47. His best-known books are* A Munster Twilight *(1916) and* The Threshold of Quiet *(1917). He also wrote many plays. Professor Corkery opened many readers' eyes to the forgotten riches of eighteenth-century Gaelic poetry and the ancient Irish cultural heritage.*

THE opera company which I had accompanied as first violinist on so many tours suddenly collapsing, I found myself rather unexpectedly out of an engagement. I communicated with my society, and after a day's delay I was ordered to go at once to Clonmoyle.

I was in the worst of humours. Clonmoyle was one of those places in Ireland which, instead of increasing in size and importance as places ought, seem to have become accustomed to doing the very opposite. Once a city, it was now but a straggling town. What had brought an opera company to try its fortunes there I could make no guess at, yet there it was, and with difficulties accumulating about it. Here was I myself, for instance, in Clonmoyle because the manager had found it impossible to supplement his scanty travelling orchestra with local players; and several others as well as I had had to travel day and night to be in time for the opening performance. Only one local musician had been dug up; and of him this story.

In everything he stood apart from us. He was old, well over sixty, however young in appearance. He was large and heavy in build, easy-going, ruminative. We, the others in the band, were rather meagre, high-strung, irritable, worried – as is the way of our tribe; on this trip particularly so (consider my own case: a first-class violinist in such surroundings!). He, on the other hand, smiled the whole day long, and his voice whispered rather than spoke. It did not seem to trouble him that the old ramshackle theatre was mouldy, damp, foul-smelling. He did not seem to notice the cruel draughts that swept us while we played, and benumbed our fingers. It made no difference to him if the manager was in a vile temper over the receipts, and our conductor still worse, his rheumatism playing old Harry with him.

At our first rehearsal I discovered he could not play in tune. 'I'm in for it!' I said, for a week of such fellowship I knew only too well would leave me a wreck. And even as I said this I saw the conductor staring hard at where the two of us were sitting side by side; was it possible he thought it was I who was playing like that! He might well have thought so, for my companion's face was not a guilty face; how any one could play so consistently flat and still smile was a problem beyond me. Yes, Ignatius O'Byrne, such was his name, still smiled and still flattened. The fact is, he was the happiest alive; it was as if he had come into an inheritance. Here he was fiddling away in his beloved operas, and it was thirty years since he had last done so. These long thirty years, he explained to me in an interval, he had been rehearsing them in his untidy lodgings in a back street, and more than that, he had been thinking them out, phrase by phrase, 'walking in the mists upon these rain-soaked hills' – I give his very words. As he spoke he swept his hand in a half-circle as if even there in the theatre he could still behold them, the dreary hills that surround Clonmoyle on every side and overlay it, as it were, with a sort of perpetual gloom. And then he added: 'Behind music is the breath of life.' A curious man, surely; I watched his face. It was glowing, glowing, as long as the music held. And once when in some happy passage the whole band was singing like one, 'Bravo, Bravo!' I heard him whisper, and later on 'Bravissimo!' and he ceased playing, ceased, until I thought of nudging him with my elbow. And so, little by little, I came to forgive him his flat playing and his awkward bowing.

Our conductor, a brute of a man, his body twisted into a knot by rheumatism, was now constantly looking in our direction; but whenever I saw him doing so I would make my violin sing for all it was worth; were we not brothers in the same craft, this old man and I? At rehearsal the second day my efforts to cover his wretched playing failed; the conductor left his place, tied up and all as he was in that knot of pain, shuffled over to where we sat, and stood between us! That settled for him which of us was playing flat. He scowled at the old resurrected musician, hissed out a fierce, wicked word under his breath, and hobbled back to his place. That night, just to make matters worse, I suppose, old Byrne played altogether vilely! He had a scarce a phrase in tune. When the curtain fell he had to face a little tragic opera of his own – the tragedy of old age and failing powers. He took it all without a word. 'The breath of life is behind music,' he whispered to me as he came from the interview; then he bent down, carefully wrapped his fiddle in a piece of braize cloth, put it in his case and made off.

The final explosion came at the rehearsal next day. He and I were the first to arrive. The score of last night's opera, it was the *Marriage of Figaro*, still lay on the conductor's stand. He turned the pages. They were pencilled all over with directions as to the tempos of the various movements. Along these pencillings old Bryne ran his finger. I could see he was having his revenge. I could see him lift his brows – just a little – as if he were amused, partly astonished. But no word escaped him. Soon the conductor came in and we began. We had not got far when we heard 'Get out!' roared in a terrible voice, the voice of one who had not slept for several nights. The old man rose up, wrapped his baize cloth around his instrument, and moved between the chairs. As he went how still the house was, only a chair moving, and his own almost silent feet! And how we watched him! But when he got as far as the conductor's chair he paused, glanced once more at the open score, once again ran his finger along the pencillings, and laughed a tiny little laugh!

I felt his going more than I should care to tell. Will you believe me? I had told that old musician, that stranger, the whole story of the sorrows of my life. Yes, I told him things I had hardly ever made clear even to myself! And he replied: 'Is it not behind music, the breath of life?' as if sorrow was there for the one purpose of being transmuted into sweet sound! I recalled his words as I went to my task that night.

And that night the extraordinary thing happened; our conductor failed to make an appearance: his rheumatism had conquered. There was then a call for our leader. He was found. Alas, he was not in a condition to conduct anything. He could scarcely stand. And he became quite cross about it; we had to leave him there in his corner, resining his bow like anything and scowling like mad. What between principals, chorus, and band, all thinking they stood a chance of losing a night's pay, and the manager flustering about like a whirlwind, our little den beneath the stage was deafening; I slipped quietly out into the house. There outside the rail was old Byrne! 'What's the matter?' he whispered. As I told him, up came the manager.

'Mr Melton,' he said to me, 'will you please take the baton to-night?'

A very flattering compliment, indeed, and I should have taken that baton, if our band did not happen to be the scraggiest ever scraped together from the ends of the earth; our leader was in the condition I have mentioned. As we spoke I saw the players getting into their places, a tempting sight, yet still I hesitated, foreseeing collapse and ignominy.

'It is not possible,' I began, but over the rail old Byrne was climbing like a boy. He had clutched the baton from the manager's hand. He had leaped into the conductor's chair. He gave but one glance to the right, to the left. 'Now, boys,' he said, and at the words we swam, sank, buried ourselves in the rich, broad, gentle strains of the overture to *Faust*. Some wide gesture he had used, some thrill in his tone had bidden us to do so – to lose ourselves in the soul of the music. At the first chord we had got within the skin of it, as the saying is. And never was the mood broken; every progression told, and not a colour tone was faulty or blurred. That memorable waltz, which use has almost spoiled, he made a new thing of it – we were all spirits in thin air, so lightly it went. But our triumph was the tremendous trio at the close.

The old man stood up to it, hiding the stage from a large sector of the house. What did he care! We felt his huge shabby figure above us as a darkness, a vastness of great potency. It commanded stage, orchestra, house, with a strong yet benign power. The voices, tenor, soprano, bass – all the instruments, strings, brass, wood, drums, the very shell of the old house itself, became as one instrument and sang the great strain with such strength and perfection that some of us trembled lest we should fall down with excitement and spoil everything.

'Oh!' we all sighed when it was over. For such moments does the artist live. I was so glad I had told him the story of my sorrows!

Now, sir, around Clonmoyle, as I have said, is a rampart of dark hills, bleak and rain-sodden, treeless and desolate. Why do I again mention them? 'Wherever did you learn to conduct?' I asked him, as we made for our lodgings.

'There!' he answered, and his outstretched hand gestured around the deserted hills, 'behind music we must get at the breath of life.' Bare, wind-swept hills! – curious place to find out the secrets of life! Or what he did he mean by 'Life'? It cannot be that the breath of life that is behind all great music is the sigh of loneliness?

'And you took him with the company?'

'No, sir; an opera company, like any other company, must pay its way.'

# SEAMUS O'KELLY

## The Rector

*Seamus O'Kelly (1875–1918) was born in County Galway. He was a playwright as well as a short story writer. His novel,* The Lady in the Deerpark, *was published in 1917. He was the editor of the Sinn Fein newspaper,* Nationality, *in Dublin. He died of a heart attack when British troops raided the offices in 1918.*

THE Rector came round the gable of the church. He walked down the sanded path that curved to the road. Half-way down he paused, meditated, then turning, gazed at the building. It was square and solid, bulky against the background of the hills. The Rector hitched up his cuffs as he gazed at the structure. Critical puckers gathered in little lines across the preserved, peach-like cheeks. He put his small, nicely-shaped head to one side. There was a proprietorial, concerned air in his attitude. One knew that he was thinking of the repairs to the church, anxious about the gutters, the downpipe, the missing slates on the roof, the painting of the doors and windows. He struck an attitude as he pondered the problem of the cracks on the pebble-dashed walls. His umbrella grounded on the sand with decision. He leaned out a little on it with deliberation, his lips unconsciously shaping the words of the ultimatum he should deliver to the Select Vestry. His figure was slight, he looked old-world, almost funereal, something that had become detached, that was an outpost, half-forgotten, lonely; a man who had sunk into a parish where there was nothing to do. He mumbled a little to himself as he came down to the gate in the high wall that enclosed the church grounds.

A group of peasants was coming along the yellow, lonely road, talking and laughing. The bare-footed women stepped with great active strides, bearing themselves with energy. They carried heavy baskets from the market town, but were not conscious of their weight. The carded-wool petticoats, dyed a robust red, brought a patch of vividness to the landscape. The white 'bauneens' and soft black hats of the men afforded a contrast. The Rector's eyes gazed upon the group with a schooled detachment. It was the look of a man who stood outside of their lives, who did not expect to be recognized, and who did not feel called upon to seem conscious of these peasant folk. The eyes of the peasants were unmoved, uninterested, as they were lifted to the dark figure that stood at the rusty iron gate leading into the enclosed church grounds. He gave them no salutation. Their conversation, voluble, noisy, dropped for a moment, half through embarrassment, half through a feeling that something alive stood by the wayside. A vagueness in expression on both sides was the outward signal that two conservative forces had met for a moment and refused to compromise.

One young girl, whose figure and movements would have kindled the eye of an artist, looked up and appeared as if she would smile. The Rector was conscious of her vivid face, framed in a fringe of black hair, of a mischievousness in her beauty, some careless abandon in the swing of her limbs. But something in the level dark brows of the Rector, something that was dour, forbade her smile. It died in a little flush of confusion. The peasants passed and the Rector gave them time to make some headway before he resumed his walk to the Rectory.

He looked up at the range of hills, great in their extent, mighty in their rhythm, beautiful in the play of light and mist upon them. But to the mind of the Rector they expressed something foreign, they were part of a place that was condemned and lost. He began to think of the young girl who, in her innocence, had half-smiled at him. Why did she not smile? Was she afraid? Of what was she afraid? What evil thing

had come between her and that impulse of youth? Some consciousness – of what? The Rector sighed. He had, he was afraid, knowledge
of what it was. And that knowledge set his thoughts racing over their
accustomed course. He ran over the long tradition of his grievances –
grievances that had submerged him in a life that had not even a place
in this wayside countryside. His mind worked its way down through
all the stages of complaint until it arrived at the Ne Temere decree. The
lips of the Rector no longer formed half-spoken words; they became
two straight, tight little thin lines across the teeth. They would remain
that way all the afternoon, held in position while he read the letters in
the Irish Times. He would give himself up to thoughts of politics, of
the deeds of wicked men, of the transactions that go on within and
without governments, doping his mind with the drug of class opiates
until it was time to go to bed.

Meantime he had to pass a man who was breaking stones in a ditch
by the roadside. The hard cracks of the hammer were resounding on
the still air. The man looked up from his work as the Rector came
along; the grey face of the stone-breaker had a melancholy familiarity
for him. The Rector had an impulse – it was seldom he had one. He
stood in the centre of the road. The Ne Temere decree went from his
mind.

'Good-day, my man,' he said, feeling that he had made another
concession, and that it would be futile as all the others.

'Good-day, sir,' the stone-breaker made answer, hitching himself
upon the sack he had put under his haunches, like one very ready for a
conversation.

There was a pause. The Rector did not know very well how to
continue. He should, he knew, speak with some sense of colloquial-
ism as if he was to get on with this stone-breaker, a person for whom
he had a certain removed sympathy. The manner of these people's
speech was really a part of the grievances of the Rector. Their conversation, he often secretly assured himself, was peppered with
Romish propaganda. But the Rector made another concession.

'It's a fine day, thank God,' he said. He spoke like one who was
delivering a message in an unfamiliar language. 'Thank God' was local,

and might lend itself to an interpretation that could not be approved. But the Rector imported something into the words that was a protection, something that was of the pulpit, that held a solemnity in its pessimism.

'A fine day, indeed, glory be to God!' the stone-breaker made answer. There was a freshness in his expression, a cheerfulness in the prayer, that made of it an optimism.

The Rector was so conscious of the contrast that it gave him pause again. The peach-like colourings on the cheeks brightened, for a suspicion occurred to him. Could the fellow have meant anything? Had he deliberately set up an optimistic Deity in opposition to the pessimistic Deity of the Rector? The Rector hitched up the white cuffs under his dark sleeves, swung his umbrella, and resumed his way, his lips puckered, a little feverish agitation seizing him.

'A strange, down-hearted kind of a man,' the stone-breaker said to himself, as he reached out for a lump of limestone and raised his hammer. A redbreast, perched on an old thorn bush, looking out on the scene with curious eyes, stretched his wing and his leg, as much as to say, 'Ah, well,' sharpened his beak on a twig, and dropped into the ditch to pick up such gifts as the good earth yielded.

The Rector walked along the road pensive, but steadfast, his eyes upon the alien hills, his mind travelling over ridges of problems that never afforded the gleam of solution. He heard a shout of a laugh. Above the local accents that held a cadence of the Gaelic speech he heard the sharp clipped Northern accent of his own gardener and general factotum. He had brought the man with him when he first came to Connacht, half as a mild form of colonization, half through a suspicion of local honesty. He now saw the man's shaggy head over the Rectory garden wall, and outside it were the peasants.

How was it that the gardener got on with the local people? How was it that they stood on the road to speak with him, shouting their extravagant laughter at his keen, dry Northern humour?

When he first came the gardener had been more grimly hostile to the place than the Rector himself. There had been an ugly row on the road, and blows had been struck. But that was some years ago. The gardener now appeared very much merged in the life of the place; the gathering outside the Rectory garden was friendly, almost a family party. How was it to be accounted for? Once or twice the Rector found himself suspecting that at the bottom of the phenomenon there might be all unconscious among these people a spirit of common country, of a common democracy, a common humanity, that forced itself to the surface in course of time. The Rector stood, his lips working, his nicely-shaped little head quivering with a sudden agitation. For he found himself thinking along unusual lines, and for that very reason dangerous lines – frightfully dangerous lines, he told himself, as an ugly enlightenment broke across his mind, warming it up for a few moments and no more. As he turned in the gate at the Rectory it was a relief to him – for his own thoughts were frightening him – to see the peasants moving away and the head of the gardener disappear behind the wall. He walked up the path to the Rectory, the lawn dotted over with sombre yew trees all clipped into the shape of torpedoes, all trained directly upon the forts of Heaven! The house was large and comfortable, the walls a faded yellow. Like the church, it was thrown up against the background of the hills. It had all the sombre exclusiveness that made appeal to the Rector. The sight of it comforted him at the moment, and his mental agitation died down. He became normal enough to resume his accustomed outlook, and before he had reached the end of the path his mind had become obsessed again by the thought of the *Ne Temere* decree. Something should, he felt convinced, be done, and done at once.

He ground his umbrella on the step in front of the Rectory door and pondered. At last he came to a conclusion, inspiration lighting up his faded eyes. He tossed his head upwards.

'I must write a letter to the papers,' he said. 'Ireland is lost.'

# JAMES JOYCE

## The Dead

*James Joyce (1882–1941). Dubliners published in 1914 was Joyce's first published work except for* Chamber Music *(1907), a volume of verse. 'The Dead' is an unquestioned masterpiece – a matchless evocation of an evening party in Dublin before the First World War.*

LILY, the caretaker's daughter, was literally run off her feet. Hardly had she brought one gentleman into the little pantry behind the office on the ground floor and helped him off with his overcoat, than the wheezy hall-door bell clanged again and she had to scamper along the bare hallway to let in another guest. It was well for her she had not to attend to the ladies also. But Miss Kate and Miss Julia had thought of that and had converted the bathroom upstairs into a ladies' dressing-room. Miss Kate and Miss Julia were there, gossiping and laughing and fussing, walking after each other to the head of the stairs, peering down over the banisters and calling down to Lily to ask her who had come.

It was always a great affair, the Misses Morkan's annual dance. Everybody who knew them came to it, members of the family, old friends of the family, the members of Julia's choir, any of Kate's pupils that were grown up enough, and even some of Mary Jane's pupils too. Never once had it fallen flat. For years and years it had gone off in splendid style, as long as anyone could remember: ever since Kate and Julia, after the death of their brother Pat, had left the house in Stoney

Batter and taken Mary Jane, their only niece, to live with them in the dark, gaunt house on Usher's Island, the upper part of which they had rented from Mr Fulham, the corn-factor on the ground floor. That was a good thirty years ago if it was a day. Mary Jane, who was then a little girl in short clothes, was now the main prop of the household, for she had the organ in Haddington Road. She had been through the Academy and gave a pupils' concert every year in the upper room of the Antient Concert Rooms. Many of her pupils belonged to the better-class families on the Kingstown and Dalkey line. Old as they were, her aunts also did their share. Julia, though she was quite grey, was still the leading soprano in Adam and Eve's, and Kate, being too feeble to go about much, gave music lessons to beginners on the old square piano in the back room. Lily, the caretaker's daughter, did housemaid's work for them. Though their life was modest, they believed in eating well; the best of everything: diamond-bone sirloins, three-shilling tea and the best bottled stout. But Lily seldom made a mistake in the orders, so that she got on well with her three mistresses. They were fussy, that was all. But the only thing they would not stand was back answers.

Of course, they had good reason to be fussy on such a night. And then it was long after ten o'clock and yet there was no sign of Gabriel and his wife. Besides they were dreadfully afraid that Freddy Malins might turn up screwed. They would not wish for worlds that any of Mary Jane's pupils should see him under the influence; and when he was like that it was sometimes very hard to manage him. Freddy Malins always came late, but they wondered what could be keeping Gabriel: and that was what brought them every two minutes to the banisters to ask Lily had Gabriel or Freddy come.

'O, Mr Conroy,' said Lily to Gabriel when she opened the door for him, 'Miss Kate and Miss Julia thought you were never coming. Good night, Mrs Conroy.'

'I'll engage they did,' said Gabriel, 'but they forget that my wife here takes three mortal hours to dress herself.'

He stood on the mat, scraping the snow from his goloshes, while Lily led his wife to the foot of the stairs and called out:

'Miss Kate, here's Mrs Conroy.'

Kate and Julia came toddling down the dark stairs at once. Both of them kissed Gabriel's wife, said she must be perished alive, and asked was Gabriel with her.

'Here I am as right as the mail, Aunt Kate! Go on up, I'll follow,' called out Gabriel from the dark.

He continued scraping his feet vigorously while the three women went upstairs, laughing, to the ladies' dressing-room. A light fringe of snow lay like a cape on the shoulders of his overcoat and like toecaps on the toes of his goloshes; and, as the buttons of his overcoat slipped with a squeaking noise through the snow-stiffened frieze, a cold, fragrant air from out-of-doors escaped from crevices and folds.

'Is it snowing again, Mr Conroy?' asked Lily.

She had preceded him into the pantry to help him off with his overcoat. Gabriel smiled at the three syllables she had given his surname and glanced at her. She was a slim, growing girl, pale in complexion and with hay-coloured hair. The gas in the pantry made her look still paler. Gabriel had known her when she was a child and used to sit on the lowest step nursing a rag doll.

'Yes, Lily,' he answered, 'and I think we're in for a night of it.'

He looked up at the pantry ceiling, which was shaking with the stamping and shuffling of feet on the floor above, listened for a moment to the piano and then glanced at the girl, who was folding his overcoat carefully at the end of a shelf.

'Tell me, Lily,' he said in a friendly tone, 'do you still go to school?'

'O no, sir,' she answered. 'I'm done schooling this year and more.'

'O, then,' said Gabriel gaily, 'I suppose we'll be going to your wedding one of these fine days with your young man, eh?'

The girl glanced back at him over her shoulder and said with great bitterness:

'The men that is now is only all palaver and what they can get out of you.'

Gabriel coloured, as if he felt he had made a mistake, and, without looking at her, kicked off his goloshes and flicked actively with his muffler at his patent-leather shoes.

He was a stout, tallish young man. The high colour of his cheeks
pushed upwards even to his forehead, where it scattered itself in a few
formless patches of pale red; and on his hairless face there scintillated
restlessly the polished lenses and the bright gilt rims of the glasses
which screened his delicate and restless eyes. His glossy black hair was
parted in the middle and brushed in a long curve behind his ears where
it curled slightly beneath the groove left by his hat.

When he had flicked lustre into his shoes he stood up and pulled his
waistcoat down more tightly on his plump body. Then he took a coin
rapidly from his pocket.

'O Lily,' he said, thrusting it into her hands, 'it's Christmas-time,
isn't it? Just ... here's a little ...'

He walked rapidly to the door.

'O no, sir!' cried the girl, following him. 'Really, sir, I wouldn't
take it.'

'Christmas-time! Christmas-time!' said Gabriel, almost trotting to
the stairs and waving his hand to her in deprecation.

The girl, seeing that he had gained the stairs, called out after him:
'Well, thank you, sir.'

He waited outside the drawing-room door until the waltz should
finish, listening to the skirts that swept against it and to the shuffling of
feet. He was still discomposed by the girl's bitter and sudden retort. It
had cast a gloom over him which he tried to dispel by arranging his
cuffs and the bows of his tie. He then took from his waistcoat pocket a
little paper and glanced at the headings he had made for his speech. He
was undecided about the lines from Robert Browning, for he feared
they would be above the heads of his hearers. Some quotation that
they would recognize from Shakespeare or from the Melodies would
be better. The indelicate clacking of the men's heels and the shuffling
of their soles reminded him that their grade of culture differed from
his. He would only make himself ridiculous by quoting poetry to
them which they could not understand. They would think that he was
airing his superior education. He would fail with them just as he had
failed with the girl in the pantry. He had taken up a wrong tone. His
whole speech was a mistake from first to last, an utter failure.

Just then his aunts and his wife came out of the ladies' dressing-room. His aunts were two small, plainly dressed old women. Aunt Julia was an inch or so the taller. Her hair, drawn low over the tops of her ears, was grey; and grey also, with darker shadows, was her large flaccid face. Though she was stout in build and stood erect, her slow eyes and parted lips gave her the appearance of a woman who did not know where she was or where she was going. Aunt Kate was more vivacious. Her face, healthier than her sister's, was all puckers and creases, like a shrivelled red apple, and her hair, braided in the same old-fashioned way, had not lost its ripe nut colour.

They both kissed Gabriel frankly. He was their favourite nephew, the son of their dead sister, Ellen, who had married T.J. Conroy of the Port and Docks.

'Gretta tells me you're not going to take a cab back to Monkstown tonight, Gabriel,' said Aunt Kate.

'No,' said Gabriel, turning to his wife, 'we had quite enough of that last year, hadn't we? Don't you remember, Aunt Kate, what a cold Gretta got out of it? Cab windows rattling all the way, and the east wind blowing in after we passed Merrion. Very jolly it was. Gretta caught a dreadful cold.'

Aunt Kate frowned severely and nodded her head at every word.

'Quite right, Gabriel, quite right,' she said. 'You can't be too careful.'

'But as for Gretta there,' said Gabriel, 'she'd walk home in the snow if she were let.'

Mrs Conroy laughed.

'Don't mind him, Aunt Kate,' she said. 'He's really an awful bother, what with green shades for Tom's eyes at night and making him do the dumb-bells, and forcing Eva to eat the stirabout. The poor child! And she simply hates the sight of it! . . . O, but you'll never guess what he makes me wear now!'

She broke out into a peal of laughter and glanced at her husband, whose admiring and happy eyes had been wandering from her dress to her face and hair. The two aunts laughed heartily, too, for Gabriel's solicitude was a standing joke with them.

'Goloshes!' said Mrs Conroy. 'That's the latest. Whenever it's wet underfoot I must put on my goloshes. Tonight even, he wanted me to put them on, but I wouldn't. The next thing he'll buy me will be a diving suit.'

Gabriel laughed nervously and patted his tie reassuringly, while Aunt Kate nearly doubled herself, so heartily did she enjoy the joke. The smile soon faded from Aunt Julia's face and her mirthless eyes were directed towards her nephew's face. After a pause she asked:

'And what are goloshes, Gabriel?'

'Goloshes, Julia!' exclaimed her sister. 'Goodness me, don't you know what goloshes are? You wear them over your ... boots, Gretta, isn't it?'

'Yes,' said Mrs Conroy. 'Gutta-percha things. We both have a pair now. Gabriel says everyone wears them on the Continent.'

'O, on the Continent,' murmured Aunt Julia, nodding her head slowly.

Gabriel knitted his brows and said, as if he were slightly angered:

'It's nothing very wonderful, but Gretta thinks it very funny, because she says the word reminds her of Christy Minstrels.'

'But tell me, Gabriel,' said Aunt Kate, with brisk tact. 'Of course, you've seen about the room. Gretta was saying ... '

'O, the room is all right,' replied Gabriel. 'I've taken one in the Gresham.'

'To be sure,' said Aunt Kate, 'by far the best thing to do. And the children, Gretta, you're not anxious about them?'

'O, for one night,' said Mrs Conroy. 'Besides, Bessie will look after them.'

'To be sure,' said Aunt Kate again. 'What a comfort it is to have a girl like that, one you can depend on! There's that Lily, I'm sure I don't know what has come over her lately. She's not the girl she was at all.'

Gabriel was about to ask his aunt some questions on this point, but she broke off suddenly to gaze after her sister, who had wandered down the stairs and was craning her neck over the banisters.

'Now, I ask you,' she said almost testily, 'where is Julia going? Julia! Julia! Where are you going?'

Julia, who had gone half-way down one flight, came back and announced blandly:

'Here's Freddy.'

At the same moment a clapping of hands and a final flourish of the pianist told that the waltz had ended. The drawing-room door was opened from within and some couples came out. Aunt Kate drew Gabriel aside hurriedly and whispered into his ear:

'Slip down, Gabriel, like a good fellow and see if he's all right, and don't let him up if he's screwed. I'm sure he's screwed. I'm sure he is.'

Gabriel went to the stairs and listened over the banisters. He could hear two persons talking in the pantry. Then he recognized Freddy Malins' laugh. He went down the stairs noisily.

'It's such a relief,' said Aunt Kate to Mrs Conroy, 'that Gabriel is here. I always feel easier in my mind when he's here . . . Julia, there's Miss Daly and Miss Power will take some refreshment. Thanks for your beautiful waltz, Miss Daly. It made lovely time.'

A tall wizen-faced man, with a stiff grizzled moustache and swarthy skin, who was passing out with his partner, said:

'And may we have some refreshment, too, Miss Morkan?'

'Julia,' said Aunt Kate summarily, 'and here's Mr Browne and Miss Furlong. Take them in, Julia, with Miss Daly and Miss Power.'

'I'm the man for the ladies,' said Mr Browne, pursing his lips until his moustache bristled, and smiling in all his wrinkles. 'You know, Miss Morkan, the reason they are so fond of me is—'

He did not finish the sentence, but, seeing that Aunt Kate was out of earshot, at once led the three young ladies into the back room. The middle of the room was occupied by two square tables placed end to end, and on these Aunt Julia and the caretaker were straightening and smoothing a large cloth. On the sideboard were arrayed dishes and plates, and glasses and bundles of knives and forks and spoons. The top of the closed square piano served as a sideboard for viands and sweets. At a smaller sideboard in one corner two young men were standing, drinking hop-bitters.

Mr Browne led his charges thither and invited them all, in jest, to some ladies' punch, hot, strong, and sweet. As they said they never took anything strong, he opened three bottles of lemonade for them. Then he asked one of the young men to move aside, and, taking hold of the decanter, filled out for himself a goodly measure of whisky. The young men eyed him respectfully while he took a trial sip.

'God help me,' he said, smiling, 'it's the doctor's orders.'

His wizened face broke into a broader smile, and the three young ladies laughed in musical echo to his pleasantry, swaying their bodies to and fro, with nervous jerks of their shoulders. The boldest said:

'O, now, Mr Browne, I'm sure the doctor never ordered anything of the kind.'

Mr Browne took another sip of his whisky and said, with sidling mimicry:

'Well, you see, I'm the famous Mrs Cassidy, who is reported to have said: "Now, Mary Grimes, if I don't take it, make me take it, for I feel I want it."'

His hot face had leaned forward a little too confidentially and he had assumed a very low Dublin accent, so that the young ladies, with one instinct, received his speech in silence. Miss Furlong, who was one of Mary Jane's pupils, asked Miss Daly what was the name of the pretty waltz she had played; and Mr Browne, seeing that he was ignored, turned promptly to the two young men, who were more appreciative.

A red-faced young woman, dressed in pansy, came into the room, excitedly clapping her hands and crying:

'Quadrilles! Quadrilles!'

Close on her heels came Aunt Kate, crying:

'Two gentlemen and three ladies, Mary Jane!'

'O, here's Mr Bergin and Mr Kerrigan,' said Mary Jane. 'Mr Kerrigan, will you take Miss Power? Miss Furlong, may I get you a partner, Mr Bergin. O, that'll just do now.'

'Three ladies, Mary Jane,' said Aunt Kate.

The two young gentlemen asked the ladies if they might have the pleasure, and Mary Jane turned to Miss Daly.

'O, Miss Daly, you're really awfully good, after playing for the last two dances, but really we're so short of ladies tonight.'

'I don't mind in the least, Miss Morkan.'

'But I've a nice partner for you, Mr Bartell D'Arcy, the tenor. I'll get him to sing later on. All Dublin is raving about him.'

'Lovely voice, lovely voice!' said Aunt Kate.

As the piano had twice begun the prelude to the first figure Mary Jane led her recruits quickly from the room. They had hardly gone when Aunt Julia wandered slowly into the room, looking behind her at something.

'What is the matter, Julia?' asked Aunt Kate anxiously. 'Who is it?'

Julia, who was carrying in a column of table-napkins, turned to her sister and said, simply, as if the question had surprised her:

'It's only Freddy, Kate, and Gabriel with him.'

In fact, right behind her Gabriel could be seen piloting Freddy Malins across the landing. The latter, a young man of about forty, was of Gabriel's size and build, with very round shoulders. His face was fleshy and pallid, touched with colour only at the thick hanging lobes of his ears and at the wide wings of his nose. He had coarse features, a blunt nose, a convex and receding brow, tumid and protruded lips. His heavy-lidded eyes and the disorder of his scanty hair made him look sleepy. He was laughing heartily in a high key at a story which he had been telling Gabriel on the stairs and at the same time rubbing the knuckles of his left fist backwards and forwards into his left eye.

'Good evening, Freddy,' said Aunt Julia.

Freddy Malins bade the Misses Morkan a good evening in what seemed an off-hand fashion by reason of the habitual catch in his voice and then, seeing that Mr Browne was grinning at him from the sideboard, crossed the room on rather shaky legs and began to repeat in an undertone the story he had just told to Gabriel.

'He's not so bad, is he?' said Aunt Kate to Gabriel.

Gabriel's brows were dark, but he raised them quickly and answered:

'O, no, hardly noticeable.'

'Now, isn't he a terrible fellow!' she said, 'And his poor mother made him take the pledge on New Year's Eve. But come on, Gabriel, into the drawing-room.'

Before leaving the room with Gabriel she signalled to Mr Browne by frowning and shaking her forefinger in warning to and fro. Mr Browne nodded in answer and, when she had gone, said to Freddy Malins:

'Now, then, Teddy, I'm going to fill you out a good glass of lemonade just to buck you up.'

Freddy Malins, who was nearing the climax of his story, waved the offer aside impatiently, but Mr Browne, having first called Freddy Malins' attention to a disarray in his dress, filled out and handed him a full glass of lemonade. Freddy Malins' left hand accepted the glass mechanically, his right hand being engaged in the mechanical readjustment of his dress. Mr Browne, whose face was once more wrinkling with mirth, poured out for himself a glass of whisky while Freddy Malins exploded, before he had well reached the climax of his story, in a kink of high-pitched bronchitic laughter and, setting down his untasted and overflowing glass, began to run the knuckles of his left fist backwards and forwards into his left eye, repeating words of his last phrase as well as his fit of laughter would allow him.

Gabriel could not listen while Mary Jane was playing her Academy piece, full of runs and difficult passages, to the hushed drawing-room. He liked music, but the piece she was playing had no melody for him and he doubted whether it had any melody for the other listeners, though they had begged Mary Jane to play something. Four young men, who had come from the refreshment-room to stand in the doorway at the sound of the piano, had gone away quietly in couples after a few minutes. They only persons who seemed to follow the music were Mary Jane herself, her hands racing along the keyboard or lifted from it at the pauses like those of a priestess in momentary imprecation, and Aunt Kate standing at her elbow to turn the page.

Gabriel's eyes, irritated by the floor, which glittered with beeswax under the heavy chandelier, wandered to the wall above the piano. A picture of the balcony scene in *Romeo and Juliet* hung there and beside

it was a picture of the two murdered princes in the Tower which Aunt
Julia had worked in red, blue, and brown wools when she was a girl.
Probably in the school they had gone to as girls that kind of work had
been taught for one year. His mother had worked for him as a
birthday present a waistcoat of purple tabinet, with little foxes' heads
upon it, lined with brown satin and having round mulberry buttons. It
was strange that his mother had had no musical talent, though Aunt
Kate used to call her the brains carrier of the Morkan family. Both she
and Julia had always seemed a little proud of their serious and matronly
sister. Her photograph stood before the pier-glass. She had an open
book on her knees and was pointing out something in it to Constantine who, dressed in a man-o'-war suit, lay at her feet. It was she
who had chosen the names of her sons, for she was very sensible of the
dignity of family life. Thanks to her, Constantine was now senior
curate in Balbriggan and, thanks to her, Gabriel himself had taken his
degree in the Royal University. A shadow passed over his face as he
remembered her sullen opposition to his marriage. Some slighting
phrases she had used still rankled in his memory; once she had spoken
of Gretta as being country cute and that was not true of Gretta at all. It
was Gretta who had nursed her during all her last long illness in their
house at Monkstown.

He knew that Mary Jane must be near the end of her piece, for she
was playing again the opening melody with runs of scales after every
bar, and while he waited for the end the resentment died down in his
heart. The piece ended with a trill of octaves in the treble and a final
deep octave in the bass. Great applause greeted Mary Jane as, blushing
and rolling up her music nervously, she escaped from the room. The
most vigorous clapping came from the four young men in the
doorway who had gone away to the refreshment-room at the
beginning of the piece but had come back when the piano had
stopped.

Lancers were arranged. Gabriel found himself partnered with Miss
Ivors. She was a frank-mannered, talkative young lady, with a freckled
face and prominent brown eyes. She did not wear a low-cut bodice,

and the large brooch which was fixed in the front of her collar bore on it an Irish device and motto.

When they had taken their places she said abruptly:

'I have a crow to pluck with you.'

'With me?' said Gabriel.

She nodded her head gravely.

'What is it?' asked Gabriel, smiling at her solemn manner.

'Who is G.C.?' answered Miss Ivors, turning her eyes upon him.

Gabriel coloured and was about to knit his brows, as if he did not understand, when she said bluntly:

'O, innocent Amy! I have found out that you write for *The Daily Express*. Now aren't you ashamed of yourself?'

'Why should I be ashamed of myself?' asked Gabriel, blinking his eyes and trying to smile.

'Well, I'm ashamed of you,' said Miss Ivors frankly. 'To say you'd write for a paper like that. I didn't think you were a West Briton.'

A look of perplexity appeared on Gabriel's face. It was true that he wrote a literary column every Wednesday in *The Daily Express*, for which he was paid fifteen shillings. But that did not make him a West Briton surely. The books he received for review were almost more welcome than the paltry cheque. He loved to feel the covers and turn over the pages of newly printed books. Nearly every day when his teaching in the college had ended he used to wander down the quays to the second-hand booksellers, to Hickey's on Bachelor's Walk, to Webb's or Massey's on Aston's Quay, or to O'Clohissey's in the by-street. He did not know how to meet her charge. He wanted to say that literature was above politics. But they were friends of many years' standing and their careers had been parallel, first at the University and then as teachers: he could not risk a gradiose phrase with her. He continued blinking his eyes and trying to smile and murmured lamely that he saw nothing political in writing reviews of books.

When their turn to cross had come he was still perplexed and inattentive. Miss Ivors promptly took his hand in a warm grasp and said in a soft friendly tone:

'Of course, I was only joking. Come, we cross now.'

When they were together again she spoke of the University question and Gabriel felt more at ease. A friend of hers had shown her his review of Browning's poems. That was how she had found out the secret: but she liked the review immensely. Then she said suddenly:

'O, Mr Conroy, will you come for an excursion to the Aran Isles this summer? We're going to stay there a whole month. It will be splendid out in the Atlantic. You ought to come. Mr Clancy is coming, and Mr Kilkelly and Kathleen Kearney. It would be splendid for Gretta too if she'd come. She's from Connacht, isn't she?'

'Her people are,' said Gabriel shortly.

'But you will come, won't you?' said Miss Ivors, laying her warm hand eagerly on his arm.

'The fact is,' said Gabriel, 'I have just arranged to go – '

'Go where?' asked Miss Ivors.

'Well, you know, every year I go for a cycling tour with some fellows and so –'

'But where?' asked Miss Ivors.

'Well, we usually go to France or Belgium or perhaps Germany,' said Gabriel awkwardly.

'And why do you go to France and Belgium,' said Miss Ivors, 'instead of visiting your own land?'

'Well,' said Gabriel, 'it's partly to keep in touch with the languages and partly for a change.'

'And haven't you your own language to keep in touch with – Irish?' asked Miss Ivors.

'Well,' said Gabriel, 'if it comes to that, you know, Irish is not my language.'

Their neighbours had turned to listen to the cross-examination. Gabriel glanced right and left nervously and tried to keep his good humour under the ordeal, which was making a blush invade his forehead.

'And haven't you your own land to visit,' continued Miss Ivors, 'that you know nothing of, your own people, and your own country?'

'O, to tell you the truth,' retorted Gabriel suddenly, 'I'm sick of my own country, sick of it!'

'Why?' asked Miss Ivors.

Gabriel did not answer, for his retort had heated him.

'Why?' repeated Miss Ivors.

They had to go visiting together and, as he had not answered her, Miss Ivors said warmly:

'Of course, you've no answer.'

Gabriel tried to cover his agitation by taking part in the dance with great energy. He avoided her eyes, for he had seen a sour expression on her face. But when they met in the long chain he was surprised to feel his hand firmly pressed. She looked at him from under her brows for a moment quizzically until he smiled. Then, just as the chain was about to start again, she stood on tiptoe and whispered into his ear:

'West Briton!'

When the lancers were over Gabriel went away to a remote corner of the room where Freddy Malins' mother was sitting. She was a stout, feeble old woman with white hair. Her voice had a catch in it like her son's and she stuttered slightly. She had been told that Freddy had come and that he was nearly all right. Gabriel asked her whether she had had a good crossing. She lived with her married daughter in Glasgow and came to Dublin on a visit once a year. She answered placidly that she had had a beautiful crossing and that the captain had been most attentive to her. She spoke also of the beautiful house her daughter kept in Glasgow, and of all the friends they had there. While her tongue rambled on Gabriel tried to banish from his mind all memory of the unpleasant incident with Miss Ivors. Of course the girl, or woman, or whatever she was, was an enthusiast, but there was a time for all things. Perhaps he ought not to have answered her like that. But she had no right to call him a West Briton before people, even in joke. She had tried to make him ridiculous before people, heckling him and staring at him with her rabbit's eyes.

He saw his wife making her way towards him through the waltzing couples. When she reached him she said into his ear:

'Gabriel, Aunt Kate wants to know won't you carve the goose as usual. Miss Daly will carve the ham and I'll do the pudding.'

'All right,' said Gabriel.

'She's sending in the younger ones first as soon as this waltz is over so that we'll have the table to ourselves.'

'Were you dancing?' asked Gabriel.

'Of course I was. Didn't you see me? What row had you with Molly Ivors?'

'No row. Why? Did she say so?'

'Something like that. I'm trying to get that Mr D'Arcy to sing. He's full of conceit, I think.'

'There was no row,' said Gabriel moodily, 'only she wanted me to go for a trip to the west of Ireland and I said I wouldn't.'

His wife clasped her hands excitedly and gave a little jump.

'O, do go, Gabriel,' she cried. 'I'd love to see Galway again.'

'You can go if you like,' said Gabriel coldly.

She looked at him for a moment, then turned to Mrs Malins and said:

'There's a nice husband for you, Mrs Malins.'

While she was threading her way back across the room Mrs Malins, without adverting to the interruption, went on to tell Gabriel what beautiful places there were in Scotland and beautiful scenery. Her son-in-law brought them every year to the lakes and they used to go fishing. Her son-in-law was a splendid fisher. One day he caught a beautiful big fish and the man in the hotel cooked it for their dinner.

Gabriel hardly heard what she said. Now that supper was coming near he began to think again about his speech and about the quotation. When he saw Freddy Malins coming across the room to visit his mother Gabriel left the chair free for him and retired into the embrasure of the window. The room had already cleared and from the back room came the clatter of plates and knives. Those who still remained in the drawing-room seemed tired of dancing and were conversing quietly in little groups. Gabriel's warm, trembling fingers tapped the cold pane of the window. How cool it must be outside! How pleasant it would be walk out alone, first along by the river and then through the park! The snow would be lying on the branches of the trees and formimg a bright cap on the top of the Wellington

Monument. How much more pleasant it would be there than at the supper-table!

He ran over the headings of his speech: Irish hospitality, sad memories, the Three Graces, Paris, the quotation from Browning. He repeated to himself a phrase he had written in his review: 'One feels that one is listening to a thought-tormented music.' Miss Ivors had praised the review. Was she sincere? Had she really any life of her own behind all her propagandism? There had never been any ill-feeling between them until that night. It unnerved him to think that she would be at the supper-table, looking up at him, while he spoke, with her critical quizzing eyes. Perhaps she would not be sorry to see him fail in his speech. An idea came into his mind and gave him courage. He would say, alluding to Aunt Kate and Aunt Julia: 'Ladies and Gentlemen, the generation which is now on the wane among us may have had its faults, but for my part I think it had certain qualities of hospitality, of humour, of humanity, which the new and very serious and hyper-educated generation that is growing up around us seems to me to lack.' Very good: that was one for Miss Ivors. What did he care that his aunts were only two ignorant old women?

A murmur in the room attracted his attention. Mr Browne was advancing from the door, gallantly escorting Aunt Julia, who leaned upon his arm, smiling and hanging her head. An irregular musketry of applause escorted her also as far as the piano and then, as Mary Jane seated herself on the stool, and Aunt Julia, no longer smiling, half turned so as to pitch her voice fairly into the room, gradually ceased. Gabriel recognized the prelude. It was that of an old song of Aunt Julia's – 'Arrayed for the Bridal'. Her voice, strong and clear in tone, attacked with great spirit the runs which embellish the air, and though she sang very rapidly she did not miss even the smallest of the grace notes. To follow the voice, without looking at the singer's face, was to feel and share the excitement of swift and secure flight. Gabriel applauded loudly with all the others at the close of the song, and loud applause was borne in from the invisible supper-table. It sounded so genuine that a little colour struggled into Aunt Julia's face as she bent to replace in the music-stand the old leather-bound song-book that had her initials on the cover. Freddy Malins, who had listened with his head perched sideways to hear her better, was still applauding when everyone else had ceased and talking animatedly to his mother, who nodded her head gravely and slowly in acquiescence. At last, when he could clap no more, he stood up suddenly and hurried across the room to Aunt Julia whose hand he seized and held in both his hands, shaking it when words failed him or the catch in his voice proved too much for him.

'I was just telling my mother,' he said, 'I never heard you sing so well, never. No, I never heard your voice so good as it is tonight. Now! Would you believe that now? That's the truth. Upon my word and honour that's the truth. I never heard your voice sound so fresh and so . . . so clear and fresh, never.'

Aunt Julia smiled broadly and murmured something about compliments as she released her hand from his grasp. Mr Browne extended his open hand towards her and said to those who were near him in the manner of a showman introducing a prodigy to an audience:

'Miss Julia Morkan, my latest discovery!'

He was laughing very heartily at this himself when Freddy Malins turned to him and said:

'Well, Browne, if you're serious you might make a worse discovery. All I can say is I never heard her sing half so well as long as I am coming here. And that's the honest truth.'

'Neither did I,' said Mr Browne. 'I think her voice has greatly improved.'

Aunt Julia shrugged her shoulders and said with meek pride:

'Thirty years ago I hadn't a bad voice as voices go.'

'I often told Julia,' said Aunt Kate emphatically, 'that she was simply thrown away in that choir. But she never would be said by me.'

She turned as if to appeal to a good sense of the others against a refractory child, while Aunt Julia gazed in front of her, a vague smile of reminiscence playing on her face.

'No,' continued Aunt Kate, 'she wouldn't be said or led by anyone, slaving there in that choir night and day, night and day. Six o'clock on Christmas morning! And all for what?'

'Well, isn't it for the honour of God, Aunt Kate?' asked Mary Jane, twisting round on the piano-stool and smiling.

Aunt Kate turned fiercely on her niece and said:

'I know all about the honour of God, Mary Jane, but I think it's not at all honourable for the Pope to turn out the women out of the choirs that have slaved there all their lives and put little whipper-snappers of boys over their heads. I suppose it is for the good of the Church, if the Pope does it. But it's not just, Mary Jane, and it's not right.'

She had worked herself into a passion and would have continued in defence of her sister, for it was a sore subject with her, but Mary Jane, seeing that all the dancers had come back, intervened pacifically.

'Now, Aunt Kate, you've giving scandal to Mr Browne, who is of the other persuasion.'

Aunt Kate turned to Mr Browne, who was grinning at this allusion to his religion, and said hastily:

'O, I don't question the Pope's being right. I'm only a stupid old woman and I wouldn't presume to do such a thing. But there's such a thing as common everyday politeness and gratitude. And if I were in Julia's place I'd tell that Father Healey straight up to his face ... '

'And besides, Aunt Kate,' said Mary Jane, 'we really are all hungry and when we are hungry we are all very quarrelsome.'

'And when we are thirsty we are also quarrelsome,' added Mr Browne.

'So that we had better go to supper,' said Mary Jane, 'and finish the discussion afterwards.'

On the landing outside the drawing-room Gabriel found his wife and Mary Jane trying to persuade Miss Ivors to stay for supper. But Miss Ivors, who had put on her hat and was buttoning her cloak, would not stay. She did not feel in the least hungry and she had already overstayed her time.

'But only for ten minutes, Molly,' said Mrs Conroy. 'That won't delay you.'

'To take a pick itself,' said Mary Jane, 'after all your dancing.'

'I really couldn't,' said Miss Ivors.

'I am afraid you didn't enjoy yourself at all,' said Mary Jane hopelessly.

'Ever so much, I assure you,' said Miss Ivors, 'but you really must let me run off now.'

'But how can you get home?' asked Mrs Conroy.

'O, it's only two steps up the quay.'

Gabriel hesitated a moment and said:

'If you will allow me, Miss Ivors, I'll see you home if you are really obliged to go.'

But Miss Ivors broke away from them.

'I won't hear of it,' she cried. 'For goodness' sake go in to your suppers and don't mind me. I'm quite well able to take care of myself.'

'Well, you're the comical girl, Molly,' said Mrs Conroy frankly.

'*Beannacht libh*,' cried Miss Ivors, with a laugh, as she ran down the staircase.

Mary Jane gazed after her, a moody puzzled expression on her face, while Mrs Conroy leaned over the banisters to listen for the hall-door. Gabriel asked himself was he the cause of her abrupt departure? But she did not seem to be in ill humour – she had gone away laughing. He stared blankly down the staircase.

At the moment Aunt Kate came toddling out of the supper-room, almost wringing her hands in despair.

'Where is Gabriel?' she cried. 'Where on earth is Gabriel? There's everyone waiting in there, stage to let, and nobody to carve the goose!'

'Here I am, Aunt Kate!' cried Gabriel, with sudden animation, 'ready to carve a flock of geese, if necessary.'

A fat brown goose lay at one end of the table, and at the other end, on a bed of creased paper strewn with sprigs of parsley, lay a great ham, stripped of its outer skin and peppered over with crust crumbs, a neat paper frill round its shin, and beside this was a round of spiced beef. Between these rival ends ran parallel lines of side-dishes: two little minsters of jelly, red and yellow; a shallow dish full of blocks of blancmange and red jam, a large green leaf-shaped dish with a stalk-shaped handle, on which lay bunches of purple raisins and peeled almonds, a companion dish on which lay a solid rectangle of Smyrna figs, a dish of custard topped with grated nutmeg, a small bowl full of chocolates and sweets wrapped in gold and silver papers and a glass vase in which stood some tall celery stalks. In the centre of the table there stood, as sentries to a fruit-stand which upheld a pyramid of oranges and American apples, two squat old-fashioned decanters of cut glass, one containing port and the other dark sherry. On the closed square piano a pudding in a huge yellow dish lay in waiting, and behind it were three squads of bottles of stout and ale and minerals drawn up according to the colours of their uniforms, the first two black, with brown and red labels, the third and smallest squad white, with transverse green sashes.

Gabriel took his seat boldly at the head of the table and, having looked to the edge of the carver, plunged his fork firmly into the goose. He felt quite at ease now, for he was an expert carver and liked nothing better than to find himself at the head of a well-laden table.

'Miss Furlong, what shall I send you?' he asked. 'A wing or a slice of the breast?'

'Just a small slice of the breast.'

'Miss Higgins, what for you?'

'O, anything at all, Mr Conroy.'

While Gabriel and Miss Daly exchanged plates of goose and plates of ham and spiced beef, Lily went from guest to guest with a dish of hot floury potatoes wrapped in a white napkin. This was Mary Jane's idea and she had also suggested apple sauce for the goose, but Aunt Kate had said that plain roast goose without apple sauce had always been good enough for her and she hoped she might never eat worse. Mary Jane waited on her pupils and saw that they got the best slices, and Aunt Kate and Aunt Julia opened and carried across from the piano bottles of stout and ale for the gentlemen and bottles of minerals for the ladies. There was a great deal of confusion and laughter and noise, the noise of orders and counter-orders, of knives and forks, of corks and glass-stoppers. Gabriel began to carve second helpings as soon as he had finished the first round without serving himself. Everyone protested loudly, so that he compromised by taking a long draught of stout, for he had found the carving hot work. Mary Jane settled down quietly to her supper, but Aunt Kate and Aunt Julia were still toddling round the table, walking on each other's heels, getting in each other's way and giving each other unheeded orders. Mr Browne begged of them to sit down and eat their suppers and so did Gabriel, but they said there was time enough, so that, at last, Freddy Malins stood up and, capturing Aunt Kate, plumped her down on her chair amid general laughter.

When everyone had been well served Gabriel said, smiling:

'Now, if anyone wants a little more of what vulgar people call stuffing let him or her speak.'

A chorus of voices invited him to begin his own supper, and Lily came forward with three potatoes which she had reserved for him.

'Very well,' said Gabriel amiably, as he took another preparatory draught, 'kindly forget my existence, ladies and gentlemen, for a few minutes.'

He set to his supper and took no part in the conversation with which the table covered Lily's removal of the plates. The subject of talk was the opera company which was then at the Theatre Royal. Mr Bartell D'Arcy, the tenor, a dark-complexioned young man with a smart moustache, praised very highly the leading contralto of the company, but Miss Furlong thought she had a rather vulgar style of production. Freddy Malins said there was a Negro chieftain singing in the second part of the Gaiety pantomine who had one of the finest tenor voices he had ever heard.

'Have you heard him?' he asked Mr Bartell D'Arcy across the table.

'No,' answered Mr Bartell D'Arcy carelessly.

'Because,' Freddy Malins explained, 'now I'd be curious to hear your opinion of him. I think he has a grand voice.'

'It takes Teddy to find out the really good things,' said Mr Browne familiarly to the table.

'And why couldn't he have a voice too?' asked Freddy Malins sharply. 'Is it because he's only a black?'

Nobody answered this question and Mary Jane led the table back to the legitimate opera. One of her pupils had given her a pass for

*Mignon.* Of course it was very fine, she said, but it made her think of poor Georgina Burns. Mr Browne could go back farther still, to the old Italian companies that used to come to Dublin – Tietjens, Ilma de Murzka, Campanini, the great Trebelli, Giuglini, Ravelli, Aramburo. Those were the days, he said, when there was something like singing to be heard in Dublin. He told too of how the top gallery of the old Royal used to be packed night after night, of how one night an Italian tenor had sung five encores to 'Let me like a Soldier fall', introducing a high C every time, and of how the gallery boys would sometimes in their enthusiasm unyoke the horses from the carriage of some great *prima donna* and pull her themselves through the streets to her hotel. Why did they never play the grand old operas now, he asked, *Dinorah, Lucrezia Borgia*? Because they could not get the voices to sing them: that was why.

'O, well,' said Mr Bartell D'Arcy, 'I presume there are as good singers today as there were then.'

'Where are they?' asked Mr Browne defiantly.

'In London, Paris, Milan,' said Mr Bartell D'Arcy warmly. 'I suppose Caruso, for example, is quite as good, if not better than any of the men you have mentioned.'

'Maybe so,' said Mr Brown. 'But I may tell you I doubt it strongly.'

'O, I'd give anything to hear Caruso sing,' said Mary Jane.

'For me,' said Aunt Kate, who had been picking a bone, 'there was only one tenor. To please me, I mean. But I suppose none of you ever heard of him.'

'Who was he, Miss Morkan?' asked Mr Bartell D'Arcy politely.

'His name,' said Aunt Kate, 'was Parkinson. I heard him when he was in his prime and I think he had then the purest tenor voice that was ever put into a man's throat.'

'Strange,' said Mr Bartell D'Arcy. 'I never even heard of him.'

'Yes, yes, Miss Morkan is right,' said Mr Browne. 'I remember hearing old Parkinson, but he's too far back for me.'

'A beautiful, pure, sweet, mellow English tenor,' said Aunt Kate with enthusiasm.

Gabriel having finished, the huge pudding was transferred to the table. The clatter of forks and spoons began again. Gabriel's wife served out spoonfuls of the pudding and passed the plates down the table. Midway down they were held up by Mary Jane, who replenished them with raspberry or orange jelly or with blancmange and jam. The pudding was of Aunt Julia's making, and she received praises for it from all quarters. She herself said that it was not quite brown enough.

'Well, I hope, Miss Morkan,' said Mr Browne, 'that I'm brown enough for you because, you know, I'm all Brown.'

All the gentlemen, except Gabriel, ate some of the pudding out of compliment to Aunt Julia. As Gabriel never ate sweets the celery had been left for him. Freddy Malins also took a stalk of celery and ate it with his pudding. He had been told that celery was a capital thing for the blood and he was just then under doctor's care. Mrs Malins, who had been silent all through the supper, said that her son was going down to Mount Melleray in a week or so. The table then spoke of Mount Melleray, how bracing the air was down there, how hospitable the monks were and how they never asked for a penny-piece from their guests.

'And do you mean to say,' asked Mr Browne incredulously, 'that a chap can go down there and put up there as if it were a hotel and live on the fat of the land and then come away without paying anything?'

'O, most people give some donation to the monastery when they leave,' said Mary Jane.

'I wish we had an institution like that in our Church,' said Mr Browne candidly.

He was astonished to hear that the monks never spoke, got up at two in the morning and slept in their coffins. He asked what they did it for.

'That's the rule of the order,' said Aunt Kate firmly.

'Yes, but why?' asked Mr Browne.

Aunt Kate repeated that it was the rule, that was all. Mr Browne still seemed not to understand. Freddy Malins explained to him, as best he could, that the monks were trying to make up for the sins committed by all the sinners in the outside world. The explanation was not very clear, for Mr Browne grinned and said:

'I like that idea very much, but wouldn't a comfortable spring bed do them as well as a coffin?'

'The coffin,' said Mary Jane, 'is to remind them of their last end.'

As the subject had grown lugubrious it was buried in a silence of the table, during which Mrs Malins could be heard saying to her neighbour in an indistinct undertone:

'They are very good men, the monks, very pious men.'

The raisins and almonds and figs and apples and oranges and chocolates and sweets were now passed about the table, and Aunt Julia invited all the guests to have either port or sherry. At first Mr Bartell D'Arcy refused to take either, but one of his neighbours nudged him and whispered something to him, upon which he allowed his glass to be filled. Gradually as the last glasses were being filled the conversation ceased. A pause followed, broken only by the noise of the wine and by unsettling of chairs. The Misses Morkan, all three, looked down at the tablecloth. Someone coughed once or twice, and then a few gentlemen patted the table gently as a signal for silence. The silence came and Gabriel pushed back his chair and stood up.

The patting at once grew louder in encouragement and then ceased altogether. Gabriel leaned his ten trembling fingers on the tablecloth and smiled nervously at the company. Meeting a row of upturned faces he raised his eyes to the chandelier. The piano was playing a waltz tune and he could hear the skirts sweeping against the drawing-room door. People, perhaps, were standing in the snow on the quay outside, gazing up at the lighted windows and listening to the waltz music. The air was pure there. In the distance lay the park, where the trees were weighted with snow. The Wellington Monument wore a gleaming cap of snow that flashed westwards over the white field of Fifteen Acres.

He began:

'Ladies and Gentlemen,

'It has fallen to my lot this evening, as in years past, to perform a very pleasing task, but a task for which I am afraid my poor powers as a speaker are all too inadequate.'

'No, no!' said Mr Browne.

'But, however that may be, I can only ask you tonight to take the will for the deed, and to lend me your attention for a few moments while I endeavour to express to you in words what my feelings are on this occasion.

'Ladies and Gentlemen, it is not the first time that we have gathered together under this hospitable roof, around this hospitable board. It is not the first time that we have been the recipients – or perhaps, I had better say, the victims – of the hospitality of certain good ladies.'

He made a circle in the air with his arm and paused. Everyone laughed or smiled at Aunt Kate and Aunt Julia and Mary Jane, who all turned crimson with pleasure. Gabriel went on more boldly:

'I feel more strongly with every recurring year that our country has no tradition which does it so much honour and which it should guard so jealously as that of its hospitality. It is a tradition that is unique as far as my experience goes (and I have visited not a few places abroad) among the modern nations. Some would say, perhaps, that with us it is rather a failing than anything to be boasted of. But granted even that, it is, to my mind, a princely failing, and one that I trust will long be cultivated among us. Of one thing, at least, I am sure. As long as this one roof shelters the good ladies aforesaid – and I wish from my heart it may do so for many and many a long year to come – the tradition of genuine warm-hearted courteous Irish hospitality, which our fore-fathers have handed down to us and which we must hand down to our descendants, is still alive among us.'

A hearty murmur of assent ran round the table. It shot through Gabriel's mind that Miss Ivors was not there and that she had gone away discourteously: and he said with confidence in himself:

'Ladies and Gentlemen,

'A new generation is growing up in our midst, a generation actu-ated by new ideas and new principles. It is serious and enthusiastic for these new ideas and its enthusiasm, even when it is misdirected, is, I believe, in the main sincere. But we are living in a sceptical and, if I may use the phrase, a thought-tormented age: and sometimes I fear that this new generation, educated or hyper-educated as it is, will lack those qualities of humanity, of hospitality, of kindly humour which belonged to an older day. Listening tonight to the names of all those great singers of the past it seemed to me, I must confess, that we were living in a less spacious age. Those days might, without exaggeration, be called spacious days: and if they are gone beyond recall, let us hope, at least, that in gatherings such as this we shall still speak of them with pride and affection, still cherish in our hearts the memory of those dead and gone great ones whose fame the world will not willingly let die.'

'Hear, hear!' said Mr Browne loudly.

'But yet,' continued Gabriel, his voice falling into a softer inflection, 'there are always in gatherings such as this sadder thoughts that will recur to our minds: thoughts of the past, of youth, of changes, of absent faces that we miss here tonight. Our path through life is strewn with many such sad memories: and were we to brood upon them always we could not find the heart to go on bravely with our work among the living. We have all of us living duties and living affections which claim, and rightly claim, our strenuous endeavours.

'Therefore, I will not linger on the past. I will not let any gloomy moralizing intrude upon us here tonight. Here we are gathered together for a brief moment from the bustle and rush of our everyday routine. We are met here as friends, in the spirit of good-fellowship, as colleagues, also, to a certain extent, in the true spirit of *camaraderie*, and as the guests of – what shall I call them? – the Three Graces of the Dublin musical world.'

The table burst into applause and laughter at this allusion. Aunt Julia vainly asked each of her neighbours in turn to tell her what Gabriel had said.

'He says we are the Three Graces, Aunt Julia,' said Mary Jane.

Aunt Julia did not understand, but she looked up, smiling, at Gabriel, who continued in the same vein:

'Ladies and Gentlemen,

'I will not attempt to play tonight the part that Paris played on another occasion. I will not attempt to choose between them. The task would be an invidious one and one beyond my poor powers. For when I view them in turn, whether it be our chief hostess herself, whose good heart, whose too good heart, has become a byword with all who know her; or her sister, who seems to be gifted with perennial youth and whose singing must have been a surprise and a revelation to us all tonight; or, last but not least, when I consider our youngest hostess, talented, cheerful, hard-working and the best of nieces, I confess, Ladies and Gentlemen, that I do not know to which of them I should award the prize.'

Gabriel glanced down at his aunts and, seeing the large smile on Aunt Julia's face and the tears which had risen to Aunt Kate's eyes, hastened to his close. He raised his glass of port gallantly, while every member of the company fingered a glass expectantly, and said loudly:

'Let us toast them all three together. Let us drink to their health, wealth, long life, happiness, and prosperity and may they long continue to hold the proud and self-won position which they hold in their profession and the position of honour and affection which they hold in our hearts.'

All the guests stood up, glass in hand, and turning towards the three seated ladies, sang in unison, with Mr Browne as leader:

> *For they are jolly gay fellows,*
> *For they are jolly gay fellows,*
> *For they are jolly gay fellows,*
> *Which nobody can deny.*

Aunt Kate was making frank use of her handkerchief and even Aunt Julia seemed moved. Freddy Malins beat time with his pudding-fork and the singers turned towards one another, as if in melodious conference, while they sang with emphasis:

> *Unless he tells a lie,*
> *Unless he tells a lie.*

Then, turning once more towards their hostesses, they sang:

*For they are jolly gay fellows,*
*For they are jolly gay fellows,*
*For they are jolly gay fellows,*
*Which nobody can deny.*

The acclamation which followed was taken up beyond the door of the supper room by many of the other guests and renewed time after time, Freddy Malins acting as officer with his fork on high.

The piercing morning air came into the hall where they were standing so that Aunt Kate said:

'Close the door, somebody. Mrs Malins will get her death of cold.'

'Browne is out there, Aunt Kate,' said Mary Jane.

'Browne is everywhere,' said Aunt Kate, lowering her voice.

Mary Jane laughed at her tone.

'Really,' she said archly, 'he is very attentive.'

'He has been laid on here like the gas,' said Aunt Kate in the same tone, 'all during the Christmas.'

She laughed herself this time good-humouredly and then added quickly:

'But tell him to come in, Mary Jane, and close the door. I hope to goodness he didn't hear me.'

At that moment the hall-door was opened and Mr Browne came in from the doorstep, laughing as if his heart would break. He was dressed in a long green overcoat with mock astrakhan cuffs and collar and wore on his head an oval fur cap. He pointed down the snow-covered quay from where the sound of shrill prolonged whistling was borne in.

'Teddy will have all the cabs in Dublin out,' he said.

Gabriel advanced from the little pantry behind the office, struggling into his overcoat and, looking round the hall, said.

'Gretta not down yet?'

'She's getting on her things, Gabriel,' said Aunt Kate.

'Who's playing up there?' asked Gabriel.

'Nobody. They're all gone.'

'O no, Aunt Kate,' said Mary Jane. 'Bartell D'Arcy and Miss O'Callaghan aren't gone yet.'

'Someone is fooling at the piano anyhow,' said Gabriel.

Mary Jane glanced at Gabriel and Mr Browne and said with a shiver:

'It makes me feel cold to look at you two gentlemen muffled up like that. I wouldn't like to face your journey home at this hour.'

'I'd like nothing better this minute,' said Mr Browne stoutly, 'than a rattling fine walk in the country or a fast drive with a good spanking goer between the shafts.'

'We used to have a very good horse and trap at home,' said Aunt Julia, sadly.

'The never-to-be-forgotten Johnny,' said Mary Jane, laughing.

Aunt Kate and Gabriel laughed too.

'Why, what was wonderful about Johnny?' asked Mr Browne.

'The late lamented Patrick Morkan, our grandfather, that is,' explained Gabriel, 'commonly known in his later years as the old gentleman, was a glue-boiler.'

'O, now, Gabriel,' said Aunt Kate, laughing, 'he had a starch mill.'

'Well, glue or starch,' said Gabriel, 'the old gentleman had a horse by the name of Johnny. And Johnny used to work in the old gentleman's mill, walking round and round in order to drive the mill. That was all very well; but now comes the tragic part about Johnny. One fine day the old gentleman thought he'd like to drive out with the quality to a military review in the park.'

'The Lord have mercy on his soul,' said Aunt Kate, compassionately.

'Amen,' said Gabriel. 'So the old gentleman, as I said, harnessed Johnny and put on his very best tall hat and his very best stock collar and drove out in grand style from his ancestral mansion near Back Lane, I think.'

Everyone laughed, even Mrs Malins, at Gabriel's manner, and Aunt Kate said:

'O, now, Gabriel, he didn't live in Back Lane, really. Only the mill was there.'

'Out from the mansion of his forefathers,' continued Gabriel, 'he drove with Johnny. And everything went on beautifully until Johnny came in sight of King Billy's statue: and whether he fell in love with the horse King Billy sits on or whether he thought he was back again in the mill, anyway he began to walk round the statue.'

Gabriel paced in a circle round the hall in his goloshes amid the laughter of the others.

'Round and round he went,' said Gabriel, 'and the old gentleman, who was a very pompous old gentleman, was highly indignant. "Go on, sir! What do you mean, sir? Johnny! Johnny! Most extraordinary conduct! Can't understand the horse!"'

The peals of laughter which followed Gabriel's imitation of the incident were interrupted by a resounding knock at the hall door. Mary Jane ran to open it and let in Freddy Malins. Freddy Malins, with his hat well back on his head and his shoulders humped with cold, was puffing and steaming after his exertions.

'I could only get one cab,' he said.

'O, we'll find another along the quay,' said Gabriel.

'Yes,' said Aunt Kate. 'Better not keep Mrs Malins standing in the draught.'

Mrs Malins was helped down the front steps by her son and Mr Browne and, after many manoeuvres, hoisted into the cab. Freddy Malins clambered in after her and spent a long time settling her on the seat, Mr Browne helping him with advice. At last she was settled comfortably and Freddy Malins invited Mr Browne into the cab. There was a good deal of confused talk, and then Mr Browne got into the cab. The cabman settled his rug over his knees, and bent down for the address. The confusion grew greater and the cabman was directed differently by Freddy Malins and Mr Browne, each of whom had his head out through a window of the cab. The difficulty was to know where to drop Mr Browne along the route, and Aunt Kate, Aunt Julia, and Mary Jane helped the discussion from the doorstep with cross-directions and contradictions and abundance of laughter. As for Freddy Malins he was speechless with laughter. He popped his head in and out of the window every moment to the great danger of his hat, and told his mother how the discussion was progressing, till at last Mr Browne shouted to the bewildered cabman above the din of everybody's laughter:

'Do you know Trinity College?'

'Yes, sir,' said the cabman.

'Well, drive bang up against Trinity College gates,' said Mr Browne, 'and then we'll tell you where to go. You understand now?'

'Yes, sir,' said the cabman.

'Make like a bird for Trinity College.'

'Right, sir,' said the cabman.

The horse was whipped up and the cab rattled off along the quay amid a chorus of laughter and adieux.

Gabriel had not gone to the door with the others. He was in a dark part of the hall gazing up the staircase. A woman was standing near the top of the first flight, in the shadow also. He could not see her face but he could see the terrcotta and salmon-pink panels of her skirt which the shadow made appear black and white. It was his wife. She was leaning on the banisters, listening to something. Gabriel was surprised at her stillness and strained his ear to listen also. But he could hear little save the noise of laughter and dispute on the front steps, a few chords struck on the piano and a few notes of a man's voice singing.

He stood still in the gloom of the hall, trying to catch the air that the voice was singing and gazing up at his wife. There was grace and mystery in her attitude as if she were a symbol of something. He asked himself what is a woman standing on the stairs in the shadow, listening to distant music, a symbol of? If he were a painter he would paint her in that attitude. Her blue felt hat would show off the bronze of her hair against the darkness and the dark panels of her skirt would show off the light ones. *Distant Music* he would call the picture if he were a painter.

The hall-door was closed, and Aunt Kate, Aunt Julia, and Mary Jane came down the hall, still laughing.

'Well, isn't Freddy Malins terrible?' said Mary Jane. 'He's really terrible.'

Gabriel said nothing, but pointed up the stairs towards where his wife was standing. Now that the hall-door was closed the voice and the piano could be heard more clearly. Gabriel held up his hand for them to be silent. The song seemed to be in the old Irish tonality and the singer seemed uncertain both of his words and of his voice. The voice, made plaintive by distance and by the singer's hoarseness, faintly illuminated the cadence of the air with words expressing grief:

> *O, the rain falls on my heavy locks*
> *And the dew wets my skin,*
> *My babe lies cold . . .*

'O,' exclaimed Mary Jane. 'It's Bartell D'Arcy singing, and he wouldn't sing all the night. O, I'll get him to sing a song before he goes.'

'O, do, Mary Jane,' said Aunt Kate.

Mary Jane brushed past the others and ran to the staircase, but before she reached it the singing stopped and the piano was closed abruptly.

'O, what a pity!' she cried. 'Is he coming down, Gretta?'

Gabriel heard his answer yes and saw her come down towards them. A few steps behind her were Mr Bartell D'Arcy and Miss O'Callaghan.

'O, Mr D'Arcy,' cried Mary Jane, 'it's downright mean of you to break off like that when we were all in raptures listening to you.'

'I have been at him all the evening,' said Miss O'Callaghan, 'and Mrs Conroy, too, and he told us he had a dreadful cold and couldn't sing.'

'O, Mr D'Arcy,' said Aunt Kate, 'now that was a great fib to tell.'

'Can't you see that I'm as hoarse as a crow?' said Mr D'Arcy roughly.

He went into the pantry hastily and put on his overcoat. The others, taken back by his rude speech, could find nothing to say. Aunt Kate wrinkled her brows and made signs to the others to drop the subject. Mr D'Arcy stood swathing his neck carefully and frowning.

'It's the weather,' said Aunt Julia, after a pause.

'Yes, everybody has colds,' said Aunt Kate readily, 'everybody.'

'They say,' said Mary Jane, 'we haven't had snow like it for thirty years, and I read this morning in the newspapers that the snow is general all over Ireland.'

'I love the look of snow,' said Aunt Julia sadly.

'So do I,' said Miss O'Callaghan. 'I think Christmas is never really Christmas unless we have the snow on the ground.'

'But poor Mr D'Arcy doesn't like the snow,' said Aunt Kate, smiling.

Mr D'Arcy came from the pantry, fully swathed and buttoned, and in a repentant tone told them the history of his cold. Everyone gave him advice and said it was a great pity and urged him to be very careful of his throat in the night air. Gabriel watched his wife, who did not join in the conversation. She was standing right under the dusty fanlight and the flame of the gas lit up the rich bronze of her hair, which he had seen her drying at the fire a few days before. She was in the same attitude and seened unaware of the talk about her. At last she turned towards them and Gabriel saw that there was colour on her cheeks and that her eyes were shining. A sudden tide of joy went leaping out of his heart.

'Mr D'Arcy,' she said, 'what is the name of that song you were singing?'

'It's called "The Lass of Aughrim",' said Mr D'Arcy, 'but I couldn't remember it properly. Why? Do you know it?'

'"The Lass of Aughrim",' she repeated. 'I couldn't think of the name.'

'It's a very nice air,' said Mary Jane. 'I'm sorry you were not in voice tonight.'

'Now, Mary Jane,' said Aunt Kate, 'don't annoy Mr D'Arcy. I won't have him annoyed.'

Seeing that all were ready to start she shepherded them to the door, where good night was said:

'Well, good night, Aunt Kate, and thanks for the pleasant evening.'

'Good night, Gabriel. Good night, Gretta!'

'Good night, Aunt Kate, and thanks ever so much. Good night, Aunt Julia.'

'O, good night, Gretta, I didn't see you.'

'Good night, Mr D'Arcy. Good night, Miss O'Callaghan.'

'Good night, Miss Morkan.'

'Good night, again.'

'Good night, all. Safe home.'

'Good night. Good night.'

The morning was still dark. A dull, yellow light brooded over the houses and the river; and the sky seemed to be descending. It was slushy underfoot, and only streaks and patches of snow lay on the roofs, on the parapets of the quay and on the area railings. The lamps were still burning redly in the murky air and, across the river, the palace of the Four Courts stood out menacingly against the heavy sky.

She was walking on before him with Mr Bartell D'Arcy, her shoes in a brown parcel tucked under one arm and her hands holding her skirt up from the slush. She had no longer any grace of attitude, but Gabriel's eyes were still bright with happiness. The blood went bounding along his veins and the thoughts went rioting through his brain, proud, joyful, tender, valorous.

She was walking on before him so lightly and so erect that he longed to run after her noiselessly, catch her by the shoulders and say something foolish and affectionate into her ear. She seemed to him so frail that he longed to defend her against something and then to be alone with her. Moments of their secret life together burst like stars upon his memory. A heliotrope envelope was lying beside his breakfast-cup and he was caressing it with his hand. Birds were twittering in the ivy and the sunny web of the curtain was shimmering along the floor: he could not eat for happiness. They were standing on the crowded platform and he was placing a ticket inside the warm palm of her glove. He was standing with her in the cold. Her face, fragrant in the cold air, was quite close to his, and suddenly he called out to the man at the furnace:

'Is the fire hot, sir?'

But the man could not hear with the noise of the furnace. It was just as well. He might have answered rudely.

A wave of yet more tender joy escaped from his heart and went

coursing in warm flood along his arteries. Like the tender fire of stars
moments of their life together, that no one knew of or would ever
know of, broke upon and illumined his memory. He longed to recall
to her those moments, to make her forget the years of their dull
existence together and remember only their moments of ecstasy. For
the years, he felt, had not quenched his soul or hers. Their children, his
writing, her household cares had not quenched all their souls' tender
fire. In one letter that he had written to her then he had said: 'Why is it
that words like these seem to me so dull and cold? Is it because there is
no word tender enough to be your name?'

Like distant music these words that he had written years before
were borne towards him from the past. He longed to be alone with
her. When the others had gone away, when he and she were in the
room in their hotel, then they would be alone together. He would call
her softly:

'Gretta!'

Perhaps she would not hear at once: she would be undressing. Then
something in his voice would strike her. She would turn and look at
him ...

At the corner of Winetavern Street they met a cab. He was glad of
its rattling noise as it saved him from conversation. She was looking
out of the window and seemed tired. The others spoke only a few
words, pointing out some building or street. The horse galloped along
wearily under the murky morning sky, dragging his old rattling box
after his heels, and Gabriel was again in a cab with her, galloping to
catch the boat, galloping to their honeymoon.

As the cab drove across O'Connell Bridge Miss O'Callaghan said:

'They say you never cross O'Connell Bridge without seeing a white
horse.'

'I see a white man this time,' said Gabriel.

'Where?' asked Mr Bartell D'Arcy.

Gabriel pointed to the statue, on which lay patches of snow. Then
he nodded familiarly to it and waved his hand.

'Good night, Dan,' he said gaily.

When the cab drew up before the hotel, Gabriel jumped out and, in spite of Mr Bartell D'Arcy's protest, paid the driver. He gave the man a shilling over his fare. The man saluted and said:

'A prosperous New Year to you, sir.'

'The same to you,' said Gabriel cordially.

She leaned for a moment on his arm in getting out of the cab and while standing at the kerb-stone, bidding the others good night. She leaned lightly on his arm, as lightly as when she had danced with him a few hours before. He had felt proud and happy then, happy that she was his, proud of her grace and wifely carriage. But now, after the kindling again of so many memories, the first touch of her body, musical and strange and perfumed, sent through him a keen pang of lust. Under cover of her silence he pressed her arm closely to his side, and, as they stood at the hotel door, he felt that they had escaped from their lives and duties, escaped from home and friends and run away together with wild and radiant hearts to a new adventure.

An old man was dozing in a great hooded chair in the hall. He lit a candle in the office and went before them to the stairs. They followed him in silence, their feet falling in soft thuds on the thickly carpeted stairs. She mounted the stairs behind the porter, her head bowed in the ascent, her frail shoulders curved as with a burden, her skirt girt tightly about her. He could have flung his arms about her hips and held her still, for his arms were trembling with desire to seize her and only the stress of his nails against the palms of his hands held the wild impulse of his body in check. The porter halted on the stairs to settle his guttering candle. They halted, too, on the steps below him. In the silence Gabriel could hear the falling of molten wax into the tray and the thumping of his own heart against his ribs.

The porter led them along a corridor and opened a door. Then he set his unstable candle down on a toilet-table and asked at what hour they were to be called in the morning.

'Eight,' said Gabriel.

The porter pointed to the tap of the electric-light and began a muttered apology, but Gabriel cut him short.

'We don't want any light. We have light enough from the street.

And I say,' he added, pointing to the candle, 'you might remove that handsome article, like a good man.'

The porter took up his candle again, but slowly, for he was surprised by such a novel idea. Then he mumbled good night and went out. Gabriel shot the lock to.

A ghastly light from the street lamp lay in a long shaft from one window to the door. Gabriel threw his overcoat and hat on a couch and crossed the room towards the window. He looked down into the street in order that his emotion might calm a little. Then he turned and leaned against a chest of drawers with his back to the light. She had taken off her hat and cloak and was standing before a large swinging mirror, unhooking her waist. Gabriel paused for a few moments, watching her, and then said:

'Gretta!'

She turned away from the mirror slowly and walked along the shaft of light towards him. Her face looked so serious and weary that the words would not pass Gabriel's lips. No, it was not the moment yet.

'You looked tired,' he said.

'I am a little,' she answered.

'You don't feel ill or weak?'

'No, tired: that's all.'

She went on to the window and stood there, looking out. Gabriel waited again and then, fearing that diffidence was about to conquer him, he said abruptly:

'By the way, Gretta!'

'What is it?'

'You know that poor fellow Malins?' he said quickly.

'Yes. What about him?'

'Well, poor fellow, he's a decent sort of chap, after all,' continued Gabriel in a false voice. 'He gave me back that sovereign I lent him, and I didn't expect it, really. It's a pity he wouldn't keep away from that Browne, because he's not a bad fellow, really.'

He was trembling now with annoyance. Why did she seem so abstracted? He did not know how he could begin. Was she annoyed, too, about something? If she would only turn to him or come to him of her own accord! To take her as she was would be brutal. No, he must see some ardour in her eyes first. He longed to be master of her strange mood.

'When did you lend him the pound?' she asked, after a pause.

Gabriel strove to restrain himself from breaking out into brutal language about the sottish Malins and his pound. He longed to cry to her from his soul, to crush her body against his, to overmaster her. But he said:

'O, at Christmas, when he opened that little Christmas-card shop, in Henry Street.'

He was in such a fever of rage and desire that he did not hear her come from the window. She stood before him for an instant, looking at him strangely. Then, suddenly raising herself on tiptoe and resting her hands lightly on his shoulders, she kissed him.

'You are a very generous person, Gabriel,' she said.

Gabriel, trembling with delight at her sudden kiss and at the quaintness of her phrase, put his hands on her hair and began smoothing it back, scarcely touching it with his fingers. The washing had made it fine and brilliant. His heart was brimming over with happiness. Just when he was wishing for it she had come to him of her own accord. Perhaps her thoughts had been running with his. Perhaps she had felt the impetuous desire that was in him, and then the yielding mood had come upon her. Now that she had fallen to him so easily, he wondered why he had been so diffident.

He stood, holding her head between his hands. Then, slipping one arm swiftly about her body and drawing her towards him, he said softly:

'Gretta, dear, what are you thinking about?'

She did not answer nor yield wholly to his arm. He said again, softly:

'Tell me what it is, Gretta. I think I know what is the matter. Do I know?'

She did not answer at once. Then she said in an outburst of tears: 'O, I am thinking about that song, "The Lass of Aughrim".'

She broke loose from him and ran to the bed and, throwing her arms across the bed-rail, hid her face. Gabriel stood stock-still for a moment in astonishment and then followed her. As he passed in the way of the cheval-glass he caught sight of himself in full length, his broad, well-filled shirt-front, the face whose expression always puzzled him when he saw it in a mirror, and his glimmering gilt-rimmed eye-glasses. He halted a few paces from her and said:

'What about the song? Why does that make you cry?'

She raise her head from her arms and dried her eyes with the back of her hand like a child. A kinder note than he had intended went into his voice.

'Why, Gretta?' he asked.

'I am thinking about a person long ago who used to sing that song.'

'And who was the person long ago?' asked Gabriel, smiling.

'It was a person I used to know in Galway when I was living with my grandmother,' she said.

The smile passed away from Gabriel's face. A dull anger began to gather again at the back of his mind and the dull fires of his lust began to glow angrily in his veins.

'Someone you were in love with?' he asked ironically.

'It was a young boy I used to know,' she answered, 'named Michael Furey. He used to sing that song, "The Lass of Aughrim". He was very delicate.'

Gabriel was silent. He did not wish her to think that he was interested in this delicate boy.

'I can see him so plainly,' she said, after a moment. 'Such eyes as he had: big, dark eyes! And such an expression in them – an expression!'

'O, then, you were in love with him?' said Gabriel.

'I used to go out walking with him,' she said, 'when I was in Galway.'

A thought flew across Gabriel's mind.

'Perhaps that was why you wanted to go to Galway with that Ivors girl?' he said coldly.

She looked at him and asked in surprise:

'What for?'

Her eyes made Gabriel feel awkward. He shrugged his shoulders and said:

'How do I know? To see him, perhaps.'

She looked away from him along the shaft of light towards the window in silence.

'He is dead,' she said at length. 'He died when he was only seventeen. Isn't it a terrible thing to die so young as that?'

'What was he?' asked Gabriel, still ironically.

'He was in the gasworks,' she said.

Gabriel felt humiliated by the failure of his irony and by the evocation of this figure from the dead, a boy in the gasworks. While he had been full of memories of their secret life together, full of tenderness and joy and desire, she had been comparing him in her mind with another. A shameful consciousness of his own person assailed him. He saw himself as a ludicrous figure, acting as a penny-boy for his aunts, a nervous, well-meaning sentimentalist, orating to vulgarians and idealizing his own clownish lusts, the pitiable fatuous fellow he had caught a glimpse of in the mirror. Instinctively he turned his back more to the light lest she might see the shame that burned upon his forehead.

He tried to keep up his tone of cold interrogation, but his voice when he spoke was humble and indifferent.

'I suppose you were in love with this Michael Furey, Gretta,' he said.

'I was great with him at that time,' she said.

Her voice was veiled and sad. Gabriel, feeling now how vain it would be to try to lead her whither he had purposed caressed one of her hands and said, also sadly:

'And what did he die of so young, Gretta? Consumption was it?'

'I think he died for me,' she answered.

A vague terror seized Gabriel at this answer, as if, at that hour when he had hoped to triumph, some impalpable and vindictive being was coming against him, gathering force against him in its vague world. But he shook himself free of it with an effort of reason and continued to caress her hand. He did not question her again, for he felt that she would tell him of herself. Her hand was warm and moist: it did not respond to his touch, but he continued to caress it just as he had caressed her first letter to him that spring morning.

'It was in the winter,' she said, 'about the beginning of the winter when I was going to leave my grandmother's and come up here to the convent. And he was ill at the time in his lodgings in Galway and wouldn't be let out and his people in Oughterard were written to. He was in decline, they said, or something like that. I never knew rightly.'

She paused for a moment and sighed.

'Poor fellow,' she said. 'He was very fond of me and he was such a gentle boy. We used to go out together, walking you know, Gabriel, like the way they do in the country. He was going to study singing only for his health. He had a very good voice, poor Michael Furey.'

'Well; and then?' asked Gabriel.

'And then when it came to the time for me to leave Galway and come up to the convent he was much worse and I wouldn't be let see him, so I wrote him a letter saying I was going up to Dublin and would be back in the summer, and hoping he would be better then.'

She paused for a moment to get her voice under control, and then went on:

'Then the night before I left, I was in my grandmother's house in Nuns' Island, packing up, and I heard gravel thrown up against the window. The window was so wet I couldn't see, so I ran downstairs as I was and slipped out the back into the garden and there was the poor fellow at the end of the garden, shivering.'

'And did you not tell him to go back?' asked Gabriel.

'I implored of him to go home at once and told him he would get his death in the rain. But he said he did not want to live. I can see his eyes as well as well! He was standing at the end of the wall where there was a tree.'

'And did he go home?' asked Gabriel.

'Yes, he went home. And when I was only a week in the convent he died and was buried in Oughterard, where his people came from. O, the day I heard that, that he was dead!'

She stopped, choking with sobs, and, overcome by emotion, flung herself face downward on the bed, sobbing in the quilt. Gabriel held her hand for a moment longer, irresolutely, and then, shy of intruding on her grief, let it fall gently and walked quietly to the window.

She was fast asleep.

Gabriel, leaning on his elbow, looked for a few moments unresentfully on her tangled hair and half-open mouth, listening to her deep-drawn breath. So she had had that romance in her life: a man had died for her sake. It hardly pained him now to think how poor a part he, her husband, had played in her life. He watched her while she slept, as though he and she had never lived together as man and wife. His curious eyes rested long upon her face and on her hair: and, as he thought of what she must have been then, in that time of her girlish beauty, a strange, friendly pity for her entered his soul. He did not like to say even to himself that her face was no longer beautiful, but he knew that it was no longer the face for which Michael Furey had braved death.

Perhaps she had not told him all the story. His eyes moved to the chair over which she had thrown some of her clothes. A petticoat string dangled to the floor. One boot stood upright, its limp upper fallen down; the fellow of it lay upon its side. He wondered at his riot of emotions of an hour before. From what had it proceeded? From his aunt's supper, from his own foolish speech, from the wine and dancing, the merry-making when saying good night in the hall, the pleasure of the walk along the river in the snow. Poor Aunt Julia! She, too, would soon be a shade with the shade of Patrick Morkan and his horse. He had caught that haggard look upon her face for a moment when she was singing 'Arrayed for the Bridal'. Soon, perhaps, he would be sitting in that same drawing-room, dressed in black, his silk hat on his knees. The blinds would be drawn down and Aunt Kate would be sitting beside him, crying and blowing her nose and telling him how Julia had died. He would cast about in his mind for some words that might console her, and would find only lame and useless ones. Yes, yes: that would happen very soon.

The air of the room chilled his shoulders. He stretched himself cautiously along under the sheets and lay down beside his wife. One by one, they were all becoming shades. Better pass boldly into that other world, in the full glory of some passion, than fade and wither dismally with age. He thought of how she who lay beside him had locked in her heart for so many years that image of her lover's eyes when he had told her that he did not wish to live.

Generous tears filled Gabriel's eyes. He had never felt like that himself towards any woman, but he knew that such a feeling must be love. The tears gathered more thickly in his eyes and in the partial darkness he imagined he saw the form of a young man standing under a dripping tree. Other forms were near. His soul had approached that region where dwell the vast hosts of the dead. He was conscious of, but could not apprehend, their wayward and flickering existence. His own identity was fading out into a grey impalpable world: the solid world itself, which these dead had one time reared and lived in, was dissolving and dwindling.

A few light taps upon the pane made him turn to the window. It had begun to snow again. He watched sleepily the flakes, silver and dark, falling obliquely against the lamp-light. The time had come for him to set out on his journey westward. Yes, the newspapers were right: snow was general all over Ireland. It was falling on every part of the dark central plain, on the treeless hills, falling softly upon the Bog of Allen and, further westward, softly falling into the dark mutinous Shannon waves. It was falling, too, upon every part of the lonely churchyard on the hill where Michael Furey lay buried. It lay thickly drifted on the crooked crosses and headstones, on the spears of the little gate, on the barren thorns. His soul swooned slowly as he heard the snow falling faintly through the universe and faintly falling, like the descent of their last end, upon all the living and the dead.